REVENUE MANAGEMENT
Maximizing Revenue in Hospitality Operations

Educational Institute Books

UNIFORM SYSTEM OF ACCOUNTS FOR THE LODGING INDUSTRY
Eleventh Revised Edition

PLANNING AND CONTROL FOR FOOD AND BEVERAGE OPERATIONS
Ninth Edition
Jack D. Ninemeier

UNDERSTANDING HOSPITALITY LAW
Fifth Edition
Jack P. Jefferies/Banks Brown

SUPERVISION IN THE HOSPITALITY INDUSTRY
Sixth Edition
Jack D. Ninemeier

MANAGEMENT OF FOOD AND BEVERAGE OPERATIONS
Sixth Edition
Jack D. Ninemeier

MANAGING FRONT OFFICE OPERATIONS
Tenth Edition
Michael L. Kasavana

MANAGING SERVICE IN FOOD AND BEVERAGE OPERATIONS
Fifth Edition
Ronald F. Cichy/Philip J. Hickey, Jr.

THE LODGING AND FOOD SERVICE INDUSTRY
Eighth Edition
Gerald W. Lattin/Thomas W. Lattin/James E. Lattin

SECURITY AND LOSS PREVENTION MANAGEMENT
Third Edition
David M. Stipanuk/Raymond C. Ellis, Jr.

HOSPITALITY INDUSTRY MANAGERIAL ACCOUNTING
Eighth Edition
Raymond S. Schmidgall

MANAGING TECHNOLOGY IN THE HOSPITALITY INDUSTRY
Seventh Edition
Michael L. Kasavana

HOTEL AND RESTAURANT ACCOUNTING
Eighth Edition
Raymond Cote

ACCOUNTING FOR HOSPITALITY MANAGERS
Fifth Edition
Raymond Cote

CONVENTION MANAGEMENT AND SERVICE
Ninth Edition
James R. Abbey

HOSPITALITY SALES AND MARKETING
Sixth Edition
James R. Abbey

MANAGING HOUSEKEEPING OPERATIONS
Revised Third Edition
Aleta A. Nitschke/William D. Frye

HOSPITALITY TODAY: AN INTRODUCTION
Eighth Edition
Rocco M. Angelo

HOSPITALITY FACILITIES MANAGEMENT AND DESIGN
Fourth Edition
David M. Stipanuk

MANAGING HOSPITALITY HUMAN RESOURCES
Fifth Edition
Robert H. Woods, Misty M. Johanson, and Michael P. Sciarini

RETAIL MANAGEMENT FOR SPAS

HOSPITALITY INDUSTRY FINANCIAL ACCOUNTING
Fourth Edition
Raymond S. Schmidgall/James W. Damitio

HOTEL INVESTMENTS: ISSUES & PERSPECTIVES
Fifth Edition
Edited by Lori E. Raleigh and Rachel J. Roginsky

LEADERSHIP AND MANAGEMENT IN THE HOSPITALITY INDUSTRY
Third Edition
Robert H. Woods/Judy Z. King

CONTEMPORARY CLUB MANAGEMENT
Third Edition
Edited by Joe Perdue and Jason Koenigsfeld for the Club Managers Association of America

HOTEL ASSET MANAGEMENT: PRINCIPLES & PRACTICES
Third Edition
Edited by Rich Musgrove, Lori E. Raleigh, and A. J. Singh

MANAGING BEVERAGE OPERATIONS
Second Edition
Ronald F. Cichy/Lendal H. Kotschevar

FOOD SAFETY AND QUALITY MANAGEMENT
Third Edition
Ronald F. Cichy and JaeMin Cha

SPA: A COMPREHENSIVE INTRODUCTION
Elizabeth M. Johnson/Bridgette M. Redman

REVENUE MANAGEMENT: MAXIMIZING REVENUE IN HOSPITALITY OPERATIONS
Second Edition
Gabor Forgacs

FINANCIAL MANAGEMENT FOR SPAS
Raymond S. Schmidgall/John R. Korpi

REVENUE MANAGEMENT
Maximizing Revenue in Hospitality Operations

Second Edition

Gabor Forgacs, Dr. oec.

Disclaimer

© Copyright 2017 by the National Restaurant Association Solutions, LLC, an Illinois limited liability company ("NRAS"). All rights reserved. Manufactured in the United States of America.

The *Revenue Management: Maximizing Revenue in Hospitality Operations* textbook (the "Textbook") contains proprietary information, including but not limited to text, photos, graphics, names, trademarks and service marks. Except where noted, NRAS owns all rights, including copyright, title and interest in and to the content of the Textbook, which may not be copied, reproduced, retransmitted, published or otherwise used for any reason other than personal use. Written permission must be obtained from NRAS prior to any reproduction, retransmission, storage in a retrieval system, or transmission in any form or any means—electronic, mechanical, photocopying, recording or otherwise. To obtain permission(s), please submit a written request to Copyright Permissions, National Restaurant Association Solutions, LLC, 175 West Jackson Boulevard, Suite 1500, Chicago, IL 60604-2814; email: permissions@restaurant.org.

The information presented in this Textbook is provided for informational purposes only and is not intended to provide legal advice or establish standards of reasonable behavior. Operators who develop policies and procedures based upon the materials in this Textbook are urged to obtain the advice and guidance of legal counsel. Although NRAS endeavors to include accurate and current information compiled from sources believed to be reliable, NRAS and its distributors and agents make no representations or warranties as to the accuracy, currency, or completeness of the information. THE INFORMATION IN THE TEXTBOOK IS PROVIDED "AS IS" WITHOUT WARRANTY OF ANY KIND, EITHER EXPRESSED OR IMPLIED, INCLUDING BUT NOT LIMITED TO THE IMPLIED WARRANTIES OF MERCHANTABILITY, FITNESS FOR A PARTICULAR PURPOSE OR NON-INFRINGEMENT. Some jurisdictions do not allow the exclusion of implied warranties, so this exclusion may not apply to you.

In no event shall NRAS, the National Restaurant Association (NRA), the American Hotel & Lodging Educational Institute (AHLEI) or any of their distributors or agents be liable for any direct, indirect, incidental special, exemplary, or consequential damages however caused and on any theory of liability, whether in contract, strict liability, or tort (including negligence or otherwise) arising in any way out of the use of the Textbook or the information contained therein, even if advised of the possibility of such damage. This disclaimer of liability applies to any damage, injury or loss resulting from inaccuracies or omissions or any actions taken or not taken based on the content of this publication.

The American Hotel & Lodging Educational Institute (AHLEI) name and logo are used under license from the American Hotel & Lodging Association (AHLA) by the National Restaurant Association Solutions, LLC, a wholly owned subsidiary of the National Restaurant Association (NRA).

ISBN: 978-0-86612-446-1 (print version)
ISBN: 978-0-86612-548-2 (e-book version)

Printed in the USA

6 7 8 9 10 22 21 20 19

Contents

Preface xi
About the Author xiii

Part I   Introduction 1

1   What Is Revenue Management? 3
   A Brief History 3
   Criteria for Effective Use 6
      Fixed-Capacity Environments • Perishable Products • Varied but Predictable Demand • High Fixed Costs and Low Variable Costs

   Revenue Management Challenges 10
      Local or Centralized • Too Much Data • Elevate from Tactical to Strategic and Embrace Total Revenue Management • Monetize Social Media • Harness the Power of Mobile

Part II   Performance Measurement 15

2   Internal Measurement Metrics 17
   Internal Measures 17
      Revenue • Occupancy Percentage • Average Daily Rate • RevPAR • Contribution Margin (Net Revenue) • Identical Net Room Revenue • Marginal Revenue Consideration • GOPPAR • Other Measures

   Case Study 30
   Data Analytics Problems 32

3   External Measurement Metrics 35
   Competitive Set 35
   Market Share 40
   The Use of Market Intelligence 43
   Measurement Challenges 44
      Big Data and Market Intelligence

   Case Studies 46

Part III   Tactical Revenue Management 49

4   Forecasting 51
   A Cornerstone of Revenue Management 51

viii Contents

  Forecasting Demand 52
   Long-Term Forecasts • Short-Term Forecasts • Unconstrained and Constrained Demand • Pace of Build

  Forecasting Room Availability 59
  Case Studies 60

5 Tactical Rate Management **65**
  Rate Structure 66
   Types of Rate
  Tactical Discounting 71
  Upselling 73
  Demand-Based Dynamic Pricing 75
  Case Studies 78

6 Stay Control and Capacity Management **81**
  Stay (Duration) Control 81
   Minimum-Stay Requirements • Stay Through • Closing a Day to Arrivals
  Capacity Management 84
   Preventive Measures • Reclaiming Rooms
  Case Studies 89

7 Displacement Analysis **97**
  Displacement Analysis Process
   Establish Net Room Revenue Differential • Establish Net Food and Beverage Revenue Differential • Determine Other Revenue Differential • Summary
  Case Study 103

Part IV Strategic Revenue Management **107**

8 Demand Generation **109**
  Demand Generation Strategies 109
   Differentiation
  Case Study 113

9 Marketing Strategies for Revenue Management **117**
  Market Segmentation Methods 117
   Mobile Commerce

	Market Targeting	121
	Market Positioning	122
	Repositioning/Rebranding	
	Promotion	122
	Customer Relationship Management	123
	Market Mix Management	124
	Case Studies	126
10	**Strategic Pricing**	**131**
	Competing on Price	131
	Rate Parity	133
	Revenue Streams Management	133
	Strategic Packaging	134
	The Package Development Process • The Objective of Packaging • Packaging and Segmentation • Packaging and Revenue Streams Management	
	Case Studies	139
	Chapter Appendix: The Emerging Trend of Hotel Total Revenue Management	143
11	**Distribution Channel Management**	**155**
	Distribution Channels	155
	Voice Channels • GDS Channel • Internet Channels	
	Social Media	161
	Mobility and Mobile Users	164
	Responsive Design	165
	Case Study	166
12	**Revenue Management's Place in Hotels**	**169**
	Automated Revenue Management Systems	169
	Capabilities of Automated Systems • Cultural Challenges • System-Integration Challenges	
	The Revenue Manager	177
	Task Lists and Competencies for Revenue Managers	
	Case Study	182

Appendix: The Top Ten Revenue Management Mistakes **185**

Index **191**

Preface

As a general manager of a small full-service property, I dreamed about hiring capable and willing maintenance staff, such as an electrician who could not only replace the cylinder of a guestroom door lock but, if push came to shove, would not shy away from unplugging a clogged guestroom toilet. As the manager ultimately responsible for everything, I had to juggle many duties and responsibilities myself, from negotiating with asphalt companies to repave our parking lot, to discussing the hotel's room upgrade policies with a loyal guest, to dealing with an unpleasant manager of a travel agency who called to complain about the menu choices at our hotel and the water temperature of our swimming pool. All of this was attended to while I wrote a report to the local fire marshal regarding the hotel's battery-renewal policies and procedures for our smoke sensors. And this was just one average morning of one average day at the hotel. So many hats to wear, so many disciplines to master—never a dull moment! The hotel business is interdisciplinary, just as life is. No wonder that the newest emerging discipline in the hotel industry, called revenue management, is also interdisciplinary in its nature. Revenue management can add new dimensions of strategic thinking and become a value-added enabler of sustainable corporate growth in the highly competitive hospitality field.

Practicing sound revenue management strategies and tactics affects almost everything a hotel does. Revenue management involves all facets of operations management—room rates, demand forecasting, and customer relations management, among many other areas. Marketing, accounting, operations management, and finances are all involved in devising revenue management strategies. Hoteliers involved in every aspect of their hotels' operations will comfortably navigate this book. Those hotel managers and employees who work for large properties and whose responsibilities are narrowed down to one particular hotel division may use this book to broaden their horizons. Hospitality students who have mastered at least introductory-level marketing, accounting, and front office management courses can build on that knowledge by reading this book. All future owners and managers of hotels will discover a discipline that will help their hotels become more profitable.

Acknowledgments

I would like to take this opportunity to express my gratitude to those who have provided help and support along the way. I have learned much—and keep learning!—from all of my students, both at the undergraduate level at the Ted Rogers School of Management at Ryerson University and also from my MBA students at the University of Guelph.

Authors need the constructive criticism and guidance of others to gain insight and inspiration, and I have received valuable help from many people, too numerous to list. I am grateful for their help.

We have entered a new era in hospitality management that is data driven: we have more data than ever before from a variety of sources that can be analyzed both by humans and machines. However, even in the era of "big data" and artificial intelligence, there is a need for well-educated people who will drive strategy based on their understanding of changing customer expectations and increased pressure for financial success. The beauty of the new challenge for revenue professionals is to develop the ability for finding optimized solutions under any set of circumstances.

I hope this book on revenue management will be followed by many others from a variety of authors, in order to build a solid theoretical foundation for this exciting new discipline—a discipline that has the potential to change the hotel industry for the better.

Dr. Gabor Forgacs
Toronto, Ontario
Canada

About the Author

GABOR FORGACS has twenty years' work experience in the hotel industry on two continents, including a management position at a Four Seasons hotel in Toronto, Ontario, Canada, and the position of president and general manager of a full-service hotel in Budapest, Hungary. Since 1997 he has taught at the Ted Rogers School of Hospitality and Tourism Management at Ryerson University in Toronto. He teaches courses in "Revenue Management for Hospitality & Tourism," "The Value of Branding in Lodging," and "Property Management Systems." He received his doctorate from the Budapest University of Economic Sciences. He also holds an undergraduate degree in economics from the same university, and he is a graduate of the College of Commerce and Hotel Management of Budapest, Hungary.

Dr. Forgacs is the editor of the online discussion series "Branding and Product Specialization in Hotels" sponsored by Henry Stewart Publications (2009), and he was invited to participate as a content expert in the development of training and educational materials on revenue management by the American Hotel & Lodging Educational Institute (2000).

Dr. Forgacs has published articles in the *International Journal of Contemporary Hospitality Management, The Hotelier Magazine* (Canada), *The Rooms Chronicle* (United States), *The Accommodator* (Canada), the *Canadian Lodging News, The Journal of Revenue and Pricing Management,* and other print magazines. He has been published in the conference proceedings of ICHRIE (International Council on Hotel, Restaurant and Institutional Education), and has published material online for Hotel-Online.com, ehotelier.com, hotelnewsresource.com, 4hoteliers.com, htrends.com, HVS International.com, and other websites. Dr. Forgacs is frequently quoted and interviewed in the Canadian media regarding revenue management and other hospitality issues.

Part I

Introduction

Chapter 1 Outline

A Brief History
Criteria for Effective Use
    Fixed-Capacity Environment
    Perishable Products
    Varied but Predictable Demand
    High Fixed Costs and Low Variable
      Costs
Revenue Management Challenges
    Local or Centralized
    Too Much Data
    Elevate to Strategic from Tactical
      and Embrace Total Revenue
      Management
    Monetize Social Media
    Harness the Power of Mobile

Competencies

1. Define revenue management and identify the basic steps of the revenue management process. (p. 3)

2. Outline the brief history of revenue management and why it has become important. (pp. 3–6)

3. Identify and describe the business traits that allow for the best use of revenue management. (pp. 7–10)

4. Identify and describe five emerging revenue management challenges. (pp. 10–13)

1

What Is Revenue Management?

REVENUE MANAGEMENT, sometimes called yield management, has become part of mainstream business theory and practice over the last three decades. Whether we call it an emerging discipline or a new management science—it has been called both—revenue management is a set of revenue maximization strategies and tactics meant to improve the profitability of certain businesses. It is complex because it involves several aspects of management control, including rate management, revenue streams management, and distribution channel management, just to name a few. Revenue management is multidisciplinary because it blends elements of marketing, operations, and financial management into a highly successful new approach. A revenue manager frequently must work with one or more other departments when designing and implementing revenue management strategies.

Quite a few managers tend to look at revenue management from a narrow perspective, seeing it as only a push-pull game with rates. When done properly, however, revenue management involves much more than just crunching numbers and adjusting price points. It encompasses product definition, competitive benchmarking, strategic pricing, demand forecasting, business mix manipulation, and distribution channel management (see Exhibit 1). The process is a dynamic and perpetual business cycle that requires all the components to be aligned and seamlessly integrated to ensure full functionality. In hotels, revenue management is used to examine how many room nights are sold (occupancy), at what rate (discounting), what else is sold (sales mix), to whom (market segmentation), and through what channel (distribution channel management). All of these components are examined and then managed with the objective of optimizing income under constantly changing supply and demand conditions.

Before we begin applying revenue management to hospitality operations, let's look briefly at how we got to where we are today.

A Brief History

Revenue management is a discipline that grew out of the airline industry's yield management initiatives of the mid-1980s. Following the deregulation of the U.S. airline industry in 1978, drastic changes took effect. Low-cost suppliers appeared that aggressively carved out a growing share of the market. The legacy carriers had a hard time figuring out how to compete successfully with the charters and the

Exhibit 1 Revenue Management as a Business Process

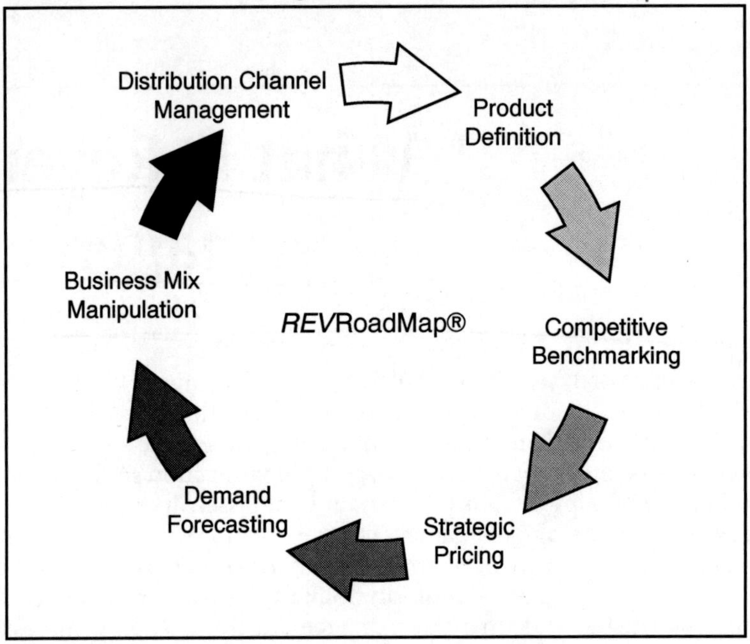

- Distribution Channel Management
- Product Definition
- Competitive Benchmarking
- Strategic Pricing
- Demand Forecasting
- Business Mix Manipulation

*REV*RoadMap®

discount airlines. By the mid-1980s, the threat became serious. Robert L. Crandall, the legendary chairman and CEO of American Airlines, fronted a new approach to tackle the problem: he used yield management to manipulate seat inventories by different fare classes on each flight. Discount allocations were based on solid data, and computers (mainframe systems at the time) were used to process massive amounts of information to deal with constantly changing market demand and competitive fares from other airlines. Forecasting became crucial. Following the successful implementation of yield management, multi-tiered rate structures (combined with forecasting accuracy and market segmentation) became the focus of strategic thinking.

A number of industries realized their business models were similar to that of the airlines in terms of product perishability, seasonality of demand, and cost structure: hotels, cruise lines, car rental agencies, broadcasters, and the entertainment industry were among the first to embrace revenue management. Hotels used tactics to increase occupancy in low-demand periods, and used premium pricing to improve income generation in high-demand periods. The financial rewards were measurable in revenue performance and increased profit.

The biggest chains traditionally take the lead on new initiatives in the hotel industry, and this was no exception. Big brands were at the forefront in implementing revenue management systems. Some companies developed proprietary systems, while others elected to purchase a system from a supplier. Quite a few corporations were content with a spreadsheet-based tool developed by their own front office and reservations people. Most tactical-level measures of revenue

> *Yield management is important to forecasting*

> ### Revenue Management or Yield Management?
>
> There is no difference between yield management and revenue management in the context of the hotel industry. The only reason the term *yield management* is still frequently used is that it was the commonly accepted term in the early years because of its airline industry origins.
>
> Initially, the European (mostly British) revenue management literature had also a preference for the term *yield management*, while the North American literature had a preference for the term *revenue management*. Today it is fair to say that there is no substantial difference between the meanings of these terms and the prevailing industry jargon has leaned toward accepting the use of *revenue management* in the context of the hotel business.
>
> Revenue management is a discipline that enables hotels to become more profitable. In order to achieve measurable outcomes, carefully selected strategies and tactics are deployed based on an analysis of supply/demand dynamics and a given hotel's products' attributes. The most successful hotels know exactly what their core competencies are, who their guests are, how to market to them, and what it takes to meet or exceed their expectations. They also control their expenses, but most importantly, they understand that the key to sustainable success in this industry is in revenue generation. Occupancy alone is not enough. Average rate alone is not enough. Today's managers need to drive both.

management can be sufficiently controlled with a simple spreadsheet designed by those who use it every day.

Today, most hotels use revenue management in one way or another. The level of automation and the degree of sophistication vary, but most hotels in competitive markets use multi-tiered rate structures that they can adjust based on key variables. The strategic understanding may differ from brand to brand, but most hotels use a variety of channels to sell their room inventory, and they are knowledgeable users of revenue management tactics at the front office level.

The hotel industry now recognizes revenue management as one of the core competencies vital to profitability. However, not everything done in the name of revenue management is new. Some revenue management tactics are as old as the industrial age. When railways gave people the ability to travel in masses, a new lodging industry started to grow. Hotels were built to accommodate travelers at frequented locations. Those who managed hotels as a profession embraced good business sense from early on. They learned the difference between seasons of high and low demand. They recognized that the selling price for one room sold to one guest needed to be different from the selling price for dozens of rooms sold to the same guest. They could distinguish the guest who spent money only on the room from others who spent much more on food, drink, and other services. Hoteliers always recognized return guests and appreciated their patronage. Hotel managers greeted those arrivals personally, offered upgrades, and devoted heightened attention to them.

Although the world has changed dramatically since hotels first came on the scene, the hospitality industry's core concept of providing accommodation for a fee has remained unchanged. The terminology may be different today, but seasonal prices, packages, volume discounts, guest loyalty programs, and average spending per stay are not new concepts at all. Hoteliers like César Ritz, Ellsworth Statler, and William Waldorf Astor knew all about these concepts, though they conducted their businesses using paper-and-pencil manual systems. The service they provided was second to none, and good hotels made decent profits. So, is there anything new under the sun?

Actually, yes, there is. While many tasks now done under the name of revenue management have been done since the nineteenth century, technology has greatly increased the amount and complexity of the information that can be analyzed as well as the speed at which it can be done. *Big data* is the term referring to this capability. Furthermore, the hotel industry is not the same as it was one hundred years ago; it has become a global industry. The complex expectations placed on today's managers far surpass the expectations of a century ago. Financial pressures have changed significantly since the trend of separating ownership and management became prevalent for midsize and larger properties in the last quarter of the twentieth century in North America. A profession called *asset management* emerged as a result: a new class of owners and investors who had no lodging operational expertise chose to hire specialists to watch over the managers of the hotels that they owned. The mandate for these asset managers was to ensure that both revenue and profit potentials were maximized.

On the supply side, the markets have become much more fragmented and competitive. On the demand side, travelers have more clout than ever, largely because they have information on virtually everything at their fingertips. Today's travelers routinely comparison shop and prefer to shorten the booking window (last-minute purchases are on the rise); this has become more convenient and thus more prevalent due to the increased functionality of mobile devices like smartphones and tablet computers. On the operational side, it is not just room service or the front desk that is expected to be available at all hours. Guests expect to be able to access hotel room availability information whenever they want it. They want to make or change reservations and make payments around the clock as well. Time has become a new currency. Guests demand that their wants and needs be met immediately. These expectations dictate a dynamic operational environment from service providers, where both people and systems must be able to handle a lot of tasks accurately and efficiently at all hours.

It is important to point out that all of the new and sophisticated revenue management technology does not replace the need for management oversight of the revenue management function. Revenue management cannot be fully automated in the way simple tasks like invoice settlement can be. Managers should see revenue management technology as an aid to their decision-making, not as a replacement for it. Savvy revenue managers use technology for data collection and analysis, but they also understand the importance of human intelligence in complex business environments and see revenue management technology as a great tool, not as a solution in and of itself.

Criteria for Effective Use

Many businesses use some revenue management elements. For example, various businesses use forecasting and seasonal pricing changes and have learned how their clientele can be segmented into clusters based on buying behavior. However, a business or industry needs to meet specific criteria to unlock the full potential of revenue management. Businesses that benefit the most from revenue management:

1. Work in fixed-capacity environments.
2. Have perishable or time-sensitive products.
3. Face varied but predictable demand over time.
4. Have a high proportion of fixed costs to variable costs.

Hospitality is one of these businesses. Let's look at these criteria more fully.

Fixed-Capacity Environment

Some businesses face few constraints on their potential sales. They can meet higher demand by producing or providing more units. If we sell consumer goods (such as clothing) and the market wants more, we can increase output as needed. If demand is high, we can stock up, increase the store's hours, and sell more. On the other hand, if demand drops, we can lower the amount we order from suppliers, decrease inventory, shorten the hours of store operation, and wait until demand strengthens.

---

110 Percent Occupancy?

Under certain conditions, hotels may seem to defy the laws of mathematics by logging occupancies of greater than 100 percent. How is this possible? First, it can only happen in a sellers' market. East European countries in the 1970s make a good illustration. There was a serious shortage in room supply at a time when incoming tourism started to grow. It rapidly became a sellers' market. Second, most of the tourists arrived in tour groups. The Hotel National, a city center hotel in Budapest, Hungary, was a typical case. Every night, the hotel was filled up to capacity with groups, most of them one-night stays. During the day, the hotel was also a popular place for locals who needed a day-use room only in the afternoon hours. The hotel rented out rooms for the day-use guests in the afternoon, then had the rooms cleaned and turned over for the groups checking in after dinner. Group contracts typically allowed a 10 percent tolerance. This meant that if the reserved room block was for 20 rooms, the invoice could be made out for 18 rooms even if the group actually needed only 17 or fewer rooms on arrival. In other words, the same room might be sold for day use, charged to a group account despite remaining unused, and sold to an actual user all on the same day. This was not unusual during those years, and it sometimes resulted in annual average occupancies of greater than 100 percent in the second half of the 1970s. Those days are long gone.

Businesses with fixed capacity do not have the luxury of these options. Fixed capacity is a significant constraint. Hotels have a finite number of hotel rooms to sell. They can't sell more than their total capacity even when the demand is there. The same capacity exists when demand is low.

Actually, given sufficient time, even fixed capacity can be changed or rearranged. Some authors use the term *relatively fixed* for this reason. Hotel managers can't change the number of rooms in a hotel overnight; however, if they see a permanent need for more units, they can always consider adding a new wing or another floor. But it would take months or years to do that. Therefore, a hotel's managers can't address short-term demand fluctuations with quick capacity changes.

A restaurant may open a patio, change its service style, or reconfigure its table mix to loosen its capacity constraints, but these measures also have limitations. Production capacity constraints limit the number of guests a restaurant can serve in a meal period. Fire safety regulations often limit the number of persons allowed on the premises at any given time.

An airline has a fixed number of seats available on a given plane regardless of demand. If the airline has too many unsold seats on its Chicago–Miami flight that departs on Tuesdays at 8:00 A.M. the airline might consider replacing its current aircraft for that flight with a smaller-capacity plane, provided one is available in its fleet. Alternatively, if the flight is always filled to capacity, the airline might consider using a higher-capacity plane. However, the decision to decrease or increase capacity cannot be implemented overnight. Likewise, a spa cannot quickly or easily increase its capacity, even if it is constantly booked and waiting lists are growing. The capacity of airlines and spas are relatively fixed, just like the capacity of hotels, cruise ships, and theaters.

Perishable Products

A hotel sells a time-sensitive product—the privilege to occupy a given room for a given time. After the time expires, the hotel has the opportunity to clean, refresh, and replenish the room and sell the privilege of staying there again to another occupant.

Tonight's room night has a short shelf life. Tonight's room night cannot be sold tomorrow. If a hotel can't sell a room night and a room remains unsold, the hotel can't store that unsold room in inventory and sell it later. Tomorrow, the hotel will sell tomorrow's room night.

Businesses that sell tangible, non-perishable products may use their inventory as a buffer. Unsold units can be inventoried. What they haven't sold one day, they might sell the following day. A clothing item like a coat or a shirt can remain on the store shelves if unsold on a Monday and sold to a customer on Tuesday. But hotels, airlines, spas, cruise ships, and theaters deal in highly perishable products. Unsold room nights, plane seats, spa treatment slots, state rooms, and show tickets can't be sold once the day, event, or trip is past. These products are called *time-sensitive* or *perishable* to reflect this special attribute. As a consequence of this fundamental trait, the pressure for businesses that sell perishable products to close a sale is significant. Lost opportunities have a strong negative impact on their profitability.

Varied but Predictable Demand

In the hotel industry, demand fluctuates all the time. Differences exist between geographical markets and property types, but virtually all hotels face some sort of seasonal demand variances. A warm winter resort hotel on a Caribbean island will have seasonal demand fluctuations that differ from those at a transient hotel in Paris, but both can identify their own main seasons, off-seasons, and shoulder seasons.

Seasonality refers to a variation of demand based on the season of the year. But demand fluctuations can be observed by days of the week as well. Saturday was the highest occupancy day in North American hotels for many years. Demand fluctuations have operational consequences: busy days and slow days dictate different rhythms in the life of a hotel. Changes can be observed even within a day: the morning rush, the midday lull, and the evening rush are characteristic of a transient hotel's life. Traffic patterns in a casino hotel differ from those in a spa hotel. Again, each hotel can describe its own seasonality within a year, a week, or a day.

Varying demand helps to put revenue management into perspective: the impacts or measures of revenue management in a hotel cannot be perceived like they would be in a static environment. The approach to revenue management is based on the understanding that everything is in permanent flux. For example, the number of reservations on the books seven days out will likely be different from the number on the books for that same day only three days out. Guests cancel or modify their reservations and new guests book at the last minute. Hotels do not provide a static operational environment.

Does this ever-changing operating environment create chaotic, unmanageable nightmares for managers? Not at all, as the fluctuations show certain patterns. This is where the concept of predictability becomes fundamental. The beginnings and endings of seasons can be identified. A hotel's records document the rush hours and the high-occupancy days and weeks. The revenue impact of statutory holidays, school breaks, and significant events in the hotel's vicinity can be predicted. This knowledge can be used to prepare demand forecasts. Accurate forecasts allow management to use appropriate pricing, product packaging (bundling), and other strategies more effectively.

One of management's challenges is finding the right tactics based on the right strategy to arrive at optimal solutions in a constantly changing environment. Revenue management can work with valuable data to identify and map out the seasonality of demand. Identifiable revenue patterns will help determine best-suited strategies and tactics to exploit revenue maximization opportunities.

High Fixed Costs and Low Variable Costs

Some expense items are not affected by occupancy. If a cost is not directly related to sales volume, it can be classified as a fixed cost. For example, mortgage payments, insurance premiums, amortization of capital assets, the payroll costs of annual salaries, energy, and maintenance are all fixed-cost items.

Some people question whether salaried payroll and energy costs should be seen as fixed items. But, according to property management literature, more than 80 percent of a hotel's energy cost depends on weather conditions rather than occupancy levels. Hot and humid days require a lot of air conditioning; cold days with strong wind-chill factors require a lot of heating. Hotels cannot necessarily seal off unoccupied rooms or floors. In that sense, most of the energy and maintenance costs are accurately considered fixed items, as they do not directly depend on sales and occupancy performance.

The only components of the payroll that can be directly related to occupancy and sales are seasonal labor, part-time employees' wages, and the overtime cost of hourly workers. Therefore, much of a hotel's labor cost also can be considered a fixed cost.

It is important to note that the fixed costs are also the big-ticket ones. They make up most of the total costs of operation. This cost structure reflects the fact that the hotel industry is capital-intensive. It takes a significant initial investment to secure a piece of land, build a hotel on it, and furnish it with all the necessary furniture, fixtures, and equipment. Once the place is ready to open, the operational costs will have to include a lot of fixed items as a result of all the required capital and resources tied up in those assets. As a real estate property, a hotel needs to carry those fixed costs, which are not reflective of the hotel's daily operating performance.

Hotels are not just capital assets, but also income-generating businesses. All those cost items that are directly related to selling a unit (room night) are classified as variable. There is no need to clean and re-supply a room if it remains vacant one night. Variable costs can also be described as the cost differential between an occupied and a vacant room.

The variable cost of a room night is the dollar amount it would cost on average to make up one room and get it ready for new occupancy. The steps involved in changing a room status from *occupied* to *vacant* vary based on the level of service and amenities a hotel provides. The housekeeping tasks of cleaning the room and providing fresh linen, towels, and bathroom supplies always contribute to the costs, as do the housekeeper's wages for the time spent on the room. High-end hotels may offer more gadgets, but they have to meet higher expectations as well. Even if a hotel does not offer designer bathrobes, the highest thread-count sheets, chocolate truffles, and remote-controlled shades, the basics that are provided to each new arriving guest can cost the hotel $10 to $40 per day. An unsold room does not incur this charge.

Revenue maximization is the logical way to address profitability challenges in the hotel business. Hotels need to drive top-line revenue to cover expenses and allow for profit. Cutting costs is seldom as effective, not only because it tends to harm the quality of service, but also because the only costs a hotel can manipulate in the short term are the variable ones, which constitute a small portion of total costs. Most hotel operational costs are fixed costs, which hotels cannot manipulate at will. The only way to achieve sustainable financial success is to maximize top-line revenue. The bottom line will be favorable only if the top line is strong and steady enough to meet financial objectives. Revenue management is critically important in helping managers meet this challenge.

Revenue Management Challenges

It is fair to say that the hotel industry has embraced revenue management.[1] It has become part of the mainstream over the years: we see more and more articles written about the various aspects of revenue management in both print and electronic media; it has become a standard agenda item at association meetings, conferences, symposia, and presentations at trade shows; colleges and universities are rolling out courses in it; and hotel executives no longer have to be persuaded that revenue management adds value to their businesses—it is accepted as evident by now.

Today offers a set of new challenges to all involved in the evolving discipline of revenue management. Let's take a look at a list of the top five emerging revenue management challenges.

Local or Centralized

There is a school of thought that revenue management is best applied if a number of individual operators of smaller hotels under the same management/ownership/brand set up a centralized regional structure where data can be processed and strategic decisions made. In this scenario, system outputs (such as rate fences) can be pushed out to the property-level managers.

According to this argument, resources are used most efficiently this way. Local expertise may be scarce, but centralized structures can use trained specialists to manage multiple units. Remote control can be effectively exercised as a result of real-time access to information and sufficient bandwidth coupled with lightning-fast processing speed. The numbers can be crunched anywhere and decisions instantly communicated, so it doesn't matter if the nerve center is down the hallway or a time zone away.

One can also propose an argument for decentralization. Provided there is qualified local expertise, all the data can be analyzed and managed locally, even on a portable device with sufficient computing power. There is no need for a centralized structure to call the play from a distance: locals may have better product knowledge and they can be more nimble if some tweaking is required when it comes to last-minute dynamic pricing and inventory allocation decisions (such as, "Instead of posting a super-saver rate on hotels.com, why don't we dump thirty rooms on priceline.com for tonight?").

There is no silver bullet. Each hotel will have to determine what works best under its given set of circumstances. The local-vs.-centralized issue will remain very much a subject of discussion.

Too Much Data

Technological improvements over the years have enabled operators to amass an ever-growing database of transactional data. Practically all important aspects of hotel operations have been digitized. We can gather valuable information not just about those guests who stay at our hotels and leave traces in the form of data with each swipe or tap of a card (whether it be to gain entry to the fitness room or to purchase a drink at the lounge); we can also collect data on those potential guests who have never even booked one of our rooms but have visited our home page. Also available are analytics on traffic sources to a landing page, time spent, abandon rate, and much more that may help us convert lookers to bookers someday. Terabytes of data are available to analyze, but we don't have enough people to do it.

Technology has outpaced the talent base. There is so much data to analyze and make sense of, but there is a shortage of well-educated revenue analysts, revenue managers, and directors of revenue to leverage the wealth of data and build strategies based on it.

Elevate to Strategic from Tactical and Embrace Total Revenue Management

Early revenue management efforts tended to focus only on tactics related to price manipulation. There is an evident need to move beyond this limited tactical approach. Leaders in the field now embrace a much more strategic approach.

Practicing strategic revenue management will separate seasoned revenue managers from novices. Total revenue management means moving from the management of room revenue only to the management of different revenue streams (including, at a minimum, function space and food and beverage). It might be a smart strategy to align total revenue management and the fast-paced field of distribution channel management, based on the logical conclusion that each revenue stream requires a different distribution strategy. Many believe that future growth will be built on strategy. One of the most fundamental issues of strategy development today is the question of whether it provides any strategic advantage for a hotel to compete on rate at all.

Monetize Social Media

Numerous ongoing discussions address the topic of measuring the effectiveness of the resources dedicated to social media. Revenue managers are a responsible bunch with analytical minds. They know how important it is to quantify the outcome of strategic decisions. *Return on engagement* and other soft measures don't seem to provide a good enough answer to owners and asset managers watching over the shoulders of revenue directors. A higher ranking on organic searches is wonderful to claim, especially if all a guest would do is organic search. More and more, travelers consult a variety of social media sites in the planning phase of a trip.

There seems to be a consensus that no responsible operator in a competitive market can justify a refusal to be part of the social media scene. No business is truly in the dark on social media; even those hotels that themselves stay mum can be discussed by others. Participation in social media is no longer an option: it is part of a hotel's curb appeal. However, the social media environment is such a fast-paced one that even a solid understanding of the rules of the game may not necessarily be rewarded with success.

How can one best justify marketing budgets when allocations to broadcast or print media compared to online are determined? Online marketing is a whole universe in its own right. Marketing spending can become quicksand as the media consumption habits of target demographics can shift relatively swiftly. The passive approach of creating awareness through marketing, then hoping to close a sale when the moment of decision to book arrives, seems so outdated. Revenue managers see the need to be at least part of the discussion at each step on the way through the purchase funnel as guests negotiate their way through. One thing is certain: new social media challenges will continue to unfold.

Harness the Power of Mobile

The battle of the screens is over; the battle between television and the computer is history. The winning screen is neither of the two, but a third one that has emerged right from our pocket (or purse) that can do more than a TV and computer combined. We call this device a smartphone for the time being, which is slightly baffling, as talk is often the last thing a smartphone is used for.

Hoteliers understand that mobile screens' dynamics are slightly different from those of the other two screens. The differences go beyond the pixel count: simplicity, speed, and functionality rule in the mobile world. More and more hoteliers are harnessing the power of location-based marketing, maximizing revenue through the mobile access to current and potential customers. The power of mobile means that a whole new marketing and sales arsenal is at the disposal of revenue managers. Quick response e-coupons or flash sales can help maximize revenue at a spa or a hotel bar, and tweets can be sent to a guest who requested adjoining rooms on arrival day. Hotels will have to master how to do that without being intrusive and disruptive. The learning process continues.

Endnote

1. This section is based on an article I wrote and published online on several websites.

Part II

Performance Measurement

Chapter 2 Outline

Internal Measures
    Revenue
    Occupancy Percentage
    Average Daily Rate
    RevPAR
    Contribution Margin (Net Revenue)
    Identical Net Room Revenue
    Marginal Revenue Considerations
    GOPPAR
    Other Measures
Case Study
Data Analytics Problems

Competency

1. Identify, define, and calculate several important internal performance measures that help to evaluate the results of operation. (pp. 17–30)

2

Internal Measurement Metrics

To MANAGE A BUSINESS EFFECTIVELY, one generally must have quantifiable goals and the means to measure how well those goals are being attained. Managers can evaluate the results of operations against internal and external measures or standards. The most useful internal measures will relate to the primary products and services a business provides. In the lodging industry, the primary product is the room night. As might be expected, most internal performance measures relate to the sales of room nights and the revenue generated from those sales.

The data that hotel analytics offers for revenue managers can be grouped into internal (property-level) data and external data that most frequently is divided into competitive set data and aggregate industry-level data. This chapter looks at a number of the most important internal measures used in managing a hotel or other lodging operation.

Internal Measures

This chapter focuses on interpreting a lodging operation's own data. The calculation and analysis that concentrate on a set of metrics derived from a hotel's own data and do not include a comparison to its competitors is termed an *internal* examination of metrics.

While revenue management is more than crunching numbers, the proper calculation of the most meaningful performance indicators is imperative. Management must be able to measure performance accurately. Hotels are capital-intensive businesses, and investors expect to be rewarded for their investments and the risks those investments entail. Investors will seek other investment options if a hotel's financial rewards do not align with their expectations. If other local properties, hotels in other markets, or other commercial real estate businesses provide better returns under substantially equal risk, investors may divest their interests in underperforming hotel assets and pursue their options elsewhere. The industry has witnessed such actions many times under such labels as "divestment of non-core assets," "diversification of investment portfolios," or "strategic re-alignment of the asset base," among others. If an asset performs up to expectations, the status quo is fine, but once an asset can't produce the expected return, the weighing of options begins. Revenue management can improve financial performance, thereby making the property a more attractive option for some investors. Conversely, some investors seek to acquire underperforming assets and turn them around by introducing revenue maximization strategies.

The only way to determine whether a hotel is underperforming is to measure the hotel's performance in comparison with some standard. Measurements are of little use without context. If a hotel has 70 percent occupancy in June, how does management decide whether this is good or bad? Internal performance measures are most commonly compared with three general standards. One standard is historical figures from comparable earlier periods. The past records of operation are crucial to have as a starting point of reference. If the above hotel has had 80 percent occupancies in the previous two Junes, the 70 percent figure for this June may be problematic. But if the hotel's previous years' figures for June were 50 percent and 60 percent, this year's figure has quite a different meaning.

The second common standard is the budget. If the hotel has budgeted for June with an expectation of 85 percent occupancy, an actual occupancy of 70 percent will likely call for investigation into the causes of the shortfall.

The third common standard is industry averages. When using industry averages, be careful to include only properties comparable in size, amenities, level of service, market orientation, age, and geographic market, if possible. Overall industry averages will include many kinds of properties that have little in common with any particular property, so those numbers will often reveal little of real use. But industry averages of comparable properties will provide an idea of how one property's performance compares with its industry segment.

New hotel developments have no historic data. In these cases, comparable hotels must be looked at and used as points of reference. There are excellent sources of information where data of this nature can be purchased.[1] These third-party sources frequently will also provide an analysis of whether the numbers need adjustment for a specific property.

When a hotel wants to improve its profitability, the first set of data to consider is the hotel's historic data. As stated earlier, the most informative variables will involve the hotel's primary product—the room night. These variables, often called key performance indicators (KPIs), include revenue, ADR, occupancy, and revenue per available room. Historical unit sales and revenue generated provide the first data set to look into.

Revenue

Revenue is the amount of sales, measured in the appropriate currency, generated from the sale of goods and services. The annual income statement has an entry for revenue for a business. It is customary to refer to revenue as a *top-line* item to reflect its position in the income statement (see Exhibit 1). This number can be broken down into quarterly, monthly, weekly, or even daily numbers if that helps managers with their analysis. The sales revenue data must be kept on file as it is generated, and it should be accessible any time management needs it. It can be compared as current year over last year, actual versus budget, the fiscal year-to-date, or any other way that serves a purpose.

Revenue can also be broken down by revenue centers. Room revenue is particularly important for revenue management and will be the first focus. Once managers have a good handle on room revenue management and implement revenue maximization strategies for rooms, they should move on to total revenue manage-

Exhibit 1   Statement of Income

STATEMENT OF INCOME

	Period	
	Current Year	**Prior Year**
REVENUE		
Rooms	$	$
Food and Beverage		
Other Operated Departments		
Miscellaneous Income		
Total Revenue		
EXPENSES		
Rooms		
Food and Beverage		
Other Operated Departments		
Administrative and General		
Information and Telecommunications Systems		
Sales and Marketing		
Property Operation and Maintenance		
Utilities		
Management Fees		
Non-Operating Expenses		
Interest Expense		
Depreciation and Amortization		
Loss or (Gain) on the Disposition of Assets		
Total Expenses		
INCOME BEFORE INCOME TAXES		
INCOME TAXES		
Current		
Deferred		
Total Income Taxes		
NET INCOME	$	$

Source: *Uniform System of Accounts for the Lodging Industry,* Eleventh Revised Edition (Lansing, Mich.: American Hotel & Lodging Educational Institute, 2014), p. 170.

ment and involve all of the other hotel revenue streams as well. These may include food and beverage, catering, function space rental, spa services, parking services, retail sales, and other revenues, depending on the particulars of a given operation.

The formula for determining room revenue is quite straightforward:

$$\text{Room revenue} = \text{Room nights sold} \times \text{Room rate charged}$$

For example, if a hotel sells 6,450 room nights at $122 per room, (gross) room revenue will equal 6,450 × $122, or $786,900. If a hotel wishes to know its room revenue total *after* any guest acquisition costs (defined below), it will use the room rate the hotel actually receives regardless of what the guests actually pay—for example, to third-party intermediaries and resellers.

Occupancy Percentage

Occupancy percentage is one of the most common performance measures in the lodging industry. It expresses the proportion of rooms sold to total rooms. The formula is:

$$\text{Occupancy percentage} = \frac{\text{Room nights sold in a period}}{\text{Room nights available in that same period}} \times 100$$

For example, consider a 300-unit hotel that has sold 1,428 room nights in one week. Total room nights available will equal 300 rooms × 7 nights, or 2,100 room nights. The weekly occupancy of this hotel is therefore 1,428 ÷ 2,100 × 100, or 68 percent.

Some hotel industry data aggregators and analysts use slightly different terminology. It is also acceptable to phrase the calculation of occupancy percentage as *demand divided by supply*, where *demand* means the number of rooms sold for a period, and *supply* refers to the number of rooms available for the same period.

Neither occupancy percentage nor revenue should be analyzed on their own. Both need to be considered when we examine a hotel's performance.

Average Daily Rate

The *average daily rate (ADR)* expresses the average room rate guests pay for rooms in a given period. It should be calculated on a daily, weekly, and monthly basis. The formula is:

$$\text{ADR} = \frac{\text{(Net) room revenue}}{\text{Number of room nights sold}}$$

For example, if total room revenue for a week is $154,240 and the hotel sold 1,428 room nights that week, the ADR is $154,240 ÷ 1,428, or $108.

In recent years, many properties have begun to calculate both an internal and an external ADR. This is due to the proliferation of distribution channels that hotels often use to help sell their rooms. These distribution channels all have costs associated with them (collectively known as *guest acquisition costs*), sometimes from agreements that let them buy hotel rooms at a discount for resale, other times for earning a commission for the sale that the hotel pays later. In such cases, the amount the guest pays for a room is not the amount the hotel receives from the sale. For internal purposes, it makes better sense to calculate the ADR based on what the hotel actually receives. The actual sales price to the guest less the guest acquisition cost provides the net room rate.

However, for external purposes, it is better to use the full amount that the guest pays. The primary use of the external ADR is to compare one hotel with other similar properties. It makes sense to compare the prices guests actually pay, since one hotel will generally not have access to its comp set's detailed internal guest acquisition costs needed to compare net room rates for a net ADR.

Tracking and benchmarking the ADR is important. A hotel makes an effort to charge rates that both provide the perception of value for the guest and allow the hotel to attain its financial objectives. The traditional expectation of ADR is that it will gradually increase from year to year. However, circumstances may at times thwart that expectation. Market pressures or the aging of a property may cause ADR to fall from one fiscal period to another. Calculating and tracking ADR changes allows management to quantify the impact of price changes, get closer to their root causes, and determine what can be done about the problem. In some cases, a declining ADR is caused by an inferior product. If management chooses not to invest in an upgrade of the hotel, the hotel can keep losing market share. When reinvestment is not chosen or available, such hotels are sometimes significantly repositioned down-market; for example, a struggling upper-tier hotel might be successfully repositioned as a competitive mid-tier hotel after reflagging the property.

The question of whether complimentary room nights should be included in the ADR calculation sometimes comes up. According to the *Uniform System of Accounts for the Lodging Industry,* Eleventh Revised Edition, they should not. Those room nights were not sold and did not generate room revenue, so including them would distort the result of an ADR calculation. If a room night was not sold for revenue, it should not be counted for sales performance analysis.

RevPAR

Occupancy percentage and ADR are both common performance measures, but sometimes they can appear to disagree. Consider a hotel's performance on two nights. The first night, the hotel has 70 percent occupancy with an ADR of $95. The second night, the hotel has 75 percent occupancy with an ADR of $90. Which appears to be the better situation? ADR suggests the first night, but occupancy percentage suggests the second night. One way to resolve this conflict is to combine occupancy percentage and ADR into a single statistic. This combined measure is called *revenue per available room (RevPAR)*. RevPAR is a way of evaluating management's success in realizing the business potential of a hotel in a given period. RevPAR calculations have become the most frequently used measure of room revenue performance. Two different formulas can calculate RevPAR:

$$\text{RevPAR} = \frac{\text{(Net) room revenue for a period}}{\text{Total rooms available for that period}}$$

$$\text{RevPAR} = \text{(Net) ADR} \times \text{Occupancy percentage}$$

The two formulas produce the same result.

In the example above, the RevPAR for the first night is $95 × 70 percent, or $66.50. The RevPAR for the second night is $90 × 75 percent, or $67.50. From a RevPAR standpoint, the second night appears to be better.

As is true for the ADR, many properties now calculate both an internal and an external RevPAR. The internal version (using net room revenue or net ADR) provides a better picture of operating results, while the external version (using total room revenue or the external ADR) is appropriate for comparisons with other properties.

RevPAR can be a useful KPI, but users must be careful not to read more into it than is there. First, RevPAR inherently appears to favor the result that produces the highest revenue. But it will not always be true that the highest revenue also produces the highest profit. RevPAR ignores cost factors that must also be considered. Second, and more interesting from a revenue management point of view, similar or even identical RevPARs may result from very different operating positions. Consider two scenarios in a 120-unit hotel. In the first scenario, the hotel sells 66 room nights at an ADR of $100. In the second scenario, the hotel sells 100 room nights at an ADR of $66. In both situations, total room revenue is $6,600 and RevPAR is $55. Are these scenarios equivalent? In terms of room revenue, yes, they are. But the total revenue earned comes from very different operating circumstances. Is one better? How might that be determined?

Before we address those questions, consider what might drive the hotel—intentionally or not—toward one result over the other. It is a management truism that a business will get the employee behavior it rewards. If the reward system is not properly aligned with management's goals, the chance of reaching those goals is diminished. If the reward system favors higher ADRs, the front office manager's incentive will be to drive ADR, resulting in a management preference for the first scenario ($100 ADR). If the reward system rewards the front office manager for filling rooms, the manager will prefer and work toward the higher occupancy percentage (83.33 percent) of the second scenario. If the reward system favors RevPAR, a manager might see the two scenarios as essentially equivalent.

So, is one scenario more desirable? The answer is almost certainly yes, but *which one* is more desirable will vary by hotel. There is no easy way to choose one scenario over the other because there are arguments for and against both. The argument for selling at a higher ADR with a lower occupancy is that the hotel will have fewer rooms to clean for the same revenue, so variable costs will be lower with the lower occupancy option. The argument for higher occupancy at a lower ADR is that having more guests could lead to additional revenue opportunities in the hotel's other revenue centers (parking, food and beverage, pay-per-view movie sales, and so on). Until we determine and compare the variable cost savings of the first scenario with the expected additional net revenue of the second scenario, we cannot identify the better option.

For that matter, even *after* we perform such a comparison, the answer may remain unresolved. This is because, despite their equivalent revenues, a revenue manager would see the two scenarios as being significantly different and the results of very different strategies. A guest willing to pay $100 for a room night is neither better nor worse than a guest willing to pay $66 per room night for the same room. But managers must recognize that these two guests belong to different market segments and targeting them requires distinctly different approaches. A hotel must identify its prime target market. Because a lot of other decisions flow from this market choice, the choice to be in the $66 ADR market or the $100 ADR market is a strategic decision.

In other words, a high ADR is not inherently better than a low ADR. The *appropriateness* of the ADR for the given hotel and target market is the central issue. Mid-market hotels might provide better profitability than luxury hotels in certain markets. The two hotel types require different investments per room and have different operational costs, staffing levels, clienteles, and revenue mixes to start with. The popularity of limited-service hotels (those offering no food service outlets) is proof that there are lucrative returns in strategic decisions to enter carefully chosen markets with the right product, regardless of price points. It would be a tremendous mistake to believe that only glamorous high-end hotels make good businesses. ADR alone is in no way indicative of financial success or failure. The answer to the question of whether the $66 or $100 ADR is better is ultimately this: it depends on the business strategy of the given hotel.

As is true with all performance measures, it is important that management track RevPAR over a period of time so that significant changes can be identified and, if necessary, investigated. A change in RevPAR can be the result of a change in either ADR or occupancy, but in real life it is unusual to have the luxury of simple scenarios. Most likely, changes tend to happen in both. Revenue managers have to look beyond the figures to see the underlying trends in order to evaluate and make strategic decisions. The revenue manager's analysis should identify which component (ADR or occupancy) is the primary driver of the change. Suppose analysis reveals that an increase in ADR was driven by rate increases rather than occupancy. Some issues to consider would then be: How long is it reasonable to expect the market to absorb further rate increases? Is there a realistic expectation of boosting occupancy in the future? What tactics should be deployed? A significant part of finding the right answers depends on asking the right questions.

Contribution Margin (Net Revenue)

The performance measures discussed so far have worked only with gross and in some cases net room revenue data. None of them has considered expenses other than guest acquisition costs. Revenue measures are a good start in revenue management analysis, but they are only a start. The next step is to consider room expenses—specifically, the variable cost of providing the product (a room night). The variable cost per unit (room night) sold has traditionally been considered the added cost incurred to clean, refresh, and resupply a guestroom. (See the sidebar on the next page for a discussion of how this traditional definition is currently faring under more complicated circumstances.) This cost is not incurred for unsold rooms. When room revenues and variable costs are known, we can calculate the *contribution margin* or *net room revenue*. The contribution margin is the amount of sales revenue left over to contribute to covering fixed costs and, once fixed costs are paid, profit. The formula for a given room's contribution margin is:

Contribution margin = (Net) room rate − Variable cost

For example, if the room rate is $138 and the variable cost of that room is $18, the contribution margin for that room night is $138 - $18, or $120. Different room types may be priced differently and incur different variable costs (for example, the variable costs for deluxe rooms and suites are likely higher than those for standard rooms). The overall rooms division contribution margin is determined by totaling the margins of the individual rooms. If a room is sold through a distribution channel that incurs a guest acquisition cost, subtract the variable costs from the net room rate.

The contribution margin of room revenue came under significant pressure during the recessionary period in North America that started in December 2007. These pressures posed a significant challenge for revenue managers, and the industry witnessed a variety of approaches to dealing with them.

> **The Changing Nature of Variable Costs**
>
> A variable cost is incurred only when an additional unit is sold. For many decades, a hotel's variable room costs have been considered to be the labor and materials costs incurred to clean and resupply a dirty room. When more than one room type is available, the cleaning costs may vary by room type. Larger and/or fancier rooms may have higher cleaning costs than basic or standard rooms.
>
> Those were simpler times. Today, the enormous growth of third-party distribution channels has created a new kind of variable cost called the guest acquisition cost. Like the cleaning costs, it is incurred only if a room is sold. But unlike cleaning costs, the amount can vary greatly and is not directly based on room type. It does not even apply to all rooms sold, since the hotel may sell its own rooms without incurring a guest acquisition cost.
>
> Since this type of variable cost does not behave like the traditional variable costs, it is common to think of it as somehow separate from variable costs, even though it meets the definition of being a cost that is only incurred if a unit is sold.
>
> Nonetheless, costs that are directly relatable to a room sales transaction are rightly referred to as variable. Today as a result of successfully digitizing all points of interaction with customers, we can accurately measure relatable costs. We know what the guest paid as a sell-rate and we know what amount the hotel actually received after all associated costs were subtracted. We pay a variety of intermediaries as well, but not like the old world 10 percent commission to a travel agent. We have dozens of arrangements with CROs, Brand.coms, OTAs, Internet platforms, search engines that charge per click or per transaction, etc. Furthermore, these fees are not constant: some are percentages, some are fixed amounts, and because of these complexities we can't even simply lump them into one convenient category like room cleaning expenses.
>
> Strictly speaking, guest acquisition costs are variable costs. They need to be measured and accounted for. But in our discussions, we will separate them from the traditional housekeeping variable costs and address them in the difference between gross or total room revenue and net room revenue.

A significant portion of revenue managers in saturated urban markets believed that decreasing their rates would help them retain market share. Therefore, discounting became rampant and even aggressive on occasion. A room night that sold for less, however, still required the same cleaning costs; thus, contribution margins fell. To mitigate the financial shortfall, many hotels downgraded the product to some extent in an effort to contain costs and provide for an acceptable margin even at discounted rates. Examples of product downgrades included the following:

- Cheaper toiletries
- Replacement of individual packages of shower gel, shampoo, and conditioner with wall-mounted dispensers
- Discontinued room service

- Morning papers no longer delivered to guestrooms (available only for pickup in the lobby)
- Free Wi-Fi Internet access offered only in common areas (such as lobbies); usage fee charged for access in guestrooms
- Refreshment of linen offered only after every second night

Some hotels took other approaches to riding out the period of softened demand for rooms. Some revenue managers were convinced that discounting rates and downgrading the product were ill-conceived ideas, so they resisted the pressures to discount and held room rates steady, but offered upgrades or value-added items at no extra charge to offer value to guests. Examples of such upgrades include the following:

- No-charge or discounted parking instead of paid parking
- Inclusion of breakfast in the room rate
- Wi-Fi Internet access provided at no charge
- No charge for local phone calls
- No charge for late check-out
- Free in-room movies instead of pay-per-view movies
- Free morning paper on request from a selection of dailies
- Free access to the business center
- Free storage of luggage for late departures

It is interesting to compare the results of these two different approaches to the same issue. Those hotels that chose to discount and dilute the quality of their value proposition were able to steal market share on occasion, but they did not benefit financially; their jump in occupancy was not large enough to compensate for the decrease in rates. They have also had a hard time rebuilding their rates and returning to pre-recession pricing levels.

Those operators who held rates steady and offered extras at no charge took a financial hit as well, but they found themselves in a much better financial position when demand started picking up again. They could opt to gradually phase out the freebies and increase their margins without changing their rates, or to keep the extras and increase their rates in line with those hotels that stopped the practice of steep discounting.

Identical Net Room Revenue

One way to apply the contribution margin is by analyzing scenarios with changing price points and occupancy levels. The objective of this calculation is to identify the occupancy percentages that will generate *identical net room revenue* at changing average daily rates. For this example, assume a hotel's ADR is $138 and its average variable cost is $18. If current occupancy is 72 percent, what occupancy would be required to generate the same net room revenue if the hotel lowered the ADR to $115? The formula is:

$$\text{Required new occupancy} = \frac{\text{Current contribution margin}}{\text{New contribution margin}} \times \text{Current occupancy \%} \times 100$$

$$= \frac{\$138 - \$18}{\$115 - \$18} \times 0.72 \times 100$$

$$= 89.07\%$$

The calculation reveals that this hotel would need 89.07 percent occupancy to generate identical net room revenue if the ADR were lowered from $138 to $115 while the variable cost per room night remained unchanged at $18. The formula works just as well for those scenarios that raise rates. If the managers in our example were considering an increase to a $143 ADR, an occupancy of 69.12 percent would generate the same contribution margin (net revenue).

This formula helps management to analyze different scenarios by quantifying the possible outcomes of pricing decisions. The revenue manager must determine whether the increase in occupancy that would be necessary following a rate reduction would be a realistic goal. In our previous example, a discount of $23 (from $138 down to $115) required a 17 percent boost in occupancy to generate the same net room revenue. Can the hotel make that happen? Management should determine what rate changes would be consistent with the financial obligations of the given hotel in light of supply/demand dynamics. A hotel's revenue manager should be best equipped to conduct an analysis of this nature and to help the management team devise a strategy for reaching the budgetary targets of the hotel.

Marginal Revenue Considerations

Marginal revenue is the additional revenue gained from selling one more product unit. *Marginal cost* is the additional cost incurred from selling one more product unit (and is basically another name for a single unit's variable cost). There are two very different situations in which marginal revenue considerations may play a role in room sales. In the first situation, it is assumed and accepted that the hotel is performing well according to its financial objectives (budget) and that it will be able to cover all its expenses as planned. Given these assumptions, a revenue manager interested in maximizing marginal revenues might advocate lowering the prices of unsold rooms to increase unit sales. In this case, the logic is that, as long as the marginal (variable) costs are covered, the rooms department will earn net revenue from such sales. Using the previous example in which the cost of preparing a room for sale was $18, any net room rate over $18 will contribute some net revenue. This is a surprisingly low dollar figure. If a hotel that is on track with regard to its performance targets wishes to generate a buzz in the market with a super saver special campaign, this approach is one to consider. This pricing is likely not sustainable in the long run as its contribution margin is probably too small to cover all costs, but if the hotel has already covered its fixed costs, this approach may generate some extra net revenue.

The second situation applies during periods of significant market pressure and might be considered the *contribution margin at any rate* calculation. There are times when extraordinary events result in a large drop in demand. In recent memory, the industry has witnessed such dramatic developments after the September 11, 2001, terrorist attacks in New York City and Washington, D.C.; after the SARS epidemic in the spring of 2003 in Toronto, Ontario; and in New Orleans after Hurricane Katrina hit in August 2005, to recall a few. When the market shrinks so quickly, hotels must compete for the business of fewer travelers. In such cases, meeting or exceeding one's budget may become less pressing than simply surviving the downturn. The fixed costs still must be paid, and operations become cash-starved very fast. The thinking in such situations is that *any* room rate higher than the *total* costs per room night would keep the hotel in business. In these cases, the room rate must generate enough to cover the variable costs per room plus all fixed costs broken down to a per-room-night basis. That is, the total costs per room night are calculated by adding up both the fixed and the variable costs per room night. To establish the pro-rated measure of fixed costs per room night, the amount of the hotel's total fixed costs is divided by the number of room nights forecasted to be sold in the same fiscal period. To generate cash flow and maintain the hope of riding out the market slump, a lot of operators resort to this thinking.

GOPPAR

Gross operating profit per available room (GOPPAR) takes the examination of profitability one step further. The GOPPAR calculation compares gross operating profit for a period—a line item appearing on the summary operating statement promulgated by the *Uniform System of Accounts for the Lodging Industry,* Eleventh Revised Edition (see Exhibit 2)—to rooms available for that period. The calculation can be done monthly, quarterly, or annually. The formula is:

$$\text{GOPPAR} = \frac{\text{Gross operating profit for a period}}{\text{Available rooms during that period}}$$

For example, a 350-unit hotel with an annual gross operating profit of $4,650,000 would have an annual GOPPAR of $13,285.71 ($4,650,000 ÷ 350 rooms).

This measure assesses cost efficiency. While RevPAR is useful for measuring revenue performance, managers are increasingly interested in evaluating overall profitability. Measuring gross profit can expose operational inefficiencies. It is one thing to be able to drive revenue and make the top line of an income statement look impressive. It is another to make the bottom line impressive as well.

The interest in gross operating profit has grown in part because of the proliferation of management contracts over the last couple of decades. The North American hotel industry in particular has embraced the trend of separating hotel ownership from hotel management. That is, it is becoming less common for hotel owners to manage their own hotels. Rather, they hire professional management companies to operate their hotels for a fee. Management contracts have undergone some changes over the years. Most early management contracts based the management company's fee on a percentage of revenue. This approach, however, did not align the interests of the owner and the manager in the most ideal manner. Managers could earn good fees by driving revenue numbers up, even when operational profits were down. One way to address this issue was the introduction of incentive fees based on gross operating profit. Another commonly used term is *EBITDA,* which refers to earnings before interest, taxes, depreciation, and

Exhibit 2 Summary Operating Statement [For Owners]

	Period Of					
	Current Period			Year-To-Date		
	Actual	Forecast/ Budget	Prior Year	Actual	Forecast/ Budget	Prior Year
Rooms Available:						
Rooms Sold:						
Occupancy:						
ADR:						
Rooms RevPAR:						
Total RevPAR:						

	Period Of											
	Current Period						Year-To-Date					
	Actual		Forecast/ Budget		Prior Year		Actual		Forecast/ Budget		Prior Year	
	$	%[1]	$	%[1]	$	%[1]	$	%[1]	$	%[1]	$	%[1]
Operating Revenue												
Rooms												
Food and Beverage												
Other Operated Departments												
Miscellaneous Income												
Total Operating Revenue												
Departmental Expenses												
Rooms												
Food and Beverage												
Other Operated Departments												
Total Departmental Expenses												
Total Departmental Profit												
Undistributed Operating Expenses												
Administrative and General												
Information and Telecommunications Systems												
Sales and Marketing												
Property Operation and Maintenance												
Utilities												
Total Undistributed Expenses												
Gross Operating Profit												
Management Fees												
Income Before Non-Operating Income and Expenses												
Non-Operating Income and Expenses												
Income												
Rent												
Property and Other Taxes												
Insurance												
Other												
Total Non-Operating Income and Expenses												
Earnings Before Interest, Taxes, Depreciation, and Amortization												
Interest, Depreciation, and Amortization												
Interest												
Depreciation												
Amortization												
Total Interest, Depreciation, and Amortization												
Income Before Income Taxes												
Income Taxes												
Net Income												

[1] All revenues and expenses should be shown as a percentage of total operating revenue, except departmental expenses, which should be shown as a percentage of their respective departmental revenue.

Source: *Uniform System of Accounts for the Lodging Industry,* Eleventh Revised Edition (Lansing, Mich.: American Hotel & Lodging Educational Institute, 2014), p. 4.

amortization. Look at Exhibit 2 again. Note that every line item above the gross operating profit is the responsibility of the management team, while every line item below gross operating profit is typically the responsibility of the owner. It makes sense to measure management's performance only on those things it can reasonably control. Gross profit calculations and GOPPAR became of interest as a consequence. GOPPAR is also consistent with the objective of revenue maximization strategies and tactics that aim to improve profitability.

Other Measures

Other measures can be calculated for the purpose of revenue performance analysis. One is *total revenue per available room (TRevPAR)*. Unlike RevPAR, which uses only room revenue, TRevPAR considers total revenue from all revenue centers. Operators that practice total revenue management will find this a meaningful indicator to track over time.

Another measure is *revenue per available customer (RevPAC)*. RevPAC is an indicator that could reveal meaningful information if tracked over time. However, managers face significant challenges related to the accuracy of RevPAC. The first challenge is to establish an accurate house count. This is problematic because many hotels do not know precisely how many hotel guests stay in-house on a given night. No universally accepted standard addresses whether double or triple occupancy rooms should command different room rates. Some hotels charge extra per person; others don't. Those that don't will perhaps have less incentive to spend time and effort gathering an accurate count. In some cases, a guest may sign in but may not fill out a registration card if his or her roommate has already signed in.

If the RevPAC calculation is based on total sales revenue, the revenue generated outside the rooms division can become an intriguing issue. Given that this formula is meant to relate revenue to the number of hotel guests, should the revenue include spending by non-guests as well—say, locals patronizing the hotel restaurant? We might believe that this would undermine the accuracy and usefulness of the RevPAC results, but it can be very difficult to accurately separate food and beverage revenues into those generated by guests and those generated by local patrons. Not every check is traceable. Some hotel guests may charge their dinners to their room folios, while others may pay cash. There may be no clear link back to a guest. Similarly, events and catering may produce significant revenue from a local clientele. Should one include that revenue when conducting a RevPAC analysis? These are questions with no easy answers. Once management makes the decisions, though, perhaps the most important aspect of RevPAC calculations is consistency. After a hotel determines a methodology for its calculations, it should consistently follow that method.

Another calculation that may help a hotel develop an in-depth understanding of its market is the analysis of spending per stay. A hotel has the data to establish how many invoices are paid in a fiscal period from the cashiers' daily reports. The combined total amount of the invoices settled can be divided by the number of payment transactions processed. Actual average dollar spending per guest visits reveals valuable data regarding the hotel's clientele. The data also expresses the effectiveness of the hotel's sales efforts. Mining the data can lead to identifying spending patterns on a variety of revenue streams and other trends.

Endnote

1. STR (formerly Smith Travel Research) offers STR Global at www.STRglobal.com. STR has a selection of market-specific reports (STAR is a great example), and it also publishes www.hotelnewsnow.com, which is a reliable source of general industry news, trends, insights, reports, and blogs. Another excellent source is TravelClick at www.travelclick.com, which has a number of products (including Hotelligence and Rate360). Hotel Valuation Services at www.hvs.com offers market reports based on aggregate data plus relevant articles and archives.

References

Banker, Rajiv D., Gordon Potter, and Dhinu Srinivasan. 2005. "Association of Nonfinancial Performance Measures with the Financial Performance of a Lodging Chain." *Cornell Hotel and Restaurant Administration Quarterly* 46 (4): 394–412.

Ingold, Anthony, Una McMahon-Beattie, and Ian Yeoman, eds. 2000. *Yield Management: Strategies for the Service Industries*. 2nd ed. London: Thomson Learning.

Case Study: KPIs and Incentives

Lance Wilkins is a retired account manager who used to work in the sales department of a television broadcaster. For decades, he made his living selling television advertising spots. He'd had a successful career, and, looking back at it, he considered himself lucky. During the last few years before retiring, he had witnessed a gradual shift in the viewing habits of the population. People started to watch less TV and spend more time online. TV program ratings took a hit, and advertisers did the logical thing: they cut their ad budgets for TV and increased them for online advertising. That meant that Lance's job got harder and harder.

Lance retired the day he reached the minimum retirement age. He decided to move on to a new phase of his life: instead of riding quietly into the sunset, he took his retirement savings and invested in something he had been considering for years—he bought a small motel on the Florida coast. Lance was convinced he could easily manage a simple business like a motel without a restaurant, and fancied becoming an owner of a resort motel where he could oversee a business and feel like he was on a perpetual vacation at the same time. The reality proved to be somewhat different from that happy dream, however.

The property that Lance purchased was a 65-room motel called The Windjammer. Lance decided to make no personnel changes and to keep all 20 of the motel's staff members, who all seemed to be decent, hard-working, reliable individuals. Lance himself had never worked in a hotel or motel before, so he studied the reports and financial statements of The Windjammer carefully in order to develop an understanding of the business.

Lance noticed that on most nights the motel had a large number of unsold rooms. It intrigued him that 25 to 30 units frequently stayed vacant while the other rooms were sold successfully. Why couldn't all or almost all of the rooms be sold? He decided to do something to address that question, and, being a former salesman, he understood the importance of motivation. He talked to Barbara, who was in charge of the front office. It was Wednesday of the first week in March. He offered her an incentive in the form of a performance bonus for each sold-out night for the rest of the month.

"I think it's possible to fill the motel, provided I have the flexibility to use different price points," suggested Barbara. Lance told her he wanted to sell out on as many nights as possible and authorized Barbara to use whatever tactics she saw fit—after all, she was the one with the industry experience. They agreed to discuss the March results early in April.

One day in the first week of April, Lance and Barbara reviewed the motel's reports for March over cups of coffee in the back office behind the front desk. The Windjammer's occupancy rate showed a record high for the whole month. The motel had produced a monthly occupancy of 86 percent! Lance could hardly contain his satisfaction. Fourteen sold-out nights! They came really close to a full house on a number of other nights as well. Lance congratulated Barbara on a job well done and handed her an envelope with a check. The performance bonus was well deserved, he thought.

Lance kept studying the monthly reports after Barbara returned to her post at the front desk. He was pleased with himself and couldn't stop smiling—until he saw the report on room rates. He cleaned his glasses and took a closer look at the printout, because he didn't believe his eyes at first. The motel's posted room rate was $75 in March. After all group discounts, senior discounts, and agency commissions were factored in, Lance expected the average net rate for March to be at least in the high $50 range. Anything over $56 would have been fine with him. However, The Windjammer's net rate was only $32.18. Lance couldn't believe it. Clearly, Barbara had discounted frequently and heavily to sell out.

After some time for reflection and more coffee, Lance realized that March's incentive for Barbara had involved only one key variable, which could account for the problem. He wanted to be a shrewd hotelier, and, after a chat with Barbara, she accepted the new challenge for the new month. Lance would pay her a performance bonus for April if the motel's ADR reached $60 or more.

April was a month of softer demand, but as far as Lance was concerned the motel had a good chance to keep its rates up. A competitor motel in the area started an extensive renovation project and closed down half of its rooms as well as its outdoor pool. Also, the new highway sign for The Windjammer was finally put up, and Lance had high hopes for that as well.

April was not as busy as March had been. Anyone could see that by simply looking at the number of cars in the motel's parking lot, which Lance had a habit of doing each night. He also noticed that the vehicle models were somewhat different in April: he saw old, beat-up cars less frequently than he had in March and noted more new-looking SUVs and import autos. He prepared for the end-of-the-month meeting with Barbara with eager anticipation.

At the meeting, Lance was impressed by the increased ADR for April. He congratulated Barbara for reaching a record ADR of $67.48, and handed her another bonus. Clearly, Barbara had stopped the practice of indiscriminate heavy discounting; this change had resulted in a dramatic ADR turnaround. In fact, she had not made any rooms available to OTAs, so the ADR was also the net rate.

Unfortunately, it was not only the ADR that changed dramatically in April. The motel's monthly occupancy took a nose dive, dropping to 41 percent—less than half of the occupancy in March!

Lance scratched his head. He was learning the lodging business the hard way, he thought ruefully. He considered reading up on room statistics and hotel data analytics. He had recently heard about a key performance indicator called RevPAR that he needed to investigate further, and he also had read about the importance of monitoring variable costs. He knew it cost him, on average, $16 to clean one guestroom. He decided he'd better run some financial reports and look them over before discussing the next performance bonus with Barbara.

Discussion Questions

1. Which RevPAR is better for a hotel owner and/or a hotel manager: the one in March or the one in April? Is there a meaningful difference?
2. Take the March hotel data (rate, occupancy, variable cost per room) and calculate it: what occupancy would be required in April with the new increased ADR to generate identical net room revenue?
3. Take the April hotel data (rate, occupancy, variable cost per room) and calculate it: what occupancy would be required to generate identical net room revenue with the lower ADR of March?
4. What did Lance learn after he developed the first and second performance incentives for Barbara?

 ## Data Analytics Problems

Problem 1

Hotel data analytics help us appreciate the pattern of changes in the daily occupancy of hotels. The following table represents a location-based breakdown of hotel occupancy percentages by the day of the week. A comparative analysis of the busiest days reveals a difference between the highest-occupancy day in an airport hotel and an urban hotel.

Occupancy Percentage by Day

Location	Sun	Mon	Tue	Wed	Thu	Fri	Sat
Urban	50.3	71.4	79.5	80.9	77.2	81.8	85.9
Suburban	44.2	62.9	70.3	71.4	67.3	74.2	79.3
Airport	51.2	70.8	79.2	81.3	77.6	77.7	78.2
Interstate	38.8	55.2	61.3	62.5	60.3	67.9	70.7
Resort	45.2	54.5	60.3	64.5	64.7	77.4	83.2
Small Metro	36.6	54.6	60.2	61.4	58.6	68.2	73.1

Discussion Questions

1. Which day of the week is the busiest for the airport property? the urban property? Are they the same?
2. What management decisions will the data analysis affect?

Problem 2

Hotel Data by Day of the Week

	Sun	Mon	Tue	Wed	Thu	Fri	Sat
Occupancy	56.3	68.2	76.5	82.9	87.2	82.2	80.9
ADR	115.21	165.80	170.95	182.62	187.38	184.52	196.83
RevPAR	64.86	113.08	130.78	151.39	163.40	151.68	159.24

Discussion Questions

1. What day has the highest RevPAR?
2. What day has the highest ADR?
3. Which performance metric is the main driver of the best day in RevPAR performance?
4. What could you suggest to improve the example hotel's revenue performance if the variable cost per room night is $19?

Chapter 3 Outline

Competitive Set
Market Share
The Use of Market Intelligence
    Big Data and Market Intelligence
Measurement Challenges
Case Studies

Competencies

1. Describe the purpose of a competitive set and the factors one must consider when creating one properly. (pp. 35–40)

2. Calculate market share and penetration indexes and explain what they reveal. (pp. 40–42)

3. Identify potential sources of market intelligence. (pp. 43–44)

4. Discuss the significant challenges that beset most forms of measurement and the efforts to interpret measurement results. (pp. 44–46)

3
External Measurement Metrics

THIS CHAPTER FOCUSES ON EXTERNAL data analytics. It discusses how to master the comparative analysis of one lodging operation's performance metrics against the key performance indicators (KPIs) of other hotels in its competitive set. While internal measures compare a hotel's performance with its own history or its budget, they do not provide a complete picture on their own. It is also important to look at various external measures. A hotel does not exist in a vacuum. Management decisions in one hotel may provoke one or more responses in competing hotels, which in turn may provoke further decisions and adjustments. Most hotels compete directly for guests with other hotels. To gain a true understanding of a hotel's performance in this dynamic marketplace, one must be able to measure that performance in a meaningful way. This chapter addresses three important external measures: the competitive set, fair market share, and market penetration. The chapter closes with a look at the use of market intelligence, including big data, and the challenges that measurement methods can present.

Competitive Set

Once a hotel's management has a clear understanding of its hotel's internal performance measures, it needs to compare its hotel with those hotels it considers its competitors. This group of hotels is referred to as the *competitive set* or *comp set*. Which hotels belong in the comp set?

Each hotel should identify its competition. Should a budget hotel located on the airport strip consider an upscale downtown hotel a competitor? It probably should not. Hotels in close proximity with similar product offerings and rates should generally constitute the comp set. The criteria for defining a comp set could be based on a fundamental question: are the hotels included in the comp set targeting the same clientele? Helpful considerations for comp set definition include the following:

- *Geographic location:* A potential guest could see hotels in close proximity as options. In metropolitan markets with a high density, this proximity can be any distance that makes sense, from a couple of blocks to a 15-minute driving distance. A hotel revenue manager can locate his or her property on a map and draw a circle around the hotel to identify competitors within a given distance. In rural or resort markets, the distances that need measurement may include not only those to nearby competing properties, but also those for any competing properties that are roughly the same distance from a main point of reference. Hotels located in opposite directions but similar driving distances away from an attraction (say, an airport or a theme park) can easily compete for the same traveler. In resort markets, the distance from the beach or from the ski runs can influence vacationers' hotel selections.

- *Amenities:* Once the geographic boundaries are set, hotels within those boundaries can be added to or eliminated from the comp set based on other criteria. Hotels offering comparable amenities should be considered competitors. Hotels without parking, fitness, and/or convention facilities will have to decide for themselves whether they compete against properties equipped with those features. Any amenity that is relevant in the eyes of the guest can matter (such as room service or pay-per-view movie channels). Full-service hotels may target travelers whose needs differ from those of travelers that limited-service hotels target. Extended-stay hotels may not include a top-tier deluxe-service boutique hotel in their comp set even if it is located on the same block, since they offer very different amenities and don't vie for the same market segment.

- *Rates:* Price range and price structure both need to be considered. Hotels in the same vicinity with similar amenities and comparable rates mean alternative hotel choices from the guest's point of view. Based on these attributes, it makes sense to include these properties in the comp set. *Price structure* refers to the existence of similar multi-tiered pricing, perhaps including seasonal rates, government rates, convention rates, and senior rates. Weekend packages and frequent guest discounts can also be included in the comparison. If both the price points and the price structure are comparable with a given hotel in the same vicinity, it definitely deserves to be considered a competitor.

- *Ratings:* Rating agencies that award diamonds (AAA/CAA) or stars (Mobil Travel Guide, Canada Select) do thorough inspections. Potential guests see the same rating in the same locale as a sign of comparable product quality. The rating services carefully look at a variety of attributes, from the curb appeal, maintenance, and cleanliness of the premises to the level of service and competency of the staff. A hotel with the same rating in the same market should be seen as a competitor.

    A Note on Ratings: Technological developments in recent years have changed the meaning and context of ratings. The consumer trend of peer-to-peer travel and sharing via social media, together with a growing public distrust of ratings agencies and promotional corporate information in general, means that increasing numbers of travelers consult the reviews of fellow travelers before booking resort or hotel accommodations. Consumer ratings on such websites as TripAdvisor.com, Hotels.com, Travelocity.com, and Expedia.com thus are rapidly changing the ratings landscape. Consumers who post reviews are not necessarily trained in rating hotels, but hotel operators cannot stop them from sharing their experiences and opinions with the world. Therefore, hotels would be wise to accept this reality and adapt to it; it is better to be part of the discussion than to be left out of it. Hotels should maintain an active presence on social media sites. Monitoring reviews and responding to comments, both positive and negative, can help to minimize the impact of negative evaluations. In addition, hotels should flag service-related complaints and promptly address them.

- <u>Brand affiliation:</u> Familiarity with a brand can drive decisions, especially in the North American market. This is true even though marketing research reveals substantial erosion in brand loyalty since the late 1990s. Customers appear to be quite willing to abandon a specific brand if a comparable product is available at a more favorable rate. But they usually switch to another brand. In the North American context, most guests prefer a branded product over a non-branded one. Convenience, familiarity, and staying in one's comfort zone are the main reasons for this strong preference. Brand affiliation helps a hotel property connect with its customers. Brands targeting similar segments of the market should be included in the comp set.

Another important consideration in identifying a comp set has to do with Internet search engines and online comparison shopping. Large numbers of potential guests use these tools to identify their hotel options. It makes sense for a hotel to run similar searches to see what properties come up. Such listings from the most popular search engines and travel websites can confirm existing comp set properties and perhaps reveal competitors that might not yet be part of the comp set. Search engines may use similar criteria to identify potential matches for key words. Better searches offer a selection in listing order by rate, classification, or amenities. Note that most searches are *not* organic (where organic means unbiased, natural results solely based on relevant search criteria); indeed, service providers can pay to be listed on the first screen or closer to the top of the list, elbowing their way into a more lucrative position on a given list. Nonetheless, such searches are still worth conducting. Revenue managers need to see hotel choices from the traveler's perspective in order to define the comp set accurately.

Markets, and therefore comp sets, are not static by nature. Comp sets need to be reevaluated on a regular basis, at least once a year. After drastic supply and demand changes, a comp set may change quickly. After a sudden drop in demand, for example, it is not unusual to see top-tier properties discount their rates to lure away the guests of mid-tier hotels. Mid-tier properties can suddenly experience competition from hotels that originally were not part of their comp sets. A bad storm, a cancelled citywide convention, or the threat of a terrorist attack can change things quickly.

As hotel properties change ownership, the new owners may reposition a hotel either up-market (a very ambitious undertaking) or down-market (which is easier and cheaper than a major overhaul). This shift may involve branding a non-branded hotel or re-flagging a branded one. Such changes may redraw the lines in a competitive market and create the need to update comp sets.

Comp set definition is vitally important. Every hotel should carefully monitor the hotels in its comp set with regard to product improvements, sales campaigns, rate changes, and so forth. Certain actions by competitors will lead a hotel to respond in one way or another. If the comp set has not been carefully determined, it may include hotels that really should not be there. This can become a problem if it leads the hotel to take actions to compete with an ill-identified competitor that actually is not targeting the same market. On the other hand, overlooked competing hotels that were wrongly kept out of the comp set may stay under the radar and take significant bites out of a given hotel's market share.

Industry Insight: Comp Sets

Defining your competition is critical to a hotel's success.
By Scott Farrell, President, InciteRevenue

As you look across your market, define who your competitors are by this measure: "What hotels can I steal share from, and which hotels can steal share from me?" If you aren't sure, ask those making the buying decisions (your guests, travel agents, meeting planners, etc.) what other hotels they are considering for future stays or what hotels they have previously stayed with. Each business segment may have a different set of competitors—for example, transient leisure customers may select from one group of hotels while a meeting planner choosing for a group may choose from among a very different group.

Always measure yourself against your prior performance and against the performance of your competitors. Performance is best measured against the market and competitors. Measuring success solely in relation to a hotel's budget can lead to suboptimal performance. For example, you may be exceeding your budget and thinking things can't get any better, but if the entire hotel market is up, you may not be winning in the market. Remember, a high tide floats all boats. You want to make sure you are rising above your competitors, not drifting with them.

Depending on your market intelligence data, your strategy may be to target sales efforts to specific channels, adjust rates, or fine-tune the timing of your promotions. Establish a plan that helps you achieve your market goals, and put it into action. But don't stop there. Continue to seek market intelligence and adjust your plans based on your findings.

Every hotel competes against someone. Sometimes it is the hotel next door, sometimes it is a hotel across town, and sometimes it is a hotel in another city or state. Too often, the competitive set a hotel uses is poorly defined. Most such competitive sets fall into one of two categories:

- Convenient: These are hotels located in a convenient zone, regardless of their actual ability to compete. These competitive sets are generally used to make a hotel look good rather than to gain any market knowledge. With the convenient category, a hotel may appear to be performing well, but not truly understand its place or its opportunity in the market.
- Aspirational: These are hotels the hotel wants to believe it competes against, but doesn't for such reasons as quality, services, or product class. Sometimes, these competitive sets can help a hotel gain market knowledge. More often, though, they cause the hotel to make pricing decisions that ultimately have a negative impact on the hotel.

As you think about your hotel, look at your current competitive set and ask yourself the following questions:

- Can I reasonably expect to steal business from this hotel?
- Does this hotel consider me a competitor?
- Do my customers consider this hotel when making a buy decision?

Industry Insight (continued)

Can you answer yes to all three of these questions? If not, it is time to revisit your competitive set and redefine whom you truly compete against. To do this, involve your entire executive team. Visit the hotels in your current comp set and other hotels that offer comparable services or products. Sometimes a hotel needs more than one comp set based on its business mix (such as one for groups and another for transients).

Understanding your comp set will help your hotel define its place in the market and ultimately benchmark itself in a way that shows how it is performing within the market. This is important, regardless of the strength of demand within the market.

In rising markets, a well-defined competitive set will enable your hotel to make sure it is growing at the same pace as or better than the market. And, in declining markets, it will help you make sure your hotel is capitalizing on all of the opportunities available.

Defining which hotels your hotel competes against can help you understand how to sell, market, price, and position your hotel. Once you have properly defined your comp set, what do you do? You should constantly watch what your competitors are doing, how they are selling, and where they are selling. By monitoring activity and positioning yourself competitively, you can capitalize on available opportunities. If you ignore what your comp set is doing, you may either leave money on the table by pricing too low or lose out on market share by pricing too high.

So, how do you leverage your well-defined comp set to make sure you are doing what you should be doing in the market? The easiest answer is to know what is going on. Use competitive data reports to watch your competitors and position your hotel accordingly. On a daily basis:

- Monitor the rates available to consumers for each hotel. This will ensure that you are neither priced too high nor too low for your market. Pricing with the market will enable you to steal share during low-demand periods and drive higher revenues during higher-demand periods. To make this process repetitive, you should invest in a rate-shopping product such as RateVIEW that delivers competitive rate information through a consistent format and process.
- Monitor your pace to make sure rate changes are having the desired effect. If your pace is slowing, you may have been too aggressive with rates. If your pace is increasing too fast, you might want to increase your rates to take advantage of the demand for certain dates.

On a weekly basis:

- Monitor your progress through specific channels. This can be done through your pace report by monitoring pick-up by channel as well as overall pick-up.
- You can also acquire data reports to help monitor your progress through the GDS. The Hotelligence FuturePACE report can help you ensure that the strategies and tactics you are using are having the desired effect.

On a monthly basis, monitor your progress in the marketplace. Many data reports are available. STR (formerly Smith Travel Research) reports can help you monitor your overall progress against your competitive set. Hotelligence reports can help you understand your position within the GDS against your competitive set. It can

(continued)

> **Industry Insight** *(continued)*
>
> also provide valuable sales leads that can lead to additional business. Understanding your position can help you determine which of your strategies and tactics are successful and which aren't.
>
> Competitive sets can be valuable resources in understanding your hotel, your marketplace, and your hotel's place in it. By defining a proper comp set, watching it, and adjusting it as needed, your hotel can perform better against the comp set regardless of the marketplace—leading ultimately to long-term growth and success. Can you afford not to have a competitive set that works for you rather than against you?

Market Share

Once a hotel has defined its comp set, the next questions to address are: (1) What is the total combined capacity of the competing hotels? and (2) How big is the portion that each competing hotel controls? Some revenue managers describe this as figuring out how big the pie is and how big the slices can get. Consider an example in which five hotels compete for the same market. Assume the following:

Hotel	Number of Rooms	Capacity Market Share
A	205	11.5%
B	225	12.7%
C	400	22.5%
D	460	25.9%
E	485	27.3%
Total	1,775	100%

Each hotel controls an easily calculated portion or share of the combined capacity of 1,775 rooms. The term *fair share* refers to the idea that, all things being equal, each hotel will get a portion of the total market that equals its capacity market share. Every property wants to earn at least its fair share of the market, and preferably more. The following example shows room nights sold during one 30-day period:

Hotel	Number of Rooms × 30	Capacity Market Share	Room Nights Sold	Room Nights Share
A	6,150	11.5%	3,936	10.1%
B	6,750	12.7%	4,590	11.8%
C	12,000	22.5%	8,520	21.9%
D	13,800	25.9%	10,626	27.3%
E	14,550	27.3%	11,204	28.8%
Total	53,250	100%	38,876	100%

The data reveals that hotels A, B, and C did not get their fair share of the room nights. That is, their room nights share is less than their capacity market share. Hotels D and E got more than their fair share: they were able to get a higher percentage of room nights spent in this market than the capacity share under their control.

But the investigation does not stop with unit sales. Revenue management examines revenue as well. Consider the following:

Hotel	Number of Rooms × 30	Capacity Market Share	Room Nights Sold	Room Nights Share	Room Revenue	Room Revenue Share
A	6,150	11.5%	3,936	10.1%	$625,824	12.3%
B	6,750	12.7%	4,590	11.8%	$679,320	13.4%
C	12,000	22.5%	8,520	21.9%	$1,158,720	22.8%
D	13,800	25.9%	10,626	27.3%	$1,285,746	25.3%
E	14,550	27.3%	11,204	28.8%	$1,333,217	26.2%
Total	53,250	100%	38,876	100%	$5,082,827	100%

Hotels A, B, and C actually exceeded their fair shares of revenue in spite of underachieving in room nights share. On the other hand, hotels D and E were not able to generate room revenue in proportion with their capacity share.

Recall that RevPAR combines occupancy and ADR. It can serve the same purpose in this analysis by combining room nights and room revenue into a single statistic.

Hotel	Number of Rooms × 30	Capacity Market Share	Room Nights Sold	Room Revenue	Occupancy Percentage	ADR	RevPAR
A	6,150	11.5%	3,936	$625,824	64%	$159	$101.76
B	6,750	12.7%	4,590	$679,320	68%	$148	$100.64
C	12,000	22.5%	8,520	$1,158,720	71%	$136	$96.56
D	13,800	25.9%	10,626	$1,285,746	77%	$121	$93.17
E	14,550	27.3%	11,204	$1,333,276	77%	$119	$91.63
Total	53,250	100%	38,876	$5,082,886	73%	$130.75	$95.45

Note that the final three cells above present the comp set market averages. These figures allow us to generate penetration indexes for these measure. A *penetration index* measures chosen indicators in relation to the market averages of the same indicators. An index that is greater than 100 percent indicates that the measure exceeds market average. An index that is lower than 100 percent is below the market average. An index of 100 percent means that the chosen indicator matches the market average. Using the figures above, we can calculate penetration factors for occupancy percentage, ADR, and RevPAR.

Chapter 3

Hotel	Capacity: Number of Rooms × 30	Capacity Market Share	Occupancy Percentage	Occupancy Penetration	ADR	ADR Penetration	RevPAR	RevPAR Penetration
A	6,150	11.5%	64%	87.7%	$159	121.6%	$101.76	106.6%
B	6,750	12.7%	68%	93.1%	$148	113.2%	$100.64	105.4%
C	12,000	22.5%	71%	97.3%	$136	104.0%	$96.56	101.2%
D	13,800	25.9%	77%	105.5%	$121	92.6%	$93.17	97.6%
E	14,550	27.3%	77%	105.5%	$119	91.0%	$91.63	96.0%
Total	53,250	100%	73%		$130.75		$95.45	

The analysis of RevPAR penetration in this comp set indicates that hotel A is the market leader in terms of RevPAR achievement. How did this hotel establish its leadership position in the comp set? Is it the result of a better website, a more aggressive sales manager, better mattresses, or more attentive guest service? We can only speculate at this point, but revenue managers shouldn't. Product knowledge and market intelligence are important, but before getting into any of those, one should start with the interpretation of hard data and determine what drove RevPAR. The above data set tells the story: the RevPAR penetration of hotel A was driven by the highest ADR penetration, which was able to compensate for the effect of the poorest occupancy penetration in the comp set. The manipulation of the two key variables, rate and occupancy, should be a result of the strategic analysis of the available options. Hotel A chose to drive ADR and got enough market acceptance to achieve 64 percent occupancy, which was enough to make hotel A the RevPAR leader in the comp set.

Considering the performance of hotel E, one can conclude that this hotel chose to drive occupancy instead of ADR. The hotel was fairly successful in this regard, as it was able to grab 28.8 percent of the total room nights during the month. Given the fact that this property controlled 27.3 percent of the room supply in the comp set (the highest), it is fair to observe that hotel E's clout makes it easier to take advantage of this market position as a fairly dominant player within the comp set.

It is always easier to drive rates down to generate cash flow than it is to drive rates up and then back it up with product quality. A RevPAR penetration index of 96 percent is not bad given the fact that filling a 485-unit hotel (hotel E) is more challenging than filling a 225-unit property (hotel B). Property size and market position are also part of the dynamics resulting in the demonstrated market penetration results per hotel.

At the end of the month, the smallest hotels in the sample comp set achieved the highest RevPAR penetrations, thus realizing their given business potential that month the most effectively. Market performance measured in market penetration is an accurate measure of competitiveness. Revenue managers need to quantify the outcome of strategic decisions through measurements. Examining the key indicators and understanding what drives them can provide the underpinning of strategy decisions for revenue managers.

The Use of Market Intelligence

A multitude of firms offer services for macro-market information on national and regional data. They also monitor trends and provide forecasts. The best known are STR, PricewaterhouseCoopers, PKF Hospitality Research, and Horwath HTL. Their big-picture market reports and other publications are useful for hotels that serve a national or international clientele. Some hotel realty firms also offer market reports that include useful information that may go beyond the real estate aspects of the industry. HVS Consulting & Valuation Services and Colliers International are examples of these.

Certain reliable sources also sell specific micro-market information. If hotels need accurate data, STR, PKF, and TravelClick are the highest profile sources in the North American hospitality industry. Their products provide daily, weekly, and monthly data on market performance using key metrics. Subscribers can get reports both on aggregate market data and on a property-specific basis. They can also request self-defined comp set data.

The reporting of the KPIs can be grouped by the following:

- Chain scales or class (luxury, upper upscale, upscale, upper midscale, midscale, and economy)
- Geographic market (regions)
- Service level (full service and limited service)
- Location (urban, suburban, airport, interstate, resort, and small metro/town)
- Size (under 75, 75–149, 150–299, 300–500, and over 500 rooms)
- Day of the week

The data in the reports can be very informative: the year-to-year, rolling-28-day, and rolling 3- and 12-month data sets offer a daily breakdown of property indicators, comp set indicators, and indexes calculated much as demonstrated in this chapter. The ADR data can be provided in major segments like transient, group contract, and others. The revenue can include other revenue as well, such as that beyond room revenue of the hotels in a chosen comp set.

Forecasting and sales information per distribution channel is also available. Each market intelligence provider has a competitive strength, a product or service that may be worth considering. Budgetary constraints will always affect purchasing decisions, so hotel managers should get the most useful information from well-selected sources. Purchasing access to relevant market information is vital. A revenue manager can determine the market intelligence needs of a given hotel and identify the best fit to meet them when selecting suppliers. Market intelligence is a critical aspect of well-informed decision-making. The money used to acquire the right set of data is well spent.

Big Data and Market Intelligence

Big data is a relatively new term that refers to the issues associated with the availability of far more data than ever before. This large volume of data is the result of successful digitization of most aspects of the interactions between service providers and their customers. Compare the decision-making process of a typical pleasure traveler two decades ago with today's process.

Two decades ago, travelers read printed media, watched television, viewed billboard ads, and listened to radio broadcasts to get ideas about possible travel destinations. Their next step involved narrowing down the options by talking to friends and colleagues and by consulting glossy printed brochures produced by travel agencies, destination marketers, and tour operators. Once travelers chose a specific destination, decided how they wanted to travel there, where they hoped to stay, and what destination activities they wanted to engage in, it was time to consult a travel professional. This professional then booked a flight, reserved a rental car, and booked accommodations and programs (such as tours and sightseeing).

Today's decision-making stages are similar, but potential travelers can now do pretty much everything for themselves, making the process much faster and much more convenient. The Internet allows travelers to narrow down alternatives and make decisions without the help of travel professionals. With just a few clicks, it is now possible to search, comparison shop, and even seek the opinions of fellow travelers by reading through blog posts, tweets, social media postings, and consumer travel reviews. Once travelers are ready to commit, they can book all transportation, accommodations, and activities for most trips online, without the help of intermediaries. The final stage of today's trips is not the travel experience itself but the sharing of trip highlights through social media and the posting of reviews on designated websites. All of this is done via the Internet, which the public increasingly accesses through mobile devices (tablet computers or smartphones) that allow convenient access to practically everything at any time.

All online activities or transactions leave a data trail, whether the user clicks through an airline's home page for seat selection, chooses a certain bed type at a hotel, charges a meal to a room, uses a debit card to pay for parking at an amusement park, or drops off a rental car at an airport. The databases that contain all this information can be unstructured and very large—and are growing more so all the time. The challenge posed by big data is to harness the power of the available data and to make business sense of it. Market intelligence will sort through all big data that is available in a variety of formats to mine it for a solid understanding of consumer choices, competition tactics, and product offerings. If revenue managers let the data tell the story, their decision-making processes will be based on fact.

While market intelligence will provide the data and even some interpretation, it will still be up to the revenue manager to analyze, interpret, and reflect in order to make wise decisions and choices. The revenue manager needs to involve other managers in this process of analyzing data and facts, sifting through and interpreting them, and assimilating them to arrive at wise decisions.[1]

Measurement Challenges

All measurement methods, formulas, calculations, and analyses present some challenges. The most frequently contested issue is the accuracy of claims that attribute a certain improvement in performance to revenue management system implementation. It is reasonable to question whether any improvement in, say,

RevPAR penetration or profitability can be conclusively attributed to a systematic practice of revenue management. The points of reference and the yardstick one might want to apply are the first subjects of challenge.

If a given hotel compares its performance measures from before and after the implementation of a systematic approach to revenue management, the following question arises: Can the hotel determine what portion of the changes result from applied revenue management and what portion would have happened anyway due to other factors? For example, if a hotel measured a 5 percent increase in year-to-year occupancy, can anyone determine if this was due to revenue management efforts, better training, renovation/refurbishment, new amenities, a redesigned website, new promotions, and so forth?

If a given hotel compares its performance measures with another hotel, the following question arises: can the hotel determine whether a hotel with a revenue management system performs better than a hotel without one? For example, hotel X and hotel Y consider each other part of their respective comp sets. Hotel X has implemented a revenue management system, while hotel Y has not. After comparing performance measures, important questions remain: Are the performance differences related to revenue management practices only or could they be related to differences in service quality? To management's abilities? To location? To room size? To the age difference of the properties? To their brand affiliations?

If a given hotel compares its performance measures to market averages, the following questions arise: Can we determine what portion of the changes result from the applied revenue management of one hotel and what changes result from seasonal or cyclical fluctuations that would have affected the whole market anyway and are beyond management's control? For example, if a hotel measures a 7 percent decline in RevPAR compared with a previous fiscal period in a market where the average decline in RevPAR in its comp set was 10 percent over the same period, is it fair to conclude that the hotel with the smallest rate of decline is the market leader or highest achiever? Can that be attributed solely to revenue management strategies and tactics? How can we tell? If we decide or assume that the answer is no, what portion of the difference between the given hotel's RevPAR and the aggregate market RevPAR results from revenue management strategies and tactics and not some other factors?

The positive impact of revenue management on profitability is increasingly recognized. However, when it comes to accurately quantifying the outcome of systematic revenue management solutions, the accuracy of measurement, tracking, and benchmarking can be problematic.

These issues make the claims of certain vendors and suppliers of revenue management systems equally problematic. Such firms sometimes promise a minimum improvement of x percent in revenue or claim a typical minimum net revenue increase of x percent from year one. Others describe product benefits as significant, measurable, and quantifiable, and offer IRR, ROI, and payback analyses. These claims may in fact be true. However, given the measuring issues just discussed, a vendor and potential user should agree at the outset on exactly what measurements will be used to determine whether the vendor's product met its guarantee. Accurate measurement can help avoid misunderstandings and disputes. It will also help substantiate the improved results of systematic revenue management practices.

Endnote

1. Robert Cross discusses the evolution of information, which starts with data (independent facts); the next level is knowledge (the assimilation of information); and the ultimate level is wisdom (the optimization of knowledge to make the best decision). See Robert G. Cross, *Revenue Management: Hard-Core Tactics for Market Domination* (New York: Broadway Books, 1997).

References

Banker, Rajiv D., Gordon Potter, and Dhinu Srinivasan. 2005. "Association of Nonfinancial Performance Measures with the Financial Performance of a Lodging Chain." *Cornell Hotel and Restaurant Administration Quarterly* 46 (4): 394–412.

Ingold, Anthony, Una McMahon-Beattie, and Ian Yeoman, eds. 2000. *Yield Management: Strategies for the Service Industries*. 2nd ed. London: Thomson Learning.

Case Studies

Case Study 1: Market Performance Analysis

Consider the market performance of Hotels A–E in the following comp set.

Hotel	Rooms	Capacity Market Share	April Occ. %	April ADR	Rooms Sold	Rooms Rev.
A	150	7%	60%	160.00	2,700	432,000
B	225	11%	68%	140.00	4,590	642,600
C	400	20%	65%	115.00	7,800	897,000
D	525	26%	80%	96.00	12,600	1,209,600
E	750	37%	83%	90.00	18,675	1,680,750
Total	2,050	100%			46,365	4,861,950

Discussion Questions

1. Calculate fair shares for occupancy and rooms revenue. Which hotels within the comp set did not get their fair share of room nights? Compare the findings to revenue share results.

2. Complete a RevPAR penetration analysis based on data provided in the table. Which hotel is the top RevPAR performer in the comp set?

3. Which hotel would you recommend as the best investment, assuming that investors have unrestricted access to financing?

Case Study 2: A Segmentation Summary

The following table lists the KPIs of My Hotel and the other hotels in its comp set. The data interpretation will provide you with an understanding of the events that unfolded during the most recent June, when My Hotel was outperformed by its competitors.

	SEGMENTATION SUMMARY—MY HOTEL vs. COMP SET JUNE							
	Transient		Group		Contract		Total	
Occupancy (%)	My Hotel	52.3	My Hotel	28.8	My Hotel	3.4	My Hotel	84.5
	Comp Set	69.5	Comp Set	15.1	Comp Set	3.2	Comp Set	87.8
	Index	75.3	Index	190.7	Index	106.25	Index	96.24
ADR ($)	My Hotel	155.2	My Hotel	124.1	My Hotel	132.8	My Hotel	143.7
	Comp Set	156.1	Comp Set	128.2	Comp Set	129.5	Comp Set	150.3
	Index	99.42	Index	96.8	Index	102.55	Index	95.59
RevPAR ($)	My Hotel	81.17	My Hotel	35.74	My Hotel	4.5152	My Hotel	121.4
	Comp Set	108.5	Comp Set	19.36	Comp Set	4.144	Comp Set	132.0
	Index	74.82	Index	184.6	Index	108.96	Index	91.99

Notes: The Comp Set data is an average of the hotels' data in the Comp Set but excludes the subject property (My Hotel).

Segmentation definitions:

Transient: Rooms booked by individual travelers. Fewer than ten rooms booked together.

Group: A block of ten or more rooms booked simultaneously.

Contract: Rooms sold by a contract that includes guaranteed payment for a significant number of room nights. Typical examples are airline crews, movie crews shooting on location, and long-staying corporate or government guests who are posted on an assignment for several months.

Index calculation: My Hotel/Comp Set × 100. An index value of less than 100 means that My Hotel underperformed the comp set average.

Discussion Questions

1. Compare the key metrics shown in the table. According to the data, why did My Hotel have a disappointing performance in June?
2. Analyze the segments and their ratios as provided in the table. What ideas can you suggest to improve My Hotel's performance, based on the analytics provided?

Part III

Tactical Revenue Management

Chapter 4 Outline

A Cornerstone of Revenue Management
Forecasting Demand
    Long-Term Forecasts
    Short-Term Forecasts
    Unconstrained and Constrained
        Demand
    Pace of Build
Forecasting Room Availability
Case Studies

Competency

1. Explain how revenue management relies on forecasting, and detail elements and components of forecasting that relate to revenue management. (pp. 51–60)

4

Forecasting

REVENUE MANAGEMENT AT THE STRATEGIC LEVEL focuses on long-term goals such as identifying desired target markets and identifying or creating factors that differentiate one hotel from its competitors. In contrast, tactical revenue management focuses on operations. Most hospitality operators have practiced tactical revenue management in one way or another. That is, most managers forecast demand, apply multi-tiered rate structures, and run scenarios to compare bookings. Tactical revenue management is in fact how most revenue managers start their careers in the field. Unfortunately, some managers tend to see tactical revenue management as the whole of revenue management. In fact, strategic revenue management identifies better, more sustainable revenue positions. Tactical revenue management efforts should support strategic decisions and goals, not undermine them.

Tactical measures are distinctly different from strategic ones. Tactical measures have relatively short time horizons, usually ranging from same-day to same-quarter. Tactical actions are easily quantifiable and measureable, unlike strategic ones. Tactical measures include forecasting, rate management, stay control, capacity management, and displacement analysis. This chapter focuses on forecasting.

A Cornerstone of Revenue Management

Forecasting is one of the cornerstones of revenue management. Short-term forecasting provides vital information for *tactical* revenue management, while long-term forecasting provides the basis for *strategic* revenue management. Forecasts help management to anticipate periods of constrained and unconstrained demand and to determine expected unit sales and revenue. This information is the foundation for making sound decisions regarding operations management, resource allocation, staff scheduling, and supply chain management. Forecasts will also drive important tactical decisions regarding pricing, group capacity allocation, ideal space configuration, and much more.

It is important to point out the relationship between budgets and forecasts. A hotel's *budget* is the document that contains a detailed breakdown of all revenue and expenses that can be reasonably planned and expected for the budget period. The objective of the budget is to document how a given hotel will realize its financial objectives. A budget, once approved, is not likely to change unless dramatic unforeseen events force a revision. A *forecast* is a projection based on information available at the time of its preparation. This is the best educated guess to help anticipate the quantity of units sold and the revenue generated from those sales.

A forecast is not static. It can and should be updated on an ongoing basis as relevant new information becomes available. If the updated forecast suggests that the attainment of budget numbers is in jeopardy, management needs to intervene and decide what course of action to take.

An annual forecast may be revisited on a quarterly basis. A rolling 90-day forecast needs to be revised once a month. A 28-day forecast should be looked at on a weekly or bi-weekly basis, depending on the needs of a given hotel. These needs are affected by the season of the year, the size of the property, and the lead time and booking patterns of targeted markets. If 10-day, 7-day, or 3-day forecasts are considered necessary, they should be updated daily.

A long-term forecast (covering 12 or more months) is not expected to be completely accurate. The shorter the term, the more accurate the forecast should become. A 30-day or a 7-day forecast involves less uncertainty than the annual forecast does. Even short-term forecasts are rarely 100 percent accurate, but they can come close. As one approaches the subject period, more and more solid information becomes available regarding competitors, scheduled attendance at events, the weather, year-to-date performance numbers, the pace of booking, and other factors.

Revenue management efforts focused solely on room revenue will rely on room revenue forecasts. Total revenue management efforts will include forecasts for function space and other revenue centers as well.

Forecasting Demand

A long-term demand forecast serves as a framework and a compass to anticipate the direction in which to turn and how far one can expect to go. While long-term demand forecasting is less detailed and accurate than short-term forecasting, management needs both. The long-term forecast will be based both on historical data and on current key economic indicators (employment rate, inflation, and disposable income) of the hotel's feeder markets. The long-term forecast uses these indicators to anticipate the future economic climate. Will next year's demand be stronger than, weaker than, or the same as the current year? If change is expected, it is important to anticipate which segments will show growth or decline, because this information drives the hotel's response. Different tactics are used for different markets.

Long-Term Forecasts

As just mentioned, elements of long-term forecasts include historical data and key economic indicators such as employment rate, inflation, and disposable income. Let's look at each of these elements.

Historical Data. Historical data is the data on file that records the hotel's past performance. It is an important starting point to know how a business performed in at least the past five years, if that data is available. There is no guarantee that the past will repeat itself, but past performance is an important reference point and it provides at least a range for reasonable expectations. Adjustments are sometimes necessary (for example, Easter holidays can shift from early April to late March).

A forecast will also have to be adjusted if market conditions change significantly between the past year and the upcoming one. In the case of operations without sufficient historical data (such as newly opened hotels), market-specific, industry-aggregate historical data can be consulted as a substitute for the lack of property-specific records.

Key Economic Indicators. Economic growth is best measured in gross domestic product (GDP). The positive or negative year-over-year changes in GDP offer businesses a frame of reference in terms of overall expectations: is the coming year going to be better or worse in the overall output of the economy? The technical definition of an economic recession is negative GDP growth in two consecutive quarters. In such a case, forecasts should be conservative and growth in demand should not necessarily be expected in a shrinking economy. In a recessionary period, revenue managers use low-demand tactics. On the other hand, if a country or a region is forecasted to increase its economic output, the forecasting of individual business performances will often reflect this positive outlook. Various surveys published in the media regarding business confidence can help managers with their forecasting. (One such survey is available at www.tradingeconomics.com/united-states/business-confidence.)

Employment rate. If the rate of employment increases, the implications for the hospitality industry are positive: when more people have jobs and are generating income, consumers spend more. This usually leads to an increase in people buying accommodations both for business and for pleasure, coupled with a higher propensity to purchase hospitality products (such as restaurant meals, catered social events, and so on).

Inflation. Inflation is the rate of change in the prices of goods and services that people buy. In the United States, the Consumer Price Index (CPI) is considered a key measure of inflation. Hospitality industry businesses need to follow the changes in the prices of commodities as well. Keeping an eye on inflation is important. As a hotel's cost of doing business rises with inflation, the hotel generally must increase its prices by a similar rate to keep pace. Holding rates unchanged will reduce profitability during periods of inflation, because the cost of doing business goes up, but the money coming in does not. The concept of *nominal growth* versus *real growth* highlights this negative impact of inflation. If a hotel increases its room rates by 5 percent during a period of 2 percent inflation, nominal growth is 5 percent, but, because of the inflation rate, real growth is only 3 percent (nominal growth minus the inflation rate).

Disposable income. Personal income minus income tax equals *disposable income*. Income earners use their disposable income to meet basic needs for food, housing, clothing, and transportation. A portion of disposable income, called *discretionary income*, is money people have left over after meeting their basic requirements. Consumers can either save or spend discretionary income, which can pay for leisure activities like vacation travel or eating out. Hospitality operators follow disposable and discretionary income statistics carefully to help them forecast demand. If the population in a given market has more discretionary income than before, the hospitality business's *value propositions* (services or product features meant to make the hotel attractive to customers) can compete for those dollars.

Industry Insight: Forecasting—An Art or a Science?

By Gopal Rao, Regional General Manager, South West Asia, InterContinental Hotels Group

For the most part, forecasting accuracy at hotels remains a challenge, due to the following reasons:

1. Improperly trained and inexperienced staff, which nevertheless is tasked with forecasting. Without any kind of formal training, the staff ends up learning by trial and error, which, at the very least, can prove extremely costly. Add to that the biggest bane of our industry—staff turnover at more than a regular pace—and the result is anything but optimal.
2. Lack of full, accurate data on which to base a proper forecast. This is caused, among other things, by the limitation of the front desk or reservation system and its reporting capabilities, a lack of recorded history, a lack of impartial knowledge of future city or market events, insufficient knowledge of a hotel's competitors' businesses, and so on.
3. Changing market conditions, like shifts in travel and market trends, new competitors, and rotation of city/hotel conferences.
4. Poor understanding and use of hotel computer systems and capabilities, including the differences between property management systems (PMS) and revenue management systems and what they can produce, such as historical reports, market segmentation reports, and group forecasts.

How can hotels get a handle on forecasting?

1. Designate a qualified staff member to be responsible for the forecasting function.
2. Properly train the designated staff member in forecasting and in the use of the PMS and revenue management systems and their reporting capabilities.
3. Make sure information about area market conditions is provided to the designated staff member. This can include feedback about competitors from the sales team, access to city and convention and visitors bureau events calendars, talks with the general manager about the impact of new competitors, and so on.
4. Send the designated staff member to all training on PMS and revenue management systems offered by the brand or corporate office to ensure that the staff member understands system capabilities and becomes proficient at using them.

If your hotel follows the four steps just listed, it will soon have an effective, highly trained staff member in charge of forecasting. The key is to pay competitively and reward accordingly.

If the hotel cannot achieve the four steps on its own, it should look to its brand or corporate office to provide revenue management services for hire, or to its

Industry Insight *(continued)*

management company to provide the services and oversight of a regional revenue manager who can forecast for the hotel.

The following list presents advice and other ideas for revenue management practitioners:

1. In recent times, the hotel industry has enjoyed strong increases in ADR year-over-year. With market conditions moderating, we may not be able to push ADR as aggressively as we have in the past. Be aware of changing conditions. RevPAR increases need to be maximized by both rate and volume (occupancy).
2. While market conditions are moderating, steep discounts or rate cutbacks are not necessary and have been proven not to increase transient volume. Always be aware of the elasticity or inelasticity of your market.
3. Continue to learn about ever-changing distribution channels (such as the Internet, global distribution systems, travel professionals organizations, convention and visitors bureaus, central reservations offices, branded hotel websites, individual hotel websites, attraction websites, travel-booking websites, and travel packagers).
4. Revenue managers need to keep in mind the differences inherent in the various market segments, their customers' buying habits, and the nuances of the various distribution channels. The simple (and easier said than done) rule of revenue management, of course, is to sell the right room at the right price to the right customer at the right time.
5. Watch for slowing demand growth, which is often accentuated by the effect of new supply coming into the market.
6. Strengthen relationships with key accounts, both local and national.
7. If conditions start to slow in your market or hotel, make sure all distribution channels are open and convey information that will compel travelers to book your hotel.

Short-Term Forecasts

Short-term forecasts are much more detailed than long-term forecasts. They provide enough specific information to justify taking specific actions. They rely on more current and accurate data: daily currency exchange rates, actual travel restrictions, price changes of complementary products (for example, airfare and gasoline) and substitute products (such as other hotels), visitor statistics, the quantifiable impact of the latest market trends, and so on. Short-term demand forecasts will not likely affect strategic directions, but they can confirm chosen strategies and help refine chosen tactics.

Daily Currency Exchange Rates. Those hospitality businesses that serve a clientele of international visitors need to track the exchange rates of the currencies of their feeder markets. The currency exchange rate is determined by the financial markets based on the strength of a country's economy compared to another. A country with a solid economy has its currency compared favorably to another that has a weaker economy, which means, to put it in simple terms, its money is worth more. The currency of a resource-rich country with high productivity is worth more than the currency of a resource-poor country that struggles with its productivity. Currencies are measured and compared in order to arrive at exchange rates. If the currency of a visitor's country is more valuable than the local currency, local goods and services become cheaper and more attractive for those travelers who earn their income in that stronger currency. The opposite also holds true: if a traveler's currency is devalued compared to the currency of the traveler's destination, travel and shopping become more expensive in that destination for the traveler, and demand declines as a result.

Actual Travel Restrictions. Health advisories or political unrest may result in travel restrictions imposed by governments to protect the safety of the traveling public. Some epidemic diseases are best brought under control if travel is restricted both to and from the affected region. Governments may issue warnings and suspend the issuing of travel visas in cases of fighting and political instability until peace and travel safety are restored. Sometimes a natural catastrophe (such as an earthquake, a flood, or a tsunami) triggers governmental measures to limit travel to the area that suffers damages. These restrictions are important for near-term forecasting of travel demand. Forecasters must work with cross-market implications as well: for example, after Hurricane Katrina devastated New Orleans in 2005, all travelers who had planned a trip to New Orleans but had to be turned away needed to find another destination. This resulted in a sudden growth in demand for comparable destinations; businesses in those destinations had to revise their forecasts in a hurry.

Price Changes of Complementary Products. If a travel destination is a fly-in destination (certain resorts, for example), price changes in airfare will influence visitation numbers. The same applies for a destination that relies on car traffic if gas prices suddenly spike. The prices of complementary products like transportation or other travel products (such as travel visas) can affect demand both positively and negatively. When prices go down, travel is more affordable; when prices go up, travelers may think twice about taking their trips.

Substitute Product. Travelers can choose between travel options. The availability of up-to-the-minute information that can be accessed via mobile and other devices enables customers to be nimble as well as fickle when finalizing a booking. A super-saver discount on a seven-day Caribbean cruise may suddenly make the cruise appear to be a viable alternative to a one-week resort vacation in Florida. A discounted offer of "three nights for the price of two" at an extended-stay hotel may attract guests who had been considering transient hotels in the area, since the extended-stay hotel's more spacious rooms and free breakfast for a comparable rate would appear to be the better bargain. Substitute product offerings may lure away brand-neutral, last-minute guests who never stop looking, even after they hold a confirmed reservation. If revenue managers notice the impact of nontraditional competition biting into their market share with substitute products, short-term forecasting cannot ignore that impact.

Visitor Statistics. Convention and visitors bureaus (CVBs) and travel research agencies gather and publish visitor statistics on a regular basis. Revenue managers should consult these reports for forecasting purposes. If there are shifts between markets (such as short-haul markets versus long-haul markets) or the data defies expectations in some regards, short-term forecasts will have to factor in the latest changes in visitor stats. One interesting example is the U.S. visitation numbers in Canada: starting in 2001, the number of U.S. visitors started a decade-long decline for a variety of reasons. Canadian destination marketers and hotel revenue managers had to adjust their forecasts while waiting anxiously for the decline to stop and the numbers to bottom out. The worst loss was in the category of same-day visits, but overnight visitation numbers declined as well.

Latest Market Trends. Market trends in the travel industry significantly influence forecasts. It is necessary to distinguish between trends that have long-term and short-term impacts. The overall shortening of the booking window, the preference for inclusive pricing, and an increased attention to health, fitness, and wellness are all examples of market trends that are supported by societal changes and sometimes driven by advances in technology. Such market trends are considered long-term trends. Other trends may not have the same staying power but will affect demand in the short run. Examples include the increase in small ad-hoc group bookings and emerging segments based on lifestyle (themed vacations, singles vacations, pride festivals, and the like) or life stage (gap-year travel or vacations that grandparents take with their grandkids, for example).

Characteristics of Short-Term Forecasts. A short-term forecast will identify demand generators with names and numbers (such as which convention has how many registrations, which tour operator booked how many bus tours for a trade exhibition, which new show opened successfully and how many performances are scheduled next month, and which local sports franchise has made the next round in a playoff run). The margin of error is smaller, the cutoff dates are known, and historical data can help in forecasting wash and spill factors if an event has past history on file. (In a group context, *wash factor* refers to group members who check out early rather than stay the entire length of the event; *spill factor* refers to the number of rooms set aside in the group block that do not sell to members of the group by the agreed-upon cut-off date; these rooms can then be released from the group hold and sold to others.)

Short-term forecasts are also more *granular*. Granularity refers to breaking forecast information down into clusters—for example, by market segment, price category, and/or duration of stay. Short-term forecasts can be broken down by reservation channels (voice, Internet, or global distribution systems) and by reservation methods (direct to guest, chain's call center, or third-party) as well.

The analysis of reservation inquiries helps revenue managers understand trends in call volume changes, conversion rates, and reasons for regrets and denials. (In reservation terminology, a *regret* is a potential guest who decides not to book; a *denial* is a potential guest turned away because of a lack of available space.)

For example, reservation agents can log all inquiries, not just those calls that were converted into sales. The analysis of regrets and denials can provide useful information regarding price resistance or customer needs and wants. The captured portion of demand is easier to track accurately than the uncaptured portion.

Unconstrained and Constrained Demand

Demand is considered *unconstrained* when a hotel can fully meet the total demand. This typically happens in low seasons. Hotels are unlikely to place restrictions on guests wishing to reserve rooms during periods of unconstrained demand. However, once demand levels rise above the hotel's capacity to meet it fully, demand becomes *constrained*. Only a certain portion of demand can be accommodated. In this case, the hotel may place various conditions or constraints on the sale of rooms to which prospective guests must agree in order to book the rooms. The most frequently applied constraints are capacity allocation, rate thresholds, and stay (duration) control.

From a revenue management perspective, if total demand exceeds a hotel's ability to meet it, the hotel should be selective and capture the highest-yield portion of it. Interestingly, this does not always mean booking the guests willing to pay the highest room rates. Room rates are only one element of the total yield a guest provides. The concept of *total spend* considers all revenue (rooms, food and beverage, function space, etc.) and is not restricted to considering a single visit in isolation. A broader-based strategic approach considers the *lifetime total value* of a guest or a client organization instead of the price point of a given room on a given day. For example, if a hotel could sell a room on a given day for (say) $50 more to guest A than guest B, does that justify denying the reservation to guest B? What if guest B is a frequent, loyal guest who spends on more than rooms? A guest who visits a hotel three times a year, stays multiple days, and spends on food and beverage, parking, function space rental, and entertainment is likely to be more valuable (that is, will provide a higher total yield) than an unknown guest (one with no history of staying at the hotel) with a one-night reservation who agrees to pay $50 more for that one night. It would be a mistake to displace a higher-total-yield guest in favor of a lower-yield guest. In practice, this means that revenue managers should *not* simply treat each day as a separate and distinct opportunity to maximize the daily revenue total. Revenue maximization is a long-term process, and decisions made on one day can have effects on many other days. It may seem counterintuitive, but there will likely be times when it makes better revenue management sense to turn down higher-paying guests or clients for a given night or event if accepting that business jeopardizes likely future business.

In other words, room rates are important, but they are not absolute measures. Revenue management has to maximize profitability by factoring in all available relevant revenue data. Revenue managers can improve the profitability of the whole hotel, not just the revenue of the rooms division.

Pace of Build

The *pace of build* is another important indicator in demand forecasting. Revenue managers can compare the booking pace of the current year with those of previous years. It is important to start with historical data. However, it is also important to consider current conditions and to factor in changes in booking patterns. A significant change taking place now is the shortening of lead times for all market segments.

Consider the following booking pace example showing actual group room bookings for July 20X1 and actual group room bookings through April for July 20X2 sales:

	Total Group Room Bookings, Cumulative by Month						
	January	February	March	April	May	June	July
20X1	350	680	740	860	880	920	890
20X2	360	690	700	750			

The booking pace shows that 20X2 started with stronger demand than the previous year. Based on the January and February data, the hotel was on pace to meet or exceed 20X1's volume for July. During March and April, the pace of build slowed and the hotel had 110 fewer nights booked in April for July than at the same time the previous year. A revenue manager would need to respond to this situation by either going more aggressively after the group market or reallocating some rooms being held open for group business to one or more other market segments.

To interpret the data correctly, the revenue manager must know that lead times differ for different segments of the market. Events (such as festivals, sport tournaments, and conventions) need significantly more planning and preparation time than vacation trips. Group trips require longer lead times than individual trips. Long-haul travel markets have longer lead times than near-market travel markets. Reservation managers have to know intimately well the booking patterns of their feeder markets.

For some markets, the shortening of lead times and the growing number of last-minute bookings have a lot to do with changing lifestyles and travel habits.[1] In the United States, the average length of vacations is getting shorter, and these shorter vacations are taken more frequently than before. The ease of access to travel information coupled with the ability to make instant online transactions feeds this consumer trend. Consumers also have noticed the prevalent revenue management practice of discounting distressed inventory. More and more travelers take advantage of special deals offered by airlines, cruise lines, car rental companies, resorts, and hotels that attempt to offload unsold inventory by capturing demand from flexible last-minute bookers.

Carefully monitoring the pace of build will help revenue managers avoid a fire sale of unsold inventory at heavy discounts. Group booking pace can be a useful early indicator of the future market demand trends due to its longer lead time. Timely intervention can be started relatively early if the booking pace gives reason for concern.

Forecasting Room Availability

The forecasting of room availability for any future date starts with the number of available units. That number is then adjusted to account for the various factors that will affect the number of rooms available for sale on the date in question. From total rooms, we subtract rooms already occupied by previous arrivals staying beyond the day in question (*stayovers*), any rooms that are out of order, expected arrivals on the given day, expected walk-ins, and guests who are scheduled to check out but extend their stay (*overstays*). A hotel cannot know with certainty how many walk-in guests will show up on a given day, nor can it know in advance which or how many guests are likely to extend their stays. But the hotel can look at its historical records and make educated estimates for planning purposes. After subtracting all these elements, the forecaster adds in expected cancellations, expected no-shows, and expected early departures (*understays*). Again, these numbers cannot be known in advance with certainty, but percentages can be reasonably estimated from historical data.

The calendar date is a good starting point when mining historical data, but the day of the week is just as important. For example, the current year's July 8 forecast may consider the previous year's July 8 figures, but if last year July 8 fell on a Thursday and this year it is a Friday, the comparison may not be as useful, especially to a hotel with very different weekday and weekend occupancy patterns. In this case, it will likely be more appropriate to look at the second Thursday in July for comparison.

How far into the future does a revenue manager forecast room occupancy? The most frequently prepared forecasts are 3-day, 5-day, weekly, 10-day, monthly, quarterly, and annual forecasts. Each revenue manager will choose a system best suited to a given property based on markets and property types.

Endnote

1. Yesawich, Pepperdine, Brown, and Russel, *National Travel Monitor 2003.* Presented at the International Hotel, Motel & Restaurant Show, New York, N.Y., November 2005.

References

Canina, Linda, and Cathy A. Enz. "Why Discounting Still Doesn't Work: A Hotel Pricing Update." *CHR Reports* 6, no. 2 (2006).

Enz, Cathy A. "Hotel Pricing in a Networked World." *Cornell Hotel and Restaurant Administration Quarterly* 44, no. 1 (2003).

Enz, Cathy A., and Linda Canina. "An Examination of Revenue Management in Relation to Hotels' Pricing Strategies." *CHR Reports* 5, no. 6 (2005).

Case Studies

Case Study 1: Forecasting in the Hotel Monroe

Monroe is a small town not too far from Detroit, Michigan, which has long been nicknamed the Motor City. The region's main source of employment used to be the automobile industry. The Detroit Red Wings hockey team sold out all of its home games in the Joe Louis Arena in the years the Wings contended for the Stanley

Cup. Hotels and restaurants also did well in the Detroit metropolitan area when people had jobs and money to spend. But those days were over.

The Hotel Monroe saw better times as well before the economic collapse and the Great Recession of 2007–2009. When the car manufacturers all suffered huge losses, the night shifts and the weekend shifts were the first to be cancelled in the car assembly plants. New car sales declined and import models competed hard with domestic ones. As a result, layoffs and plant closures decimated the work force. People lost their jobs by the thousands at first, by the tens of thousands later. Businesses that made their money selling their wares to the auto workers and their families closed down in big numbers, people left Detroit and the surrounding towns in droves, and the bad economy brought Detroit to its knees. The recovery was painstakingly slow, and the city had to declare bankruptcy in the summer of 2013.

During this tough economic period, the Hotel Monroe struggled to keep the lights on. Renovation plans were shelved and staffing levels were reduced in the 120-room suburban hotel. The hotel was downgraded from four stars to three. The monthly occupancy rarely reached 50 percent, and cash flow was a contentious issue. The hotel tried to make up for its weathered appearance by offering personal attention and hospitable, intuitive service.

Trevor, the general manager of the hotel, is a college-educated man in his mid-thirties. His family owns the Monroe. He worked most jobs in the hotel during his summer vacations as a boy growing up, starting out as a bellhop and a busboy. He runs the business now. He has the habit of pitching in where he can on the occasional busy afternoon: he parks cars, carries luggage for arriving guests, and answers the phone at the front desk to help out. After he had to let go of the assistant hotel manager, he took on more administrative duties as well. Since he can't afford to buy a season ticket anymore to see his beloved Red Wings play, he watches the games on TV in his office, after a dinner of pizza and beer.

Trevor was struggling with the forecast for next week. While looking at the Running 10-Day Occupancy Report during the intermission between the first and second periods of the hockey game, he was astonished to see that the forecast was way off. The previous week had been forecasted to have an occupancy of between 45 and 55 percent, but the report showed remarkable occupancy numbers. In fact, the Monroe's occupancy had been over 75 percent most days of the past week.

Trevor knew they had been busy and he remembered asking some of the housekeeping staff to take extra shifts, asking a maintenance employee to put in some overtime, and even calling in part-time help to clean rooms. He was looking for clues to explain this dramatic increase in business before finalizing the forecast for the following week; he wasn't sure if the sudden spike in occupancy would hold. To find out what was happening, he needed more information.

Trevor decided to do some research instead of watching the second period of the hockey game. He left his office, got into his car, and glanced down at his watch: it was 8:45 P.M. He decided to drive around town and check the parking lots of the hotels in his comp set. All of them were full, indicating that it was a busy time for all of the hotels in town. A number of the licence plates he saw were from out of state. Why were so many people visiting Monroe in October?

Trevor returned from his tour and parked his car in the back of the Hotel Monroe's parking lot. As he walked through the hotel lobby on the way to his office, he saw Gary behind the front desk and stopped to chat for a minute. He learned from Gary that the Monroe had only 18 vacant rooms for the night. He asked if Gary knew what was going on. Why the unexpected surge in demand for rooms?

"I guess this is all about that latest YouTube sensation, boss. Everybody wants to try the well water at Old Mike's Farm. That video went viral. Have you seen it?"

The telephone at the front desk rang, and Trevor quickly thanked Gary for the input before moving on as Gary reached to answer the phone. The truth was that Trevor had no idea what Gary was talking about. He wasn't a YouTube watcher at all. He went back to his office and fired up his laptop. He got on YouTube and searched for "Mike's Farm in Monroe." There were hundreds of matches for his search, and on top of the list he found a video that was less than two minutes long. Mike, the elderly person in the video, talked about a miracle cure that not only healed his skin condition but also rejuvenated him in general. He was widowed but now he was interested in getting married again to someone much younger. It all began with drinking his well water. He had never used that water before for more than watering his garden. However, this past summer he noticed that every plant and flower in the garden grew much taller and bigger than before. He tried the water himself, drinking a cup or two a day at first. It tasted good and made him feel good. Now he was drinking four or five cups a day and he never felt better in his life. He was delighted to offer his well water to anyone without charge, although donations to the local fire department were welcome. A donation box was put out by the well. "Bring your own bottles, and limit two bottles per person, please," Mike suggested as he closed his message.

Trevor understood now why suddenly a lot of folks wanted to come to Monroe. Trevor wished all the believers in the miracle cure the best, and he also hoped that the wish of the local fire fighters to be able to afford to buy a new fire engine would come true as well. But what should he do about his forecast for next week?

Discussion Questions

1. Should Trevor revise his short-term forecast for the following week?
2. Is there reason to revise the long-term forecast?

Case Study 2: Forecast Adjustment

Hotel Churchill is an upscale hotel in downtown Toronto, Ontario, Canada, with a capacity of 260 rooms. The hotel is close to the Old City Hall, the theater district, and Toronto's main shopping district. A very close competitor, the Hotel Harmony, is on the same street less than a block away. The Harmony has 360 rooms and is an upper-midscale hotel that has struggled during the last couple of years with changes in brand affiliation and ownership. The Harmony is included in the Churchill's comp set.

The revenue manager of the Churchill got some interesting news in a tweet from a hotel realty company: the Harmony had been sold, and the new owner was not a hotel corporation but the University of Toronto, which has a chronic shortage of student housing. The tweet said the university planned to convert the hotel into a student-housing facility. The conversion would take place in the coming quarter.

Discussion Question

Does the Churchill need to make changes in its forecasting? What changes, if any?

Chapter 5 Outline

Rate Structure
    Types of Rates
Tactical Discounting
Upselling
Demand-Based Dynamic Pricing
Case Studies

Competencies

1. Identify and describe the various components of tactical rate management. (pp. 65–73)

2. Discuss the advantages of upselling. (pp. 73–75)

3. Summarize the concept of demand-based dynamic pricing. (pp. 75–78)

5
Tactical Rate Management

MANY PEOPLE CONSIDER rate management to be the heart and soul of revenue management. Managers who hold a simplistic view of revenue management often wrongly perceive price control as revenue management itself. Revenue management involves much more than rate control. Nonetheless, the pricing of the room night is a pivotal issue that has both tactical and strategic aspects.

Price setting in the lodging industry, if it is done by revenue professionals, is not cost-based but demand-based. Many industries, including the consumer goods and even the restaurant industry, have a traditional cost-based approach to price setting: after the production costs of goods are determined, a mark-up (margin) is applied in order to cover the costs of bringing the goods to market and allow for profit. This is a simplified description of how the sales price is determined for a piece of furniture, a toothbrush, a car, or a bowl of chicken noodle soup. However, those industries that (1) have a high portion of fixed costs and a low portion of variable costs, and (2) deal in intangible and perishable products have realized over the years that switching from cost-based to demand-based pricing allows for more flexibility to respond to changing market conditions and can lead to higher profitability. Practitioners of revenue management in the lodging industry have embraced demand-based pricing.

The strategic approach to pricing has a long-term view. Its main objective is revenue growth through successful price positioning in a given comp set and through maintaining or growing market share. On balance, the tactical approach to room rate management has a short-term operational focus that considers same-day and same-week rate management issues. Its main objective is cash flow generation from revenue growth.

A hotel's tactical rate management should align with its strategic pricing approach. Inconsistencies between tactical and strategic pricing spell trouble. If, for example, a hotel positions itself as a pricey upper-upscale property with high service quality (a strategic choice) and then reacts to a market hiccup by offering huge discounts and other significant incentives (two-for-ones, double loyalty points, and the like), these tactical measures could seriously undermine the integrity of the hotel's strategic positioning. A deviation like this from strategic objectives also makes it very hard to maintain the coveted upper-tier image and rates.

The strategic rate level and market position that are the results of dedicated efforts and hard work can be very easily compromised by the wrong tactical choices. It is not that unusual to see four-diamond full-service hotels suddenly going head-to-head against three-diamond limited-service hotels. If they become cash starved during a market slump, higher-ranked hotels may choose to compete on price by offering a better value at comparable price points. This desperate measure will probably cost them more in the long run than the revenue they grab from other properties. Diluting a brand name and devaluing a product have consequences. Revenue managers should think carefully before they decide to go after a market segment that has never been theirs and that, if the market recovers, will never be considered as a target again. Discounting has not proven to be a successful method of RevPAR growth. Maintaining the consistency of tactics and strategy is a lot more important than most managers would like to admit.

What revenue managers need to consider is that customers prefer clarity: they prefer to know what they can expect from a given brand or service provider. At the least, this involves rate level, amenities, and service quality. Consistency in these categories means a lot to guests. Hotels that never deviate from their positioning, never jerk their rates too far up or down, and keep the same target markets every season are rewarded with a steadier flow of revenue and a more loyal customer base.

Tactical rate management requires a multi-tiered rate structure. What is a rate structure and what is not? When different room types are priced differently in a hotel, that reflects a certain selection rather than a rate structure. Differences in room size, location, view, and so forth may and should be reflected in rates (physical rate fences). In contrast, a multi-tiered rate structure means that the same room night can be sold at varying price points.

Some hotels can afford to have a very simple pricing approach. For example, a solitary roadside motel located at the off-ramp of a major highway may deal exclusively with traveling guests who arrive without reservations and never stay more than one night. This motel might have one rate only and would sell the first room of the night at the same rate as the last room that completes a full house. This operator may never need or want to practice revenue management. On the other hand, most hotels in competitive, saturated markets choose a more complex approach to pricing their room nights to reflect seasonality and the fact that their clienteles are not necessarily homogeneous.

Rate Structure

A rate structure can be as complex or as simple as the hotel believes makes the most sense. Hotel A may offer nine different rates for the same room, while Hotel B offers sixteen and Hotel C offers thirty-nine. A surprising number of revenue managers may have two dozen or more. There is no conclusive evidence that thirty-nine different rates work better than sixteen. One might wonder if there are really thirty-nine distinctly different clusters of guests that a given hotel might want to cater to.

Is there a meaningful difference between a room rate of, for example, $158 and $155? How can one characterize the buying behavior differences associated with a $3 rate difference within the $150–$160 range? If this $3 difference would really make or break a possible sale, then by all means a revenue manager should consider it. However, a manageable system with more well-defined and distinctly different offerings would make much more sense. The differences between price points should be a reflection of buying behavior, customer needs, and purchase power balanced with the perception of value from the guests' perspective.

Types of Rates

Types of rates include rack rate, corporate and special corporate rates, group rates, promotional rates, government rates, event rates, employee rate, complimentary rate, and hurdle rate/best available rate.

Rack Rate. The *rack rate* is the highest rate a hotel would like to charge for unconstrained demand. It is also referred to as the walk-in rate, the premium rate, and the posted rate. This is the rate that is quoted first when a potential guests asks, "Do you have a room for tonight?" Most jurisdictions require hotels to display each room's rack rate conspicuously inside the room. According to research, more than 80 percent of guests claim they try to negotiate a lower room rate than the one quoted.[1] The research also noted that potential guests often try to get perks and extras without paying extra. A rack rate is the rate that most guests would like to bargain down. The chances of collecting the rack rate will depend on supply and demand. A hotel is in a stronger bargaining position to hold its rack rate in periods of excess demand.

A statistic known as the *rate achievement factor (RAF)* measures the hotel's efficiency in achieving the rack rate. The calculation of rate efficiency can be done by comparing actual ADR for a room type to the rack rate for that room type. For example, if a room type has a rack rate of $120 and an ADR of $84, the RAF is $84 ÷ $120, or 70 percent. The RAF indicates how heavily the rack rate was discounted in a given period and serves as a constant reminder that we are now living in an age of comparison shopping, price transparency, and well-informed, hard-bargaining customers.

The term "rack rate" originated from the days when there was a physical room rack at the front desk of hotels. Today, hotels with actual room racks are hard to find. Computerized property management systems (PMS) are affordable and user-friendly enough that even small operators can buy and use them. The PMS assigns rate codes to all the different rates a hotel has, with rack rate as the top rate. All other rates are lower, reflecting some form of a discount for one reason or another.

Corporate and Special Corporate Rates. Transient hotels offer volume discounts to provide an incentive for potential buyers of a lot of room nights. While leisure travelers spend after-tax (i.e., disposable or discretionary) income in order to travel and are more price-sensitive than business travelers, leisure travelers usually lack the purchase power to justify a special rate. Corporate travelers are a lot less price-sensitive for a variety of reasons, but corporations have more leverage as volume purchasers. Corporations having a lot of business activity in a given locale are in a good position to negotiate preferential treatment.

Corporate rate as a category can include many corporate rates based on the volume of room nights. If a corporation buys enough room nights per year to qualify for a corporate discount, the hotel will generally offer a basic corporate rate. If the volume is significant enough to warrant an even greater discount, a preferred corporate rate is customary. Corporations that have a manufacturing plant, headquarters, training facility, or main unit in the hotel's vicinity can have a significant and more or less steady need for hotel rooms over the years. In such cases, a corporate-specific rate can be negotiated—for example, an IBM rate or a Ford rate.

There are also special corporate deals involving contract rooms. For example, an airline may want to reserve twelve guestrooms every night in order to allow various airline personnel to check in and check out as needed. The hotel will invoice the airline for the rooms rather than the airline personnel. The assigned rooms will always be available, and a contract will govern the fixed amount charged for the rooms and the frequency of invoicing.

The negotiation of a corporate rate can happen at a property level or at a corporate (chain) level. A certain annual volume of room nights can be included in an agreement. From management's perspective, it is important to work out the fine details: who qualifies for the corporate rate—employees only, or business associates as well? Does the corporation have a dedicated position or office to coordinate and place bookings? What room type is offered? Are there seasonal rate adjustments? Is the same rate recognized on holidays or high-demand citywide event days? Are there blackout dates? Is there a required minimum lead time per booking?

Another important issue that can arise has to do with who has priority. Suppose a reservations manager determines that she could get the rack rate for all the rooms normally allotted to corporate guests for the coming week. She wants to not offer corporate rates next week because charging the higher rack rate for the rooms will mean more revenue. The real question for a revenue manager is, what is more profitable for the hotel in the long run? Guests who enjoy a corporate rate have a history that can be analyzed. Such guests may pay a lower room rate, but spend more in the hotel's other revenue centers than typical transient guests. Even if they don't, though, there may be more at stake. A revenue manager can determine a corporate account's total annual room nights and revenue generated, and compare this with the minor revenue increase that could be achieved by turning away corporate guests in favor of rack-rate-paying guests during the coming week. Based on the larger picture, the answer is usually quite clear: turning away corporate guests (or forcing them to pay the rack rate rather than the corporate rate) could endanger the corporate accounts, and it does not make good business sense to lose a significant volume of revenue in the long term just to get a small increase in revenue in the short term. Short-term objectives and long-term objectives need to be aligned. Short-term thinking can be dangerous in a business like a hotel that is built for the long haul.

Problems can come up for both hotels and corporate guests when a fixed corporate rate is offered by a hotel. Hotels sometimes offer last-minute discounts to the public that are lower than their corporate rates. Corporate travelers who notice this may object and point out that they could have paid a lower rate if they had held out until the last minute. They might feel abused rather than rewarded for the loyalty shown to the hotel; they might even question the need for a negotiated corporate discount when travelers can get lower rates without any demonstrated loyalty. Hotels, on the other hand, may feel they should have the flexibility to not honor negotiated corporate rates on occasion. They question the rationale of charging a corporate room rate much lower than the going ADR on excess demand days when comparable hotels may be sold out charging premium rates. These considerations have led more and more hotels and corporate partners to negotiate a certain percentage off the best available rate (BAR) as a corporate discount instead of a fixed corporate rate. Those operators who practice demand-based dynamic pricing (discussed later in the chapter) benefit most from this approach by gaining additional flexibility in tactical rate control without irritating loyal corporate clients.

Group Rates. The significance attributed to group revenue in a given hotel is a strategic decision. Whatever the strategic approach to group business might be, tactical rate management requires a selective pricing approach consistent with the specific nature of this segment. Group bookings are usually handled by the sales department, where agents and managers are highly specialized in dealing with this line of customers. The revenue manager and the director of sales and marketing need daily coordination and a close working relationship to succeed in maximizing group revenue.

Selling many room nights at once instead of selling the same number one booking at a time is a lot less resource-intensive and costly. It also generates more revenue per booking on the sales side.

Group rates depend on a number of variables, including the season of the year, the number of room nights wanted (based on group size and duration of stay), other revenue generated (food and beverage, function room rentals, golf, spa, etc.), and the group's history.

The group business segment has a number of sub-segments: corporate meetings, conventions, associations, incentive groups, leisure groups, and SMERF groups (social, military, educational, religious, and fraternal organizations). There are also ad-hoc groups (such as a circle of friends getting together for a bachelor party or an alumni reunion group that does not meet yearly and does not plan to return to the same hotel again) and series groups (such as a bus tour operator arriving each Tuesday for two nights between April and October with overseas tourists).

Group contracts govern room rates, as well as the prices of other services such as catering. Revenue managers need to consider the margins on each revenue stream generated by a group. Some groups bargain hard for a lower room rate but are more flexible in accepting additional charges (like charges for baggage handling), while other groups may accept a higher room rate but negotiate for inclusive, "no charge" services like breakfast, drink coupons, transportation, and so on.

The importance of managing all potential revenue streams falls under the heading of "total revenue management." This strategic concept helps managers achieve revenue optimization, which is a step beyond revenue maximization. Instead of thinking only in the silos of one revenue stream at a time and attempting to maximize the revenue potential of each revenue stream considered in isolation, the holistic total revenue management approach allows revenue managers to optimize the total revenue impact of a booking if it involves multiple revenue streams. Some revenue streams are more profitable than others; for example, the margin on function space revenue is different than the margin on a meal. Total revenue management gives revenue professionals a higher degree of flexibility in negotiating a more profitable contract for groups that are interested in booking multi-day stays involving multiple revenue streams. Shifting groups toward higher-margin revenue streams would certainly produce more favorable results for a hotel or resort than simply being content to generate revenue through revenue streams with lower contribution margins. Total revenue management improves not just revenue, but also profitability.

Promotional Rates. Certain organizations can significantly influence buying. Automobile associations (such as AAA/CAA), organizations representing retired persons (such as AARP), and the publishers of coupon books (such as Entertainment Coupon Book) will negotiate a discount on behalf of their membership, typically in the form of a percentage off the rack rate. Hotels are usually allowed to exclude the highest occupancy dates of the year, during which the hotel has the right to charge full rates even to qualifying members of the various organizations that have negotiated discounted rates.

Government Rates. Municipal, provincial/state, and federal governments employ tens of thousands. Their need for accommodation while traveling on business provides a significant revenue source for some hotels. Hotels that are interested in catering to this market will have to honor the government-set rate established for each fiscal year. Negotiations are not necessary, because the government will issue its own directives of per diem spending limits for each budget cycle per market. Note that rates and per diems can vary by location in response to local differences in the cost of living.

Event Rates. In North America, meeting planners are commonly in charge of event management. Professional meeting planners are experienced and knowledgeable regarding the lodging industry and the complexity of a meeting contract. Event rates may fluctuate based on seasonality and the size and overall revenue impact of the event in question.

A meeting planner may carefully negotiate the room rate as a key element of the contract. Revenue managers should not concentrate on the room rate to the exclusion of all other considerations. They need to keep in mind the total revenue impact of an event. Based on how it is spent, the same total revenue amount can have a very different profit margin for the hotel.

Employee Rate. Most hotel companies charge a discounted rate to their employees who are on a business or vacation trip if they are staying at a hotel of the same brand or company. Rates and corporate policies vary, and employee rates (as well as related "friends and relatives" rates) are always subject to room availability.

Complimentary Rate. Offering free accommodations to clients, potential clients, and dissatisfied guests is considered a cost of doing business. A room night can be made complimentary on the spot to help mollify an unhappy guest. Sometimes the offer of a complimentary future stay is more practical.

There are many other reasons for hotels to offer complimentary rates. Hotel managers sometimes offer free accommodations to marketers in exchange for publicity. Some brands use complimentary room nights as a reward to their employees. Many hotels offer room nights as a product donation to support causes and charitable events. Hotels may also offer comp rooms when employees need overnight accommodation when given back-to-back shifts or when weather emergencies prevent employees from getting home safely.

Hurdle Rate/Best Available Rate. Traditionally, the *hurdle rate* has been the lowest rate a hotel is willing to offer on a given day or week. It may be a flexible amount subject to varying market conditions. There may be different hurdle rates on Monday and Friday of the same week, subject to market changes and the cash flow needs of a given fiscal period.

As industry jargon, the term "hurdle rate" is in the process of being replaced by *best available rate (BAR)*, a newer term that means nearly the same thing. In fact, the terms are often used interchangeably today, even though they have slightly different connotations. Strictly speaking, the hurdle rate was more static, because, until recently, hotels held information, pricing, and positional power over customers, so they could determine a lowest price point and were able to hold firm. As customers have come in recent years to hold much more information power than in the past, the industry's approach to pricing has shifted. The BAR gradually took over as a rate that a service provider believes is the lowest price point that offers an attractive enough value proposition to generate a sufficient volume of business. Unlike the hurdle rate, however, a BAR can be quickly and easily adjusted if dynamic market conditions justify the change. In practical application, the BAR is the best price until something forces a hotel to rethink it.

A hotel may also use a *stay-sensitive hurdle rate*. This tactic's objective is to maximize revenue by offering price incentives for longer stays. Simply stated, with a stay-sensitive hurdle rate, the longer a guest agrees to stay, the lower the nightly rate will get. For example, the BAR for a one-night stay might be quoted as $140, but if the guest agrees to stay two nights, a BAR of $129 will be offered for each night of the two-night stay. A three-day stay might get a BAR of $115. These price options should be pointed out to guests at the time of booking. Guests who accept the option to stay longer generate higher total revenue at lower unit prices. Unfortunately, most guests show little flexibility with their dates. Travel arrangements are often already finalized by the time a guest begins booking the accommodations portion of a trip. Therefore, guests' lack of flexibility will often limit the effectiveness of this tactical measure.

Tactical Discounting

Tactical discounting is done to generate revenue in the short term. If a hotel believes that downward rate adjustments will provide price incentives for their potential guests to book same-day or same-week room nights, this tactic may help to hold or boost occupancy. However, selling more room nights at reduced room rates will not necessarily generate higher room revenue. The unknown variable is how much occupancy will be gained because of the reduced rate.

Researchers analyzed data from more than 6,000 hotels regarding the effects of discounting from 2001 to 2003.[2] According to the researchers' key findings, hotels can increase market share within their comp set by discounting, but it is done at the cost of declining revenue performance. Hotels in the study that chose to discount their rates by more than 2 percent (compared with their comp set's average) achieved lower RevPAR performance than their competitors. There were minor differences identified in the level of price sensitivity (elasticity) between the clienteles of upper-upscale and economy hotels. In 2003, other researchers concluded from data gathered during 1989–2000 by 480 hotels in twenty-two U.S. metropolitan areas that, on average, for every 10 percent decrease in room rates, demand rose by only 1.3 percent.[3] The evidence to date clearly shows that discounting room rates does not improve profitability. These findings were consistent with research pointing out that the corporate segment is less likely than the leisure segment to respond to a room rate discount.[4]

Overall, it appears that tactical discounting can accomplish a number of things. It can fill rooms that would have stayed vacant. It can capture market share from competitors. It can attract leisure travelers, who are more likely to respond to discounts and perceptions of a better deal. It can get the business of brand-neutral, price-sensitive customers. But it does all this by reducing revenue and diluting RevPAR, as the impact of selling more units at lower rates is usually negative.

Late discounting has led to another noticeable and unfortunate trend for hotels. More and more guests with reservations are calling to cancel their rooms one or two days before arrival if last-minute discounts have been offered either on third-party websites or on the hotel's website for the date(s) the guests booked. These guests cancel their old reservation, then make a new one at the newly available discounted rate. What has become evident is that many guests never stop looking for deals, even after they have booked their room nights. Hotels that post discounts for last-minute bookings may watch already booked business become less profitable when attentive guests discover and switch to the lower rate. This revenue "leakage" may further dilute room revenue.

Despite its often negative impact, the discounting tactic is still frequently used to sell distressed inventory. When a weekly, 3-day, or same-day forecast shows disappointing demand, the revenue manager may believe the only way to boost occupancy is to drop rates. Demand-based dynamic pricing (discussed later in the chapter) is applied in order to gauge what price point the market will accept.

Given the drawbacks of discounting, we might reasonably wonder why any revenue manager would ever use it as a tactic. The answer can be complex. Low occupancy has always been considered a reflection of less-than-satisfactory sales performance. Low occupancy reduces a hotel's ability to pay its fixed costs as they come due, so owners tend to want some sort of intervention to ensure those costs will be covered. The factor that managers can most easily control is room rates, so it is often their first choice—even though discounting should probably be their last choice. Developing a convincing value proposition by creating more value without discounting is harder work: package development (bundling), better-defined differentiation, better websites, and product improvements (such as better service, better mattresses, better shower heads, better amenities, better breakfasts, etc.) all require more work, more creativity, and need some ramp-up time to take effect. Owners may put pressure on revenue managers to show short-term results, and holding or boosting occupancy through discounting may temporarily assuage owners and get them off the manager's back.

Another argument is that, although room revenue is likely to fall, the increased occupancy may generate revenue increases in the hotel's other revenue centers. Increasing occupancy also helps maintain the level of employment the hotel needs to uphold service quality and sustain staff morale. Capturing market share from competitors can also be a consideration, but this goal presents a serious issue to deal with. Can a hotel retain the captured clientele? The answer is probably not. Deal-driven bargain hunters always go where the best deals are, so there is no protection against a competitor's steeper discount next time. Therefore, even if a short-term battle can be won by using discounting, there is no chance to win the long-term war by using this tactic. Any discounted price can be undercut by someone more desperate.

There are times when discounting is used for entirely the wrong reasons. After the terrorist attacks of September 11, 2001, the New York hotel market saw a drastic decline in demand. Following the SARS outbreak in the spring of 2003, the bottom of the market fell out in Toronto. In both cases, the steep decline in demand had nothing to do with the pricing level of hotel rooms. Travelers stayed away for a variety of reasons, but high room rates were not one of them. Why did hoteliers expect heavy discounting to fix their occupancy problem when room rates were not part of the problem in the first place? If travelers avoid an area because of safety, security, or health concerns, can low rates really persuade them to disregard those concerns? The answer seems obvious. Nonetheless, discounting became so rampant in both cities that it took years for their hotel markets to recover.

By definition, at the day-to-day operational level, hotels take a tactical approach to rate management versus a strategic one.[5] But tactics should never ignore the larger strategy. To avoid confusing the market by saying one thing and doing another, strategy and tactics should be aligned. Unfortunately, many managers use tactics that conflict with their larger strategy. When we see hotel brands that promote service quality as their strategic choice for market positioning start to discount and promote value instead in their day-to-day operations, there is a clear misalignment. Driving attention to discounts will undermine a coveted strategic choice of being a brand differentiated by service quality—a market position that takes extended effort to achieve. Consumers must not be confused in this way: brand clarity is vital. If a hotel chooses to be a price- or value-driven choice, it should support that strategy consistently with its tactics.

All of this does *not* mean that discounting should never be used. However, managers who consider tactical discounting need to understand the complexity and dangers of the issue.

Upselling

The sales technique of *upselling* is considered an effective tool for revenue maximization. Upselling is used on those customers who either purchased a product already and are yet to begin using/consuming it, or are in the process of finalizing their purchase; a room night, a vacation, a state room on a cruise, a seat on a flight, and a car rental are just a few of the many hospitality products that are conducive to upselling. If a sales agent is successful in proposing a premium suite instead of a regular guestroom, a full-size luxury car instead of a midsize sedan, or a business class ticket on a flight instead of a ticket for a seat in coach, such upselling results in more revenue and higher margins.

There is an important distinction between an upsell and an upgrade. To upgrade means to give a higher category (or premium) product to the customer at

Industry Insight: Upselling at Shangri-La

By Julian Darisse, Shangri-La Hotels & Resorts

Our model for an upselling program in Shanghai was unique. Our hotel had two towers with 952 rooms and nineteen room categories. When I first transferred to Shanghai, I identified two fundamental problems with the program at my new hotel. First, the program was not staff-friendly. Second, it was not revenue-friendly. The question was how to rectify both problems.

Step one was to discuss this challenge with our director of revenue. I showed her how the existing upsell grid was difficult to follow and unclear for the staff. An employee only has a split second to quote a new rate to a client at reception. The director was concerned that we were underselling higher room categories. Results were indicating that the average rate gap between lower and mid-tier categories was too close.

I started by asking her what she had in mind. Her goal was to ensure rate integrity. We started at the high end with our best available rate and she would discount a percentage from each room category. The implied benefit for guests is that they can enjoy a better room category for less than the published rate. Then, I had to review the difference in price per upsell, something that would be easy for staff to sell. Chinese RMB was best served in denominations of 50 and 100, because it's easier to sell in that currency.

Our grid system was reworked to meet both staff and revenue goals. It was approved by the director of sales and marketing, the director of rooms, the director of human resources, and the general manager. Here is how it worked.

Our incentive program for staff was comprehensive and rewarding. Staff received 8.5 percent per qualified incremental upsell. There was an individual incentive for achieving more than twenty, thirty, and forty upsells in one month (staff members were given a choice of spa or food and beverage vouchers). A team incentive was also devised, as follows: if there was an increase of 3 percent in RevPAR over the previous year and the team had achieved its total incremental upsell, then it would receive a departmental cash bonus of 2 percent of that total.

Two months after this new grid system was introduced, we again met to review the previous two months' results. Total upsells had started to increase, but the incremental total was stagnating. This meant that the average revenue per upsell had decreased and was not a significant contributor to RevPAR. It was determined that many upsells during the past two months had been made to corporate guests, whose starting point was much lower than the best available rate. This had to change.

We worked on a tier system with a minimum upsell threshold. The tier system was based on occupancy (tiers 1 and 2, occupancy under 65 percent; tiers 3 and 4, occupancy over 65 percent). The threshold forced the staff to use a minimum starting point to upsell. This eliminated the issues with corporate rates. For example, as opposed to ABC Corporation guest being upsold from a RMB1250 standard room for RMB200 to a club room, it was now to be from RMB1250 to the tier 1 (less than 65 percent occupancy) threshold rate of RMB1650, then the RMB200 increment to a club room. This translated to an upsell increment of RMB600 as opposed to RMB200.

Industry Insight *(continued)*

Staff members were afraid that it would be too difficult to sell to corporate guests at reception. The threshold tier system needed to happen and ended up doing two things. First, it encouraged those who were willing to pay for a club room to continue to do so, with an increased margin for the hotel (and larger incentive for staff). Second, it ensured that corporate-rate guests were not shrinking the price gap between lower and higher room categories.

Further modifications were made to the upselling program. They included the following:

- The exclusion of upselling to certain corporate guests per contract;
- Analysis of "frequently upsold guests" to prevent them from upselling to the same room category twice within a month, which allowed them to enjoy a lower than BAR and only permitting these guests to upsell to a higher room category; and
- Offering staff an added incentive to upsell underperforming room categories.

By working closely with our director of revenue and making the selling easier for frontline staff, we managed to increase year-over-year contributions to RevPAR by a minimum of 4 percent, upsell more than 10 percent of daily arrivals, and have the most successful upsell program in the company.

---

no extra charge. After paying for a compact rental car, a customer can be upgraded to a midsize car at no extra charge at management's discretion; after paying for a regular guestroom, a guest may be given a suite, if for whatever reason management decides to give this upgrade to the guest. Upgrading may impress a customer, but it does not generate extra revenue. Upselling does.

The hoped-for outcomes of upselling are increased revenue and margins for the business and a more satisfying experience for the customer. An appealing value proposition, an interested buyer, and a well-trained sales agent who knows when to propose an alternative product or service—these are all components of successful upselling. Incentivizing the sales agents is probably the most important element of a successful upselling program. It is the responsibility of management to configure an effective incentive program for upselling.

Demand-Based Dynamic Pricing

Dynamic pricing means that a hotel will change its room rates daily or even within a day if up-to-the-minute market information reveals the need for adjustments. It is based on the recognition that the right rate to charge for a room night is what the customer is able and willing to pay. By underpricing, the revenue manager leaves money on the table; by overpricing, the hotel may price itself out of the market. Those who practice dynamic pricing believe that the hotel has to continually adjust rates in response to ever-changing supply/demand conditions. The constant challenge is trying to determine the optimal price on a given day.

Industry Insight: Dynamic Pricing

By Bill Winzer, Vice President, Pricing and Analysis, Marriott International

Dynamic pricing can be a very effective approach to maximizing hotel performance. The key to dynamic pricing is to understand the projected demand for your hotel, overall demand for the market, and demand in your local competitive set.

As demand-changing events occur (group bookings, severe weather, etc.) at your hotel and the competition, the revenue leader needs to determine the impact of the event and any pricing or rate program restrictions that need to be modified.

You must be careful also to understand the pricing and mix of business of your competition. If a competitor raises its benchmark rate, you need to know how much of its business is being sold at these price points. Just because a competitor raises its price point does not mean it is correct. You need to be aware of any pricing changes by your key competitors, fully understand the positioning of your hotel, and make the appropriate pricing changes.

For example, a 200-room hotel was forecasting 90 percent occupancy for a three-day time period. The hotel sales team just booked a corporate group with a strong catering contribution that exceeded the group target rates and contribution over this time period. The hotel has just gone from an unconstrained forecast of 90 percent to 120 percent. Based on this booking, the revenue leader would review the forecasted transient demand by segment and determine what length of stay of restrictions should be applied during this week and if any increase to the benchmark rate is appropriate. All premium rooms would be strongly promoted during these high-demand days. The goal of the pricing and length-of-stay restrictions is to increase revenue and profit for the entire week, not just on the three forecasted sellout nights.

A very popular pricing principle that applies dynamic pricing is called *demand-based pricing*. In low-demand periods, lower rates are offered. As demand increases, lower rate categories are closed and higher rates are quoted. Demand-based pricing as a principle is not new. Its prevalent use today has been made possible by high-speed connectivity, broadband integrated networks, and lightning-speed data processing. Revenue managers can keep their fingers on the pulse of the market, since a lot of information can now be accessed in real time. Room rate adjustments can be implemented at the click of a mouse, and updated rates can be posted across multiple distribution channels with ease.

A simple example will help to demonstrate the difference between dynamic, demand-based pricing and static pricing. Assume, for example, that on a given day, the 300-room Astoria Hotel sells 250 rooms. In scenario A, the hotel has two-tiered pricing with a group rate of $90 and a transient rate of $130. In scenario B, the hotel has multi-tiered pricing: a low-demand rate of $90 and other rates of $110, $130, and $150, offered at increasing occupancy levels. Both scenarios sell the same number of total rooms, with sales at each rate broken down as follows:

A: Rate	Group Rate $90	Transient Rate $130	Total
Rooms sold	150	100	250
Revenue	$13,500	$13,000	$26,500

B: Rate	$90	$110	$130	$150	Total
Rooms sold	80	60	60	50	250
Revenue	$7,200	$6,600	$7,800	$7,500	$29,100

In comparing scenarios A and B, note that B produced $2,600 more in revenue, an ADR increase of $10.40, and a RevPAR increase of $8.67. In scenario B, the revenue manager closed the $90 rate after eighty rooms were booked and set the rate at $110. After sixty more rooms were booked, this rate was closed and the next sixty rooms were booked for $130. When the next sixty units were booked and the hotel had 200 rooms booked, a rate of $150 was offered for the last fifty bookings. This approach increased room revenue, ADR, and RevPAR by 9.8 percent without selling more units.

Dynamic pricing does not adjust room rates only upward or only downward. Price changes can go either way. Assume a revenue manager has forecasted 75 percent occupancy for the day, but she opens the day looking at only 65 percent ROB (rooms on the book) with a $160 BAR. She wonders if that missing 10 percent occupancy can be realized from walk-ins and same-day bookers. By early afternoon, there is no demonstrated new demand out there at the posted rate. At 2 P.M. she decides to intervene. She lowers the BAR to $139. The phone lines start buzzing. By 6 P.M., the hotel has picked up enough same-day bookings to expect 80 percent occupancy. By shopping her comp set, she learns that some of the other hotels are starting to sell out of certain room types. The revenue manager at this point decides to change tactics. At 6:15 P.M., she closes down the discounted rate and posts a new rate for walk-ins of $170. Such is dynamic pricing at work.

How dynamic must one become to be dynamic *enough*? There are no simple answers. The above example raises many questions. Would the originally forecasted occupancy have been achieved without dynamic pricing, just by staying the course with the starting BAR of $160? Did the hotel encounter price resistance or resentment from guests who had booked their room at the higher rates?

There are arguments for and against frequent price changes. A revenue manager will weigh the notion of consistency and price integrity against possible revenue gains through frequent tweaking. There is also the issue of "who's in charge?" Should revenue managers stress consistency or should they go with the flow and let the perceived market forces dictate pricing levels? Are a hotel's service quality, location, brand name, and amenities suddenly worth much less or much more just because market demand shifted one afternoon?

There are dangers in approaching rate controls with a narrow perspective that focuses on one key variable only—usually occupancy. If a hotel reacts to surpassing 80 percent occupancy by closing out its government rate while not forecasting to fill, that decision can be questionable. If, for example, a government-related event takes place in the region and the hotel stops honoring that rate, revenue opportunities will not be maximized. If demand came mostly from that particular segment, competitors that keep their government rate open may pick up the rejected volume. The point is to be selective in closing rate categories. Revenue managers must look beyond the volume of demand to see segment dynamics as well before applying rate controls.

Should a given hotel compete on price? That is a strategic decision. If a revenue manager makes a considered decision to use pricing as a competitive weapon, demand-based dynamic pricing can become one of the most effective tools in the battle for price-sensitive customers.

Endnotes

1. Yesawich, Pepperdine, Brown, and Russel, *National Travel Monitor 2003*. Presented at the International Hotel, Motel & Restaurant Show, New York, N.Y., November 2005.
2. Cathy A. Enz, Linda Canina, and Mark Lomanno, "Why Discounting Doesn't Work: The Dynamics of Rising Occupancy and Falling Revenue Among Competitors," *CHR Reports* 4, no. 7 (2004).
3. Linda Canina and Steven Carvell, "Lodging Demand for Urban Hotels in Major Metropolitan Markets," *CHR Reports* 3, no. 3 (2003).
4. Yesawich et al.
5. Linda Canina and Cathy A. Enz, "Revenue Management in U.S. Hotels: 2001–2005," *CHR Reports* 6, no. 8 (2006).

Case Studies

Case Study 1: Demand-Based Dynamic Pricing After Hurricane Sandy

The Press of Atlantic City, a Pleasantville, New Jersey, newspaper, reported on July 23, 2013, that two Atlantic County hotel operators had settled with the state to reimburse customers who were "excessively and unjustifiably" charged for lodging immediately after Hurricane Sandy, the deadliest and most destructive hurricane of the 2012 Atlantic hurricane season and the second-costliest hurricane in U.S. history.

These are the first reported settlements to come from New Jersey's investigation into claims of price gouging at hotels after the storm, according to a statement from the attorney general's office. Eight businesses, including gas stations as well as hotels, were part of the settlement. The settlement payment included civil penalties, attorneys' fees, and investigative costs. With these settlements and the first two price-gouging settlements announced in April, the Division of Consumer Affairs has assessed a total of $328,844.72 against companies, according to the statement.

Discussion Question

Why were hotels overcharging people who needed a place to stay after Hurricane Sandy devastated their homes? How can this be related to demand-based dynamic pricing? What seems to have gone wrong?

Case Study 2: Demand-Based Dynamic Pricing for the Super Bowl

A study that compared hotel performance during the peak days of the 2012 Mardi Gras in New Orleans, Louisiana, and the time period leading up to the Super Bowl (which was played in New Orleans on February 3, 2013) showed that the Super Bowl drew much higher rates despite similar occupancy levels. Upscale hotels had an average daily rate of $460 during the Super Bowl, compared with an ADR of $265 for Mardi Gras 2012. A similar impact was evident for midscale properties—$392 for a night's stay for the Super Bowl and $273 for Mardi Gras. The rate gaps are significant. (It's interesting to note that the midscale hotels during the Super Bowl had a higher ADR than the upscale hotels for Mardi Gras.) This differential indicates that the clientele for Mardi Gras has a distinctly different purchasing power and buying behavior than the clientele for the Super Bowl.

Hotels in New Orleans reported a boost in weekly performance results during the week of 27 January–2 February 2013 (the week leading up to the Super Bowl), according to data from STR. The market's occupancy rose 24.5 percent to 71.1 percent, its average daily rate jumped 125.9 percent to $289.03, and its RevPAR increased 181.3 percent to $205.59. The New Orleans hotel industry also benefited from weekend events leading up to Super Bowl XLVII.

Overall, during that same time period, the U.S. hotel industry's occupancy rate was up 3.6 percent to 53.5 percent, ADR rose 6 percent to $106.64, and RevPAR increased 9.8 percent to $57.06.

Discussion Question

Is what the New Orleans hotels were doing acceptable practice during the two high-profile citywide events of Mardi Gras and the Super Bowl? Were they practicing revenue management or were they price-gouging?

Chapter 6 Outline

Stay (Duration) Control
    Minimum Stay Requirements
    Stay Through
    Closing a Day to Arrivals
Capacity Management
    Preventive Measures
    Reclaiming Rooms
Case Studies

Competencies

1. Identify three tactics that can be used to maximize revenue by controlling the length of guest stays. (pp. 81–83)

2. Define capacity management and how it is used in revenue management. (pp. 84–89)

6

Stay Control and Capacity Management

STAY OR DURATION CONTROL and capacity management are two important revenue management tools. Stay control is a revenue maximization tactic that involves selecting the highest yield reservations from among all reservation inquiries by managing the availability of the product. Capacity management focuses on maximizing revenue through occupancy. This chapter addresses both of these tools.

Stay (Duration) Control

One revenue maximization tactic is to select the highest yield reservations from among all inquiries by managing the availability of the product. The assumption is that longer stays and higher revenue per stay equal higher yields. The application of *stay control* (also called *duration control*) means that instead of offering rooms on a first-come-first-served basis, the hotel attaches conditions to its room offers. Reservations that don't meet those conditions are rejected, even if rooms are still available.

Stay control measures and forecasting are closely related: the control measures or "strings attached" that a reservation agent has available when processing a booking depend upon the foundation of an accurate forecast.

Minimum-Stay Requirements

Minimum-stay requirements are one such condition. When the demand for rooms outpaces the supply, the result is a sellers' market. During such periods of excess demand, revenue managers can take advantage of the leverage they possess by means of *MLOS (Minimum Length of Stay)* restrictions. If a multi-day event attracts guests expected to stay many nights, accepting shorter reservations may prevent a hotel from selling those rooms to longer-staying guests who call later. Accordingly, the revenue manager may limit room sales to those guests who agree to stay a minimum number of days.

For example, the New York City Marathon is traditionally run on a fall weekend and it attracts many thousands. Most local hotels require a minimum of two nights because of the high demand for accommodations. Similarly, resorts that sell one-week packages may not be interested in accepting shorter bookings during their peak season. The objective of this tactic is to maximize revenue by accepting bookings that produce higher yields based on stay pattern forecasting.

The London 2012 Summer Olympic Games provided an extreme example of a sellers' market. The city's hotels applied all the excess-demand tactics that made sense, including premium pricing and minimum length of stay. Their thinking was: why waste an opportunity to book a six-day stay by accepting a two-night request for the same room? For example, if a caller requested a room for two nights only, arriving on Wednesday and leaving on Friday, that same unit could not be offered to the next caller, who might have wanted it from Sunday to Saturday. If the midweek booking for two nights were to be accepted, the hotel would need to find additional guests with complementary needs—for example, a guest for the three nights from Sunday through Tuesday, plus one for Friday night—just to match the revenue that a six-day guest would produce.

A possible downside of this tactic is that high-lifetime-value guests may be rejected. It should be possible for hotel staff to use discretion with such guests and override a given system's stay controls. It is a very good idea to log and track rejected bookings to make sure the tactic is not misapplied or used counterproductively. Corrective measures can be taken if data shows that minimum-stay requirements are leading to undesirable levels of lost revenue.

When market conditions are unfavorable, a different approach must be taken. The recession of 2007–2009, for example, produced a buyers' market in which buyers took advantage of their leverage by doing comparison shopping. This had a dramatic effect on extended-stay hotels that primarily catered to guests who needed a suite for at least one week. These hotels were not used to accepting short-staying "transient" guests, but the recession forced them to suspend their MLOS policy and offer rooms even for single-night stays. The need to generate cash flow in order to cover fixed costs was stronger than the preference for long-staying guests.

Legality of MLOS. Questions are sometimes raised about the legality of MLOS. The most common inquiry is about whether a hotel that refuses to offer an available unit for sale for one customer but then sells it to another one is guilty of illegal discrimination. The answer is simple: no illegal discrimination takes place if reasonable MLOS criteria are used to determine whether to accept a booking and the hotel will accept the business of any potential customer who qualifies, regardless of his or her protected status. The practice of MLOS is legal as long as all customers are welcome who meet the MLOS criteria.

Another MLOS issue involves how to handle guests who wish to cut their stays short. It is essential for hotels with minimum-stay requirements to spell out to guests in clear, simple terms what the consequences are for understaying a booking without a documented emergency. Such a policy should discourage customers from booking a room for multiple nights just to meet the required minimum and then trying to check out after a shorter stay. If the policy is to charge for the full stay and a guest acknowledges the policy at booking, then there is no legal ground for an understaying guest to seek reimbursement. Nevertheless, hotel managers need to be aware that enforcement of MLOS policies can create ill-will and may wish to waive such charges, especially in the case of regular guests.

Stay Through

On occasion, there are gaps in the forecast. A gap is a very low occupancy day preceded and followed by days that are not considered low occupancy. The *stay-through* tactic intends to boost occupancy for the gap day(s) by promoting reservations that arrive before and check out after the gap day(s). If successful, this tactic generates revenue both from the extra days of reservations and from filling the gap.

Unfortunately, booking extra days may not necessarily fit the travel plans of potential guests. It is not unusual for trip planning to start by booking transportation, especially if it includes air travel. Once flight arrangements are finalized, most guests are not in a position to change flight dates on a whim, regardless of any incentives a hotel might offer. These circumstances can make it difficult for reservation agents to use the stay-through tactic effectively.

Closing a Day to Arrivals

A revenue manager may choose to close a given day to arrivals if he or she believes that accepting more arrivals for that day would not benefit the hotel. After this measure is implemented, no more bookings would be accepted with an arrival on the closed day. Reasons for closing a day might include the arrival of one or more VIPs with extraordinary security arrangements (as is often the case with political figures, a famous rock band, a professional sports team, etc.) or renovating, deep cleaning, or redecorating floors or sections of a hotel. Or it could simply be a staffing and business flow decision. If the given day is both a high occupancy and high turnover day (that is, all or most of the rooms occupied the previous night will depart and all or most of the occupancy on the given day will come from new arrivals), a hotel with staffing constraints may decide at some point not to accept more bookings for the day in question. Suppose, for example, that the 350-room Rose Hotel expects 335 departures and 340 arrivals (40 individual transient guests and 300 conventioneers) on May 15. All 300 conventioneers need an in-room set-up with one of six different welcome packages corresponding to which of the six scheduled seminars they are attending. The guests will arrive as individuals from all over the world. Because the hotel believes it will have to stretch its resources to the limits to manage the turnover of 335 rooms and the arrival of the conventioneers, it decides to close the day for additional new arrivals. It believes that the revenue gained from selling its last ten rooms would probably not justify the added challenges those guests would represent. After this decision is made, all systems will display the same restriction, and no reservation agent will be authorized to override the arrival control measure. Hotel Rose is closed for arrival on May 15.

This tactic should be used with caution. The risks in applying this tactic are high. High-yield reservations (long-staying and full-rate-paying guests) or significant lifetime value guests may be turned away just because they picked the "wrong" arrival day. The revenue management thinking would suggest that the Hotel Rose in the above case should find a better way to deal with the operational challenges (such as giving both the housekeeping department and registration at the front desk additional resources). It will often be more beneficial to continue to accept bookings—possibly even overbooking and walking low-risk low-yield arrivals—and to keep the reservations that are the most important revenue source of a hotel. Revenue managers need to be selective when they have options. Closing a date to arrival is seldom the best option for revenue maximization, though it can sometimes be an appropriate response to unusual situations.

Capacity Management

Capacity management is an essential revenue management tactic. Its objective is to maximize revenue through maximum guestroom occupancy on any given night. On nights when full occupancy seems attainable, most hotels do more than leave it to chance: they overbook the hotel. *Overbooking* means accepting more bookings for a given day than the hotel has the capacity to meet (such as a 400-room hotel accepting 405 bookings). Before deciding to use this tactic, a hotel should look into its legality; in some jurisdictions, overbooking can be against the law. Some hotels choose never to use this tactic on principle, which is a decision that deserves respect. However, the majority of transient hotels in urban commercial markets use overbooking to their advantage very successfully.

The rationale for this ambitious approach is the reality that every hotel deals with cancellations, no-shows, and early departures (understays). Hotels usually have more available rooms to work with than their bookings suggest, because a number of those bookings will never materialize. Moreover, that number is reasonably predictable based on historical trends. If a hotel's records show that 2 percent of its guests with reservations typically don't show up to check in (no-shows), 1 percent cancel before arrival, and 2 percent of guests who are scheduled to check out after the day in question will in fact check out early on or before that day, the hotel can make fairly safe estimates for forecasting purposes.

Note, however, that there are also some statistics that *reduce* room availability, such as overstays and out-of-order rooms. *Overstays* are people scheduled to check out on a given day who decide to stay longer.

The total effect of these elements is sometimes called the *wash factor*. The hotel "washes" its data to remove the misleading parts. The result helps the manager estimate how many units it would be safe to overbook on a given day. The accuracy of that projection is the key. Hotels that are comfortable using the tactic can maximize revenue on high occupancy days by preventing revenue loss from understays, no-shows, and cancellations.

However, using this tactic is not without risks. There will be days when things refuse to fall into place nicely. On a day when nobody cancels, everyone shows up, and no one checks out early, management has to deal with the consequences. Those are the nights when the front office will run out of rooms before it runs out of guests holding confirmed reservations. When this occurs, the front office staff must explain that the hotel cannot honor the reservation. The industry term for this is *walking a guest*. It is fairly standard practice for the hotel to help such guests secure alternate lodging. In North America, hotels usually will also pick up the room charge of guests who are walked, but this practice cannot be taken for granted in other markets. Local customs and supply/demand dynamics may differ a great deal.

In essence, revenue managers must decide whether they prefer to manage the risk of revenue loss or the risk of overbooking. The operational consequences of this capacity management tactic may put front office employees into very delicate situations. Fortunately, proven measures exist that help manage these situations.

When it is necessary to walk guests, the front office should book adequate quantity and quality nearby. No manager should walk a guest to a lower-rated

Industry Insight: Overbooking

By Julian Darisse, Shangri-La Hotels & Resorts

Depending on how you feel about overbooking, I've had the opportunity or misfortune of experiencing it from every angle. I have had to empathize with upset guests, provide support for beleaguered staff, and had nights as a night manager when 5:00 A.M. couldn't come soon enough.

My first experience with overbooking came in Toronto at Canada's largest hotel, the 1590-room Delta Chelsea Hotel. The Chelsea is a centrally located four-star hotel with a massive lobby that was always busy. It wasn't uncommon to have 800 checkouts and 900 check-ins on a given day. As I gained more experience on reception, they would assign me to the status control supervisor position on the late shift. This meant that I would assist my colleagues with assigning rooms and would often decide whether to upgrade or downgrade a guest. I treated this situation like a jigsaw puzzle in which I had to put the right guests into the right rooms to make a perfect fit.

I remember one day in September 2002 when we went as far as -30 on rooms. In addition to our standard inventory of 1590 rooms, we also had at our disposal quite a few parlor rooms—rooms that had already been prepared by housekeeping and that featured all of the amenities of normal rooms except for a pullout bed. With the approval of my front office manager, I started to select guests who seemed likely to take these rooms: single travelers, one-nighters, and guests in their twenties. I sold at least ten of these rooms to guests who were happy to be saving money. We further washed about five tentative bookings and had a further ten pre-registration bookings for early arrival the following day to play with (that is, sometimes guests arriving earlier than normal check-in times will pre-register; if possible, those rooms are kept empty the night before arrival to avoid rushed room cleanings before the guests arrive, but they can be used if needed). By 7:00 P.M. we were about -5, and by the end of the night we had a perfect fill with five no-shows.

While working at the Langham Hotel in London, England, I had to walk guests to other hotels, making sure to avoid high-yield and regular guests. It occasionally happened that we had a large group that couldn't get their connecting flight out through Heathrow, or an unexpected storm delayed train travelers from going home, or we had a technical fault somewhere in the hotel.

Be careful with that last reason for an overbooking! One of my colleagues told a walked guest that we had a bad flood only to have the guest ask to see the flood. Luckily for him, a guest had fallen asleep while running a bath and flooded the room with water! I try to avoid saying that we are "overbooked" or "sold out"; both are clichés and can upset clients even more, so I tend to employ "we're fully committed." That seems to go over better.

London was also great for the "call around"—keeping in touch with other area duty managers and night managers and letting each other know how "deep" you are on a sold-out night. Such courtesy calls help to create an industry camaraderie and to garner good future relations. In fact, if our hotel was close to filling, I would contact a few of our competitors to let them know that we had a couple of rooms

(continued)

> **Industry Insight** *(continued)*
>
> left if they needed help. More often than not, they would take advantage of the offer when oversold. One thing to keep in mind is that the rate that you charge a competitor hotel for a walk will more than likely dictate what rate that hotel will charge you in future, so remember to be fair.
>
> Capacity management is ultimately about teamwork because it takes colleagues from various departments and areas to make sure guests are happy and that the hotel is generating revenue. If it is likely that the night manager will have to walk guests, the reservations manager, revenue manager, front office manager, or late duty manager should not leave for the night without first calling other hotels to find out how many rooms they have available.

hotel. The accommodating hotel should be of equivalent or greater service level or rating classification to mitigate the inconvenience and reduce the chance of further irritating the guest. It is common practice to schedule inexperienced staff for the evening shift, but on a night when the hotel expects to walk guests, inexperienced desk staff should never be left on their own. Managers don't want to see their hotel making the news for the wrong reason. Guests who are irate over a relocation gone bad can cause significant public relations damage. An experienced supervisor or an assistant front office manager should stay until the last walked guest is taken care of. Relocating a guest is a skill that can be perfected only through experience. Guest reactions to getting walked can be unpredictable.

One sometimes hears stories about disgruntled guests suing the hotels that walked them. Litigation has certainly been brought. However, there are no known cases of successful lawsuits against hotels for walking a guest. The existing litigation suggests that hotels should have a policy regarding walking and that under no circumstances should a hotel profit from it. Many hotels include a clause in their confirmation notes that mentions the possibility of overbooking and how it would be handled in order to create awareness regarding this possibility. A common stumbling block for litigants has been that they are unable to show that the breach of the contract (the reservation) led them to suffer specific consequences, especially when the hotel offered to help find alternate lodging and to pay for it.

Preventive Measures

Managers must try to prevent overstays on critical days. It is wise to flag the folio of those guests whose departure plans are suspect and get a commitment to an exact departure date. To communicate and ensure a definite departure date, front desks may require registering guests to initial their departure date on the registration card at arrival, especially if that date is overbooked. It never hurts to get things in writing.

Some guests may genuinely not know at check-in how long they will stay. Others may fail to inform the front office if their plans change. When overbooking is involved, it is up to the front office manager to track down the in-house guests and clearly state how long the hotel can accommodate them. With the advances of technology, a growing number of guests are able to check themselves in and bypass the front office. Technology-based check-in options include self-service kiosks, online check-in, and smart door locks using NFC (Near Field Communication) technology that enables the guest's smartphone to double as a room key. There is no chance in these cases for a guest service agent to confirm the guest's departure date, so the front office needs to contact such guests regarding the departure date, especially on those days when a hotel is in danger of running out of rooms. Texting, tweeting, and e-mailing an in-house guest are acceptable forms of communication; however, an old-fashioned handwritten note left on the table or slid under the door is still very effective.

Consider the situation carefully if guests scheduled to check out on an overbooked day decide they want to extend their stay. Can a guest decide to stay one more night than indicated at arrival? Absolutely. It happens all the time. Can the guest do that without the hotel's approval? Absolutely *not*. Both parties to a contract (written or oral) must agree to any modifications. A rate and a departure date are vital parts in the simple contract that is established between hotel and guest. Hotel managers are on solid legal ground to deny any extensions as long as their actions are reasonable. It often helps to explain the situation and to offer options.

Again, management must decide whether it prefers dealing with an unhappy guest whose extension request is denied or with an unhappy guest arriving with reservation in hand who will have to be walked. The deliberation deserves thought. If there is one revenue management rule to apply in this situation, it would simply be that the business of a known return guest should not be jeopardized for the business of an unknown guest. Revenue management thinking suggests that a high-lifetime-value customer is just too important to risk losing in order to accommodate an unknown guest that may never return. With that in mind, the decisions should always be handled on a case-by-case basis.

If guests must be walked, the decision of *which* guests to walk must be addressed. The winnowing can start by identifying those reservations the hotel would definitely *not* like to walk under any circumstances. There are the VIPs, frequent-stay club members, honeymooners, special requests, multi-night stays, and others who would not make good candidates for relocation. Guests who get walked are usually (but not exclusively) the very late arrivals. Because of the time of day, single female travelers and business travelers generally are not the best candidates to be walked. With corporate travelers, there may be a lot more riding on the decision than one arrival; the whole corporate account can be at risk if the hotel walks the wrong corporate guest. Single-night arrivals with no history and leisure guests who don't mind the apology coupled with a complimentary night elsewhere may make better potential candidates for walking.

Reclaiming Rooms

Revenue managers, front office managers, and executive housekeepers must work together to anticipate the days when a hotel may run short of rooms. With effective cooperation, a hotel might "find" enough usable rooms to significantly reduce the number of guests who must be walked. This can make a tremendous difference.

> ### Selling the Couch
>
> This is a true story of a guest who got an unusual accommodation one night instead of getting walked. It happened in the Hotel Béke in Budapest, close to one of the major railway stations. Mr. B. was a regular guest at the Béke. He was a purchaser for a small company and didn't know his way around the big city. He came once or twice a month, stayed always one night, and he wasn't picky: any room would do. After a number of years, he had earned the status of a regular guest and stopped making advance bookings. He just showed up, accepted any room, and never made a fuss.
>
> On a night when the hotel was heavily overbooked, Mr. B. walked in and matter-of-factly inquired which room could be his for the night. He was flabbergasted to learn than not one room was available. As acceptance of this bad news sank in, he suggested he would just find an armchair in a quiet corner of the lobby and spend the night right there. After all, he had a 5:15 train to catch the next morning.
>
> This gave an idea to the desk clerk, who was genuinely sorry to deny accommodations to such a loyal guest. The clerk knew there was a couch on the top guest floor in the small lobby in front of the elevator. He asked Mr. B. to come back around midnight, after things had quieted down. He would have housekeeping make a bed on that couch for Mr. B., who gladly accepted the offer.
>
> Some early-rising guests the next morning called anxiously to report a man occupying the couch of the elevator lobby on the top floor but other than that everything worked out fine. Mr. B. was charged the price of an extra bed, which he settled leaving the usual tip for the staff. When the Front Office Manager showed up, he asked whether the previous night was a full house. The night clerk said, "Boss, had record occupancy. We even sold the couch in the top floor elevator lobby."

Experienced hotel managers know that additional guestrooms for the night can often be found by looking hard enough. The first step is to compare the daily housekeeping report, which is based on a physical inspection of each guestroom at around check-out time, to the room status in the computerized property management system (PMS). It is not unusual for the front office and housekeeping to have different room statuses for the same room. If the PMS shows a given room as occupied, but housekeeping reports no luggage or other trace of occupancy, the discrepancy must be resolved.

Out-of-order (OOO) rooms should also be considered on sold-out days. The reason code (if there is one) is important in determining whether the OOO status could be changed. Some rooms may have been taken out of service for scheduled maintenance work or deep cleaning. Others may have been placed out of order because of minor defects. If a room can be assigned to a new arrival, even at a reduced rate, it makes sense to put it back in inventory instead of walking a guest. Housekeeping and engineering staff know the rooms best, so the front office needs to work with them closely. Peeling wallpaper, a torn shower curtain, or a bad carpet stain may be temporarily covered up or acknowledged by a discount if that's what it takes to prevent a walk.

Function Rooms. Some hotels have small boardrooms or executive conference rooms that could be temporarily set up for one-night stays. If these rooms have a washroom and a pull-out sofa, or if a cot or rollaway can be placed in the room, some guests may accept them for one night in exchange for a reduced room rate, a complimentary meal voucher, or other incentives. Most local health and safety regulations will require that each "temporary room" be equipped with its own toilet facilities, television set, telephone, and door with its own locking mechanism.

Parloring. If a hotel has suites where the connecting door between the parlor (sitting room) and bedroom(s) can be locked and each room has separate entrances from the hallway with locks, these units can be sold separately if the rooms have televisions, telephones, and adjoining bathrooms. Volunteers can be offered a special deal at arrival. The room also needs a pull-out sofa, a Murphy bed, or a rollaway in order to be offered to volunteers at a reduced rate.

Upgrading. A useful tactic is to offer an upgrade if the hotel is oversold for a particular room type. An upgrade to a junior suite can help satisfy a guest when the hotel is short of the non-smoking queen room originally booked. If three single reservations turn out to be three colleagues checking in at the same time, a quick-thinking guest service agent can offer an upgrade into a single multi-bedroom suite in exchange for their separate standard accommodations. The offer of a bottle of a fine drink may sweeten the deal and allow the hotel can get back three rooms.

Case Studies

Case Study 1: Playoff Time

Hotel Sport is a 250-room independent suburban hotel located close to a sports stadium. The stadium has a capacity of 25,000 and it serves as the home field of the local Major League Soccer (MLS) team, while also hosting college football games on occasion. Hotel Sport is a select service property in the midscale category.

Its rate structure is simple:

Rack	$190
Weekend	$159
Low season/Government	$140
Groups (of 15+)	$130
BAR	$120

Late August is traditionally low season in the hotel. Demand usually picks up after Labor Day, when area businesses and government offices are back in full swing. The hotel has more group business during the summer and it faces less transient demand. The sell rate in late August is the $140 Low Season rate.

In our mini-case we consider handling reservation calls on two consecutive days: on July 29 and then on July 30. On both these days we will deal with bookings for the same late August weekend. For the weekend of August 24–26 the forecasted occupancy is around 130 rooms. Reservations on the book are ninety guaranteed and twenty-five non-guaranteed reservations, plus the hotel expects fifteen walk-ins. There is no indication of any special demand drivers for late August when July 29 arrives.

Discussion Questions

1. On July 29: What rate should the revenue manager approve to quote for reservation inquiries for the weekend of August 24–26 based on the information above?

2. On July 30: There is exciting news: the Major League Soccer franchise of the city has just clinched a spot in the playoffs. The news travels fast: it is all over the sport shows on television, it is the headline news on the sports pages in all local papers, and it is all over the internet. The first game in the elimination round will be against the Los Angeles Galaxy, which features the world-famous superstar Steven Gerrard in its lineup. The first leg of the home-and-home series is going to be played in the local stadium on August 25. All the hotels in city are filling up fast and phones with reservation inquiries are ringing off the hook at the Sport. The hotel's website has crashed as the booking engine could not handle the sudden increase of volume. Things became hectic in a matter of hours at the Hotel Sport. What rate should the revenue manager approve to quote now for group reservation inquiries for the weekend of August 24–26? Are there any stay control measures that should be considered?

Case Study 2: Two Arrivals, One Room

Damien is the afternoon duty manager of the Prince Harry, a 300-room downtown property in Vancouver, British Columbia, Canada. The Prince Harry is an upper-midscale, full-service hotel frequented by both corporate travelers and leisure travelers that is known for its impressive meeting facilities. The hotel is sold out tonight, thanks to a convention. Before finishing up his shift at 12:00 midnight, Damien consults Kyla, the front office supervisor, to find out if there are any more registered guests who have yet to arrive. He learns that there are two such guests: Mr. Baum and Ms. Kerry. Both are confirmed reservations and both indicated late arrival time due to flight schedules. Damien checks the reservation records and learns the following:

- The reservation for Mr. Baum is for a double room at a rack rate of $230 for one night. Mr. Baum is a first-time guest whose mailing address is in the state of Washington. He had booked online through the hotel's website and has confirmed the reservation with a credit card in his name. No special requests were made.

- The reservation for Ms. Kerry is for a single room for two nights at a corporate rate of $165/day. Ms. Kerry is a regular guest who comes on a monthly basis and invariably stays for two nights. Her guest history file shows a wealth of orders of room service meals (breakfast always and dinner sometimes) and pay-per-view movies. Her reservation was made on the phone and it is guaranteed by her company. Her employer is known to book rooms on a regular basis and also function space (mostly board rooms for meetings) a handful of times a year.

Unfortunately, there are no more vacant double or single rooms left for the night. The only vacant room left is a junior suite, which cannot be split because the bedroom can be accessed only through the parlor. Damien did some calling around earlier in the evening and learned that comparable hotels in the vicinity of Prince Harry would pick up overflow at $240 per room (double or single).

Kyla has a suggestion for Damien: "Let's see who comes in first and just take this easy. I am not leaving until both guests are dealt with, trust me. I will check in that first arriving guest into the junior suite. Never a problem for me to give away a minor upgrade, right? If the second guest would arrive later as well, I will walk him/her and pick up the tab for all the costs as we always do if we are walking. Don't worry boss, I've done this before."

The Prince Harry's walking policy states that the hotel pays for a walked guest's cab fare, room charge, and one long-distance call. Damien has to instruct the Kyla what course of action to follow. His goal is to maximize revenue while considering both short-term and long-term implications.

Discussion Question

How should Damien advise Kyla?

Case Study 3: Walking Mr. Walker

Nick is the night manager at the Pearl, an upper-upscale hotel with 460 rooms. His shift begins at 11 P.M. and he always starts his shift by reading the log book because it is the most valuable source of information about what happened at the hotel since the end of his previous shift. He learns from the afternoon entries a frantic effort had been made to secure a couple of extra rooms at neighbor properties of the same category because the Pearl was running short on rooms. Those efforts met with limited success: only one room had been put aside by the Mandarin Hotel in case the Pearl had to walk a guest.

The hotel had been overbooked by three rooms at the start of the day, which did not look like a major problem. Unfortunately, that afternoon a family gathering occupying five rooms decided to overstay their reservation by staying for an extra night. Losing those rooms meant the Pearl was sitting at minus-eight rooms before arrivals started to trickle in. With the situation suddenly looking bleak, the evening shift logged an entry canceling the five 6 P.M. holds. When two early departures were detected by housekeeping, it looked as though the situation might work out after all.

This leaves Nick with only one potential problem, a late arrival named Mr. Walker who has no room assigned in spite of the Special Attention code. This code signifies a guest who is not a VIP, but who is a regular for whom special care is offered in the form of possible upgrades and welcoming gestures such as a fruit plate. Nick has an uneasy feeling about the situation, so he scans the afternoon room status verification report one more time in hopes of finding another discrepancy. Occasionally, a room turns out to be physically vacant even though the PMS system shows an occupied status for it, but Nick has no such luck tonight.

Nick calls the Mandarin front desk to verify that one room is still being held. He learns that it is a queen bed on a low floor, recently renovated, for $340. The night clerk promises to hold it until Nick calls to release it. They are close to filling up to capacity.

Nick is not looking forward to breaking the news to Mr. Walker that the Pearl doesn't have his room. He has heard rumors that Mr. Walker is a short-tempered business executive in the high-pressure field of hedge-fund management. Nick doesn't have long to wait. A black limousine pulls up and Mr. Walker comes walking through the main entrance, apparently agitated. He ignores the welcome of the doorman, venting his anger in a loud tirade.

"I can't believe how these airlines are still in business! It is beyond belief what they can get away with. I book my own flight, I provide the payment, I book my own seat, I check myself in, I even print my own boarding pass. I get no customer service whatsoever, they got lousy planes, rude personnel, ridiculous food and they are totally unreliable! Nobody knows where my luggage is. I'd be lucky if they locate it somewhere across the Atlantic. I should have arrived at 5:30 in the afternoon and look at this: it's almost midnight! My evening schedule got totally messed up." He reaches the front desk and angrily tells Nick that his nightmare started when his flight out of Chicago was delayed, which led him to miss his connecting flight and arrive too late for an all-important business dinner lined up for tonight. Now he just wants to get into his room so he can return a ton of messages and deal with other pressing issues. He only needs to pick up his key and be on his way.

Nick listens patiently to Mr. Walker's tale of woe, wondering if he can keep the irate guest's anger directed at the airline industry. When Mr. Walker pauses to take a breath, Nick quietly remarks, "I am so sorry for your troubles tonight, Mr. Walker. However, I'm afraid I have bad news for you."

"Don't even think about that. I've had more than my fair share of mishaps for one day."

"Well, I don't know how to say this but we have an overbooked situation right now. We are fully committed and ran out of rooms for the night. I can't give you the room we thought we would have. There were guests who decided not to check out and that has left us a number of rooms short."

"You've got to be kidding me, right? This can't be happening to me!"

"I am afraid we will have to ask you to spend your first night at another hotel and be back for your second night tomorrow. It's only today that we are short of rooms. We secured a room for you and we will fully absorb all the costs of..." Unfortunately, Nick can't complete the sentence. Mr. Walker cuts him off abruptly and loudly vents his frustration with a barrage of expletives.

Nick manages to keep his calm while Mr. Walker is yelling at him, reminding himself that the guest has had a string of misfortunes and is not mad at him personally. So he lets Mr. Walker blow off steam until he calms down enough to explain that moving to a different hotel would be a catastrophe. A number of people are likely to stop by looking for him at The Pearl, Mr. Walker explains, because all of his business associates know that this hotel is his home base. In addition, he expects to receive faxes, courier deliveries, and urgent phone messages because his hotel is his office while on the road and often gives out an office number instead of a personal mobile number. Finally, he has already ordered a 7:45 A.M. pick-up in the morning. The angry guest concludes his outburst by demanding that Nick find him a room at the Pearl immediately.

Nick has been listening attentively and taking notes all the while and suddenly an idea occurs to him. When Mr. Walker finishes, Nick asks the angry guest to accompany him to a small boardroom on the mezzanine level. He shows him that the room has a telephone and a private bathroom with a sink. Nick explains that he can have this room fitted to Mr. Walker's needs in a matter of minutes by removing the large table and the chairs and replacing them with a cot made up like a bed. He adds that the shower in the fitness room will be available all night long and that he can even roll in a night stand with a lamp or a television set, if desired. There will of course be no charges for the improvised room, Nick explains.

Mr. Walker is still not satisfied. With a frown, he declares that he is more interested in the other option offered, a room at the Mandarin. "How far is that hotel?" he demands. "Is that place any good?" Nick assures him that the Mandarin is a fine hotel located only a three-minute cab ride away and that the last room is being held for him. He promises to instruct the switchboard operator, the concierge, and all other staff members to promptly forward any messages or deliveries to the Mandarin.

Mr. Walker grudgingly accepts the taxi chit and allows Nick to personally escort him to a waiting cab. Nick assures him that things will work out and promises to call the airline and put a rush order on his missing suitcase if they manage to locate it during the night. He says he expects to see him back at the Pearl tomorrow.

Nick returns to his office and prepares a log note recording a brief summary of the events and a to-do list for all involved in dealing with Mr. Walker's needs. Then he telephones the Mandarin and asks for Mr. Walker's room. When he is put through, he inquires whether the room is satisfactory and if there is anything else he could do for him. Nick also asks Mr. Walker to give him his room number at the Mandarin in order to speed up the transfer of communications and deliveries.

Mr. Walker returns to the Pearl the following afternoon looking much more relaxed after having had a much better day. He is greeted by the afternoon duty manager but he doesn't stop to chat and heads straight for the elevator, eager to get to his room. Upon arriving in the suite that he has been upgraded to, he discovers that a handwritten welcome note is waiting for him propped up by a bottle of his favorite Bordeaux red wine and accompanied by a cheese plate, all compliments of the Pearl.

When Nick comes in to start his shift that night, he is surprised to find an internal mail envelope on his desk. There is a note inside, addressed to the General Manager of the Pearl, who has forwarded a copy to Nick with the remark, "Well done, Nick!" The note reads: "Thanks for the welcome gestures today, much appreciated. The way I was treated last night and today really goes to show how much the Pearl cares about me and this will keep me coming back here, although I was redirected to another hotel (a good choice, the Mandarin). In fact, I didn't skip a beat; got all my messages, deliveries and even my suitcase was there when I woke up! Please tell the night guy I am sorry if I got carried away a bit last night. I had a hard day and he was very professional and helpful. After this incident I will be an even more loyal Pearl guest! You guys rock! Best, P. Walker."

Discussion Questions

1. How did Nick handle the situation?
2. Is the guest always right?
3. What were the keys to turning a potential disaster into an opportunity?
4. What are the revenue management implications of dealing with a guest such as Mr. Walker?

Chapter 7 Outline

Displacement Analysis Process
    Establish Net Room Revenue
        Differential
    Establish Net Food and Beverage
        Revenue Differential
    Determine Other Revenue Differential
    Summarize
Case Study

Competency

1. Describe the function of, identify the steps of, and perform a displacement analysis. (pp. 97–103)

7
Displacement Analysis

WHEN GROUP BUSINESS COMPETES with transient business for capacity allocation, revenue managers need to conduct quick and accurate analyses that will help them decide whether to take a group booking and reject some transient business, or reject a group booking and allocate capacity to individual transient bookings instead. Quantifying the outcome of possible scenarios helps revenue managers make informed decisions.

Displacement Analysis Process

Group revenue can significantly contribute to rooms division revenue for most hotels in urban commercial markets. Management must determine the ideal capacity and rate allocation dedicated to the group market in any given period. The targeted market mix will be determined based on the hotel's strategy. These decisions are certainly subject to seasonality. A hotel may more aggressively pursue the group segment in shoulder seasons and off-seasons than in the main season, when it caters more to higher-paying transient guests. A hotel's historical data provides a good source of information about the staying and booking patterns of each market segment.

The most important partners of a hotel that relies on group business include tour operators, travel agents, convention and visitors bureaus, global distribution systems, meeting planners, and a variety of associations, to start with. There will be times when a hotel needs its partners to fill gaps or boost the occupancy in low-demand periods. Sometimes it is the other way around: groups may desperately need to find accommodations when overall demand is high. Supply/demand dynamics have a tendency to fluctuate due to the cycles of the economy (between prosperity and recession) and changes in seasonality (from peak to shoulder to off-season). Revenue managers and sales directors have learned to appreciate the significance of good working relationships with key group clients and know too well that group business cannot be ignored. If hotels would like to benefit from group revenue when overall demand is soft, groups need to be accommodated also when overall demand is strong.

Hotels will sometimes turn away transient business able and willing to pay higher room rates to allocate rooms to groups at lower rates instead. Can this decision be consistent with revenue maximization strategies? In the right circumstances, a *displacement analysis* can determine the quantifiable benefits of different options.

A displacement analysis is not always appropriate. If a hotel has unsold capacity and reliable forecasting indicates little chance of selling that block of rooms, the hotel is happy to book anything at all. In this case, it doesn't make sense to conduct a displacement analysis for a group booking. In a soft market where a hotel is delighted to get any group business, no displacement will likely take place. However, when demand is high, the revenue manager will likely have to qualify and rank bookings, then select from among potential customers. A displacement analysis should be completed if the acceptance of a group booking will result in turning away other business (transient or other groups). In such a situation, the displacement analysis is a useful tool that helps a hotel determine which booking to accept.

A hotel may use a spreadsheet-based system to compute the variables. The temptation is significant to produce a quick "yes" or "no" answer to a request. But the numeric results of the analysis should not be the only criteria for the decision. Although revenue management is a numbers-driven process, it should never be reduced simply to a push/pull game with dollar figures. It is the *interpretation* of the numbers and all other relevant factors that should drive the revenue management tactics selected.

Why is it necessary to conduct a numeric analysis when management may end up favoring a customer that would pay lower room rates? Here are some considerations:

- Other revenue streams (food and beverage, function rooms, etc.) need to be considered as well to calculate the total revenue impact.
- The lifetime business value of a group client may be an important variable.
- Management needs to know the difference in profitability between scenarios to plan and budget effectively.
- Market share, revenue mix, and other strategic objectives may play a role.

Displacement analysis is a four-step process:

1. Establish net room revenue differential.
2. Establish the net food and beverage revenue differential.
3. Determine other revenue differential.
4. Summarize.

The displacement analysis process compares the net revenue differential between scenarios.

Establish Net Room Revenue Differential

To calculate net room revenue, variable costs must be identified and subtracted from the room rate. In some cases, fees payable per reservation (as a percentage of room revenue and/or a fixed amount per booking) must also be subtracted from the room rate. Other relevant fees may include a percentage of room revenue for marketing and royalty due under a franchise agreement. Some contracts secure a central reservation office (CRO) or a call center fee per booking. Assume the following:

Transient room rate:	$150
Variable cost:	18
Franchise fee of 8%:	12
CRO if applicable:	6

In this case, net room revenue is $150 − ($18 + $12 + $6), or $114.

To establish the net room revenue differential, the following variables must be known:

- The number of group room nights
- Group room rate
- Group room revenue
- Net group room revenue
- The number of displaced transient room nights
- Displaced room rate
- Displaced room revenue
- Displaced net room revenue
- Difference between net group room revenue and net displaced room revenue

The comparison of net group room revenue and net displaced room revenue will produce the net room revenue differential. Let's look at an example.

The Windsor has 400 rooms. The average transient rate in March is $142 and the variable room cost is $17. The Windsor is affiliated with a franchisor that charges a royalty fee of 4 percent and a marketing fee of 3 percent. The combined fees are applicable to room revenue. The local university's business student alumni association plans a reunion. The group requests single rooms for $65 per room night, meals (breakfast for $10, lunch for $24, dinner for $32), and other services for a three-day event scheduled for March 6–8 as follows:

Date	Rooms	Breakfast	Lunch	Dinner	Meeting Room
March 6	85	85	0	85	—
March 7	80	80	0	0	$300
March 8	70	70	40	0	$300
Total	235	235	40	85	$600

The organizer of the alumni association believes that 70 percent of the group members will purchase one beverage per day. The revenue manager of the Windsor would like to conduct a displacement analysis before confirming or rejecting the group's request.

The forecasted occupancy of the hotel for the days in question is as follows:

March 6	March 7	March 8
365	360	310

A Note on Spreadsheet Design

A spreadsheet program is a practical tool for displacement analysis calculations. Microsoft Excel is the most commonly used spreadsheet that is able to perform all the calculations required. For any given scenario, it is simple to calculate the number of daily available rooms by subtracting the number of rooms that are forecasted to be occupied from the number of total available rooms. In our example, the Windsor has 400 rooms and, according to the forecast on March 6, only 365 will be occupied. The number of available rooms is 400 - 365 = 35.

If a group request arrives, the formula will have to calculate the shortfall or surplus in room capacity. In our case, the group needs 85 rooms on March 6, so the hotel will not be able to accommodate 50 (85 - 35 = 50) of those who are forecasted to book.

As long as the spreadsheet returns a positive value for this difference—that is, as long as the hotel will have to displace some rooms—a simple subtraction formula is sufficient (group rooms needed minus available rooms). However, there might be days during a multiple-day group-block booking when no displacement takes place at all. March 8 is such a day in our scenario. The hotel has 90 available rooms and the group-block booking needs only 70. A simple subtraction formula will return a negative value of -20 (70 - 90). However, from the displacement point of view, the number of surplus units (20 in this case) is irrelevant and even potentially misleading: on days with no displacement, the formula should show 0 instead of the actual surplus room count. Consider the following summary of the three-day booking:

- On day 1: 50 displaced rooms
- On day 2: 40 displaced rooms
- On day 3: -20 displaced rooms (that is, 20 surplus rooms)

The summary (SUM function) will calculate total displacement for the group days as: 50 + 40 - 20 = 70. But the right answer for total displaced units is 50 + 40 + 0 = 90. The hotel is displacing a total of 90 rooms (50 on the first day, plus 40 on the second).

Excel's best formula options for solving this issue involve using the "IF" logical formula that can be installed to display a value of zero instead of negative values, or the "SUMIF" function, which will disregard negative values when calculating the SUM of a range of cells. The step-by-step installation of these functions is explained in the built-in self-help feature of the spreadsheet.

Note that the Windsor can accept the group only if it displaces some of the forecasted transient demand. If the group takes 85 rooms on March 6, only 315 rooms will remain for transient guests, which is 50 fewer rooms than the number forecasted. March 7 will have 40 fewer rooms than the forecasted transient demand.

An initial comparison shows the transient room cost as $17 + ($142 × 7%), or $26.94, and the group room cost as $17.00 + ($65 × 7%), or $21.55.

The hotel's capture rate (the percentage of transient guests purchasing a meal) and other relevant data per meal period for transient guests in March is:

Meal	Price	Food Cost %	Food Cost*	Net Revenue	Transient Capture %
Breakfast	$12	30%	$3.60	$8.40	70%
Lunch	$28	34%	$9.52	$18.48	20%
Dinner	$40	32%	$12.80	$27.20	40%

*Cost of ingredients

The group meals will be calculated with the same food costs per item at discounted prices: $10 for breakfast, $24 for lunch, and $32 for dinner.

Group Meal	Breakfast	Lunch	Dinner
Price	$10.00	$24.00	$32.00
Food cost	$3.60	$9.52	$12.80

Beverage costs and prices are the same for group guests and transients. The beverage capture rate of transient guests in the Windsor is 40 percent. The average beverage price is $6.00 and the average beverage cost is 29 percent, so the variable beverage cost is $1.74.

We establish the net room revenue differential as follows:

The number of group room nights:	235	
Group room rate:	$65.00	
Group room revenue:	$15,275.00	(235 × $65)
Group room cost:	$5,064.25	($17 + [$65 × 7%]) × 235
Total net group room revenue:	$10,210.75	($65 − $21.55) × 235
The displaced transient room nights:	90	
Displaced room rate:	$142.00	
Displaced room revenue:	$12,780.00	(90 × $142)
Transient room cost:	$2,424.60	($17 + [$142 × 7%]) × 90
Total displaced net room revenue:	$10,355.40	($142 − $26.94) × 90

The room revenue analysis shows that accepting the group will result in a net room revenue *decrease* of $144.65.

Establish Net Food and Beverage Revenue Differential

We establish the net food and beverage revenue differential in much the same way, working with each revenue source separately. Recall that beverage costs and prices are no different for groups and transients at the Windsor.

Average beverage margin:	$4.26	
Total group room nights:	235	
Group beverage capture rate:	70%	
Total beverage contribution from group:	$700.77	($4.26 × 235 × 70%)
Displaced transient room nights:	90	
Transient beverage capture rate:	40%	
Total displaced beverage contribution:	$153.36	($4.26 × 90 × 40%)

Accepting the group results in a beverage contribution *increase* of $547.41. Turning to food, we determine the following:

Group breakfasts:	235	
Breakfast price for group:	$10.00	
Breakfast cost:	$3.60	
Margin on group breakfast:	$6.40	
Group breakfast contribution:	$1,504.00	(235 × $6.40)
Group lunches:	40	
Lunch price for group:	$24.00	
Lunch cost:	$9.52	
Margin on group lunch:	$14.48	
Group lunch contribution:	$579.20	(40 × $14.48)
Group dinners:	85	
Dinner price for group:	$32.00	
Dinner cost:	$12.80	
Margin on group dinner:	$19.20	
Group dinner contribution:	$1,632.00	(85 × $19.20)
Total group food contribution:	$3,715.20	($1,504 + $579.20 + $1,632)
Displaced transient room nights:	90	
Transient breakfast price:	$12.00	
Breakfast cost:	$3.60	
Margin on transient breakfast:	$8.40	
Transient breakfast capture rate:	70%	
Displaced transient breakfast contribution:	$529.20	(90 × 70% × $8.40)
Transient lunch price:	$28.00	
Lunch cost:	$9.52	
Margin on transient lunch:	$18.48	
Transient lunch capture rate:	20%	
Displaced transient lunch contribution:	$332.64	(90 × 20% × $18.48)
Transient dinner price:	$40.00	
Dinner cost:	$12.80	
Margin on transient dinner:	$27.20	
Transient dinner capture rate:	40%	
Displaced transient dinner contribution:	$979.20	(90 × 40% × $27.20)
Total displaced transient food contribution:	$1,841.04	($529.20 + $332.64 + $979.20)

Accepting the group results in a food contribution *increase* of $3,715.20 − $1,841.04, or $1,874.16 from all three meal periods.

The combined food and beverage net revenue differential is $1,874.16 + $547.41, or $2,421.51.

Determine Other Revenue Differential

The third step in the displacement analysis process is to determine any other revenue. In this case, the group wants to rent a meeting room for two days, generating total other revenue of $600.

Summarize

The fourth and final step is to summarize the results. Doing so reveals the results of accepting the group to be the following:

Net room revenue differential:	($144.65)
Beverage contribution differential:	$547.41
Food contribution differential:	$1,874.16
Other revenue contribution:	$600.00
Total increase from group:	$2,876.92

Accepting the group results in an overall net revenue gain of $2,876.92, which is a combination of a decrease in net room revenue and increases in net food, beverage, and other revenue streams.

This displacement analysis shows that accepting the group will increase the hotel's profitability for the days in question, though it will come at the cost of some transient business. Management may choose to accept the group after this analysis, or it may consider other potential options based on the market conditions and the hotel's strategic objectives. For example, can the hotel persuade the group to accept alternative dates that will not displace transient business? The displacement analysis results do not dictate a simple answer, but they give management critical information it will need to make an informed decision.

Case Study: Displacement at the Hotel Fernando

The 450-room Hotel Fernando is a four-star full-service hotel in San Petresco. It is highly regarded among both locals and tourists. Its service standards and amenities complement its exquisite rooms. In addition, the hotel boasts an impressive amount of meeting and conference function space to cater to events and groups. Due to a steady increase in group bookings, management is proposing to implement new revenue management tactics to expedite its process of deciding which groups to accept. Certain techniques, such as displacement analysis, would prove very helpful, especially during the main season when the hotel operates at high-occupancy levels. By using a displacement analysis spreadsheet, management would be able to more effectively select the booking opportunities with the highest net revenue potential.

The hotel forecasts its occupancy levels for the upcoming Easter weekend, April 14–16, as follows:

Apr 14	Apr 15	Apr 16
405	420	355

The average daily transient rate for those days has been posted at $175 per room. The variable cost for cleaning any occupied room, regardless of whether it has been assigned to a transient or group guest, averages $20. A franchise fee of 8 percent, which is composed of 4 percent for a marketing fees assessment and another 4 percent for royalty fees, must be allocated to the room cost; the fees are calculated based on the room rate. The following table explains these transient room costs:

Total Transient Room Cost:	$34.00
Variable Cost:	$20.00
Franchise Fee: 8% (ADR: $175)	$14.00

After all room costs have been established, the net transient room revenue may be calculated by subtracting the total room costs from the room rate. Therefore, in this scenario, the net room revenue (also called *contribution margin*) is $175 − $34, or $141.

Hotels make a significant portion of their net revenue from rooms, but, if they have the facilities to support other revenue opportunities, such as food and beverage facilities and meeting and banquet halls, total revenue will increase. Based on historical data, the Hotel Fernando's capture rate of transient guests purchasing a meal in its food and beverage facilities is as follows:

Meal	Average Check	Food Cost %	Food Cost	Net Revenue	Transient Capture %
Breakfast	$12.00	30%	$3.60	$8.40	70%
Lunch	$25.00	35%	$8.75	$16.25	25%
Dinner	$45.00	32%	$14.40	$30.60	40%

The information in the preceding chart is based on the Hotel Fernando's purchase-ratio history. Since the hotel's capture rate is higher during breakfast, it receives more business from transient guests during that time period. It is important to point out that the average check at breakfast is $12, which is lower than the average check at either lunch or dinner. The breakfast food cost percentage is the lowest of the three meals, but breakfast also brings in the lowest net revenue per meal. Dinner, on the other hand, has a slightly higher food cost percentage, but this meal period generates a substantially higher net revenue value due to the significantly higher average check.

The Hotel Fernando's capture rate of transient guests purchasing a beverage in its food and beverage facilities is as follows:

Average Beverage Price	$5.00
Average Beverage Cost	20%
Direct Variable Beverage Cost	$1.00
Transient Capture Rate	50%

The 50 percent capture rate means that, on average, half of the transient guests staying in the hotel will purchase one beverage a day. The average beverage price is $5 and the direct variable cost associated with that one beverage is $1; therefore, the hotel would make $4 net revenue from each beverage sold. Furthermore, if 85 transient guests staying in the hotel have a capture rate of 50 percent, approximately 43 people (calculation rounded up) would purchase drinks. Consequently, the hotel would generate $170 net revenue from selling beverages to these transient guests.

The Group Request. One of the most prestigious community groups in the state is the Rotary Club, whose members are known as Rotarians. The Rotary Club meets every month in one of the Hotel Fernando's conference halls. Since the hotel has positioned itself as a leader in conference facilities, the Rotary Club has decided to host its annual Easter event at the Hotel Fernando. Rotarians from around the state will stay in the hotel to attend the conference that is being held on-site over the Easter weekend.

The event coordinator for the Rotary Club requested a three-night stay, arrival on April 14, staying the night on Good Friday, and departure on April 17, which is Easter Monday. The coordinator also inquired about receiving special group room rates of $70, breakfast coupons for $10, lunch for $22, and dinner for $41. The group also wishes to rent a conference room and audiovisual equipment for two days.

Normally, this situation would not pose a problem, but since the hotel has forecasted high-occupancy levels during that weekend, it would probably have to displace a number of its transient guests. Therefore, management has proposed that a displacement analysis spreadsheet be created so management can fully understand whether it is advantageous to accept the group booking.

Occupancies. The occupancy forecasts for the transient guests and for the group-block guests are as follows:

	Apr 14	Apr 15	Apr 16
Forecasted Occupancy	405	420	355
Group Rooms Request	75	85	90

Other Revenue. The Hotel Fernando rents conference rooms for $250 per day and audiovisual equipment for $80 per day. Costs to the hotel for these items are $60 per day for conference room setup and $30 per day for the audiovisual equipment.

Assignment

Perform a displacement analysis for the Hotel Fernando. Include a brief discussion explaining how the different revenue management tactics are applied in your scenario.

If you do so by creating a displacement analysis spreadsheet, the spreadsheet should consist of a workbook with four worksheets:

- Net room revenue differential calculation
- Net food and beverage revenue differential calculation
- Other net revenue calculation
- Summary, where all the subtotals are linked and tallied up for decision-making

Part IV

Strategic Revenue Management

Chapter 8 Outline

Demand Generation Strategies
    Differentiation
Case Study

Competency

1. Describe the role that differentiation plays in demand generation and the most frequently used differentiation strategies. (pp. 109–113)

8

Demand Generation

MANY REVENUE MANAGERS can skillfully use tactical measures to improve revenue generation in the short term. Such managers may well "hit a home run" once in a while. But to truly maximize revenue in a coherent and effective way over the long term, revenue managers must move beyond short-term tactics to embrace long-term strategic planning. Tactics are most effective when they support an overarching strategic goal. The proof of this is in the results. Hotels that use only revenue management tactics are not as consistently successful as hotels that use such tactics in support of a clear strategic goal. Hotels are long-term capital investments by nature. Revenue managers have the ability to use revenue management as a strategic tool to help lay the foundations of sustainable success.

The integration of tactical and strategic revenue management helps management generate demand with proven marketing measures. The strategic approach sees pricing in the larger context of desired target markets, rather than as a nightly race to the highest possible revenue. In addition to generating demand (the topic of this chapter), strategic revenue management topics include the overall management of all a hotel's revenue streams, as well as strategic packaging and distribution channel management.

These topics are complex and exciting because it is at the strategic level where true success can be secured. Revenue managers who recognize and apply the full array of strategic revenue management resources are able to handle any challenges offered by a dynamic marketplace. Using strategy as a guide, the best managers find optimum solutions under any set of circumstances.

Demand Generation Strategies

The objective of demand generation is to produce the most possible revenue under any supply/demand conditions. To achieve this, strategic revenue management goes beyond the management of existing demand to manipulate and increase demand. Using demand generation strategies, revenue managers can take a proactive rather than a reactive approach to maximizing revenue.

Supply/demand dynamics are driven primarily by market forces. A hotel can influence demand because it is an active player in its market. Revenue managers have a significant role in helping the members of chosen market segments to become guests of their hotels. They do this in part through product development and careful product positioning among the comparable options available to potential guests.

Ambitious hotels want their voices to stand out and be heard by targeted customers against the noise of the market. The market noise is loud and constant, as customers get bombarded by advertisements and marketing appeals of all sorts. A hotel's marketing budget is limited even in good times, and marketing managers can work only with the value proposition of a given hotel, branded or not. At the very heart of even the most creative marketing appeal, there must be a marketable product. One of the key drivers of marketability is differentiation.

Differentiation

A hotel can differentiate itself from its competitors in more meaningful ways than room rate. Two examples of successful hotel brands that got started in the early 1960s in North America illustrate this principle quite well. La Quinta Inns championed a concept called *limited service* by offering hotels without restaurants and by catering to the needs of budget-conscious business travelers by placing the telephone on a desk rather than beside the bed. The second example is Four Seasons Hotels, which was the first premium rate luxury chain in North America to offer concierges, complimentary overnight shoeshines, 24-hour room service, bathrobes, and shampoo in their hotels. Both brands became successful by differentiating their products and grew to become significant players in their fields over the years.

The success of differentiation is in eye of the guest. A feature needs to be more than simply different. Guests need to value the feature for differentiation based on that feature to work. For example, it might make little sense for an all-inclusive resort hotel to offer no-charge faxing and photocopying as a differentiating feature, because this feature would probably not be relevant to vacationing leisure guests. On the other hand, a hotel offering "one-minute check-in after 3 P.M. or the night is free" to loyalty program members might find that its time-pressed business travelers highly value this feature.

The most frequently applied differentiation strategies build on unique features, level of service, location, and brand affiliation.

Unique Features. If a hotel has a unique feature that can be successfully exploited to differentiate it, marketing communications can be built around that feature. Some hotels can be considered one-of-a-kind because of their unique locations or architecture, such as historic hotels converted from ancient buildings (castles, chateaux, palaces, monasteries, manors, etc.), underwater hotels, ice hotels, atrium hotels, and hotels with any theme from an Egyptian pyramid to Venetian lagoons to rock and roll.

If the hotel is not unique as a building, it may still develop unique amenities. A hotel may have the largest water slide in town or the only ice skating rink in a desert location. It may be the only hotel inside a baseball stadium with a field view or the place with the most famous musical dancing fountains, the best gym, or the smartest and fastest elevators. Any of these could be a unique selling point. Several years ago, Starwood Hotels and Resorts upgraded essential amenities to gain successful differentiation. This multi-brand corporation began its campaign after a commissioned sleep study concluded that many guests have unsatisfactory sleep experiences in hotels. In 1999, Starwood launched the Heavenly Bed—top-quality mattresses and bedding upgrades—at its Westin Hotels brand. The successful differentiation led to similar initiatives at other Starwood brands (such as the Sweet Sleeper at Sheraton).

Some landmark hotels are so famous and prestigious that even a brand affiliation essentially becomes a subtitle. The Waldorf Astoria New York, managed by Hilton, or The Savoy in London, managed by Fairmont, are such properties. The cachet of the name a landmark hotel has successfully established over the years can eclipse everything else. That can be the best source of differentiation, but it is also the hardest to earn.

Any unique feature not provided by default (like a location or architecture) can be difficult to establish, but, once recognized, can be the source of competitive advantage for years to come. Any hotel that can claim a unique feature is in a strong position to build on its unique value proposition through premium pricing and a high level of awareness that helps generate and sustain demand.

Level of Service. An extraordinary level of service can also be a differentiator. For example, some hotel chains have built a culture of service excellence. The challenges are significant. The approach to business must incorporate every facet of operations, from hiring to supply chain management. A high employee-to-guest ratio is one piece of the puzzle. Detailed attention must be given to the thread count of the chosen linens, the angle of pen placement on the note pad, the temperature settings in guestrooms, and the maximum number of telephone rings allowed before an employee must answer a call. In every guestroom, consistent quality must be delivered every day. Individualized "high-touch" services are offered, and empowered employees never settle for a compromise in the pursuit of perfection, whether it concerns a meal, a floral arrangement, or a last-minute ticket request for a sold-out event.

Service-related differentiation may not always be so resource-intensive. Pet-friendly hotels offer a service that typically does not require extensive investment, even when providing special menu and room service for pets. This differentiation can matter a great deal to some market segments.

An emerging category classified as *select service* (also called *focused service*) falls somewhere between full service and limited service. The intended differentiation targets business travelers who may not need the whole range of services offered by a traditional full-service hotel, but who need more services than a limited-service hotel traditionally offers. This service category offers value for the traveler through hip design, high-end technological amenities, and select food and beverage service to meet the needs of emerging customer segments. These brands (for example, Four Points by Sheraton, Holiday Inn Express, Hyatt Place, Element and Aloft from Starwood) in many cases use the halo of a well-established "mother ship" brand. The lower investment requirements help to take certain brands down-market and make them feasible options for interested franchisees. In smaller markets where a full-service hotel is not financially viable, a select-service operation with streamlined food and beverage services may be the best fit.

Location. A prime or unique location can provide a highly valuable point of differentiation in markets with high barriers to entry. The airport hotel inside the terminal building, the closest hotel to a main attraction (festival site, museum, theme park, etc.), the best ocean front among other resort hotels, and the hotel right on the slopes at a ski resort will (other things being equal) generate higher revenue than competitors in less favorable locations.

As many hotels have learned through the years, the factors that determine whether a hotel is in a prime location or not can change over time. Many one-time prime locations have become secondary over time for a variety of reasons. Hotels built near railway stations in the heart of a city have often suffered when the station relocated. For that matter, hotels near railway stations also lost a lot of their business when people began to travel primarily by automobile. U.S. hotels on important roads through towns and cities lost a lot of their business when the interstate highway system begun in the 1950s bypassed them and traffic volume dropped deeply on what came to be considered the old country roads. A fine seashore resort can be badly damaged by hurricanes, or a city famous for top-notch entertainment and fine cuisine can lose its market position as a favored destination after a tragic flood, as the industry witnessed in New Orleans after Hurricane Katrina devastated the city in 2005. These examples are humbling reminders that even the advantage of a prime location cannot be taken for granted.

Some locations offer such unique differentiation that a hotel can become an attraction in itself. Examples include under the sea in Dubai; high on the cliff wall of an ancient volcano on the Greek island of Santorini; deep in the Canadian wilderness on a lake accessible only by float plane; on a tiny private coral island in the Maldives; in the heart of Paris just steps away from the sights; or right on Times Square in New York City. These locations offer the highest barriers to entry for any possible competitor.

Brand Affiliation. A brand name can help a hotel differentiate itself from competitors. A successful brand can be the source of quantifiable competitive advantages. Most branded properties outperform non-branded ones as a result of premium pricing and efficient central reservation systems. Brands tend to have more resources for promotions and for efficiently managing their distribution channels. As the commercial lodging industry is a very competitive one, successful brands can be significant factors in revenue maximization. Brand recognition helps the guest know what to expect in terms of price level, service quality, amenities, and other product attributes.

Branding is prevalent in the lodging industry. Single- and multi-brand hotel companies capitalize on this marketing trend and continually create new brands to cater to changing lifestyles and consumer preferences. Some brands own and operate their properties, but franchising and management contracts have become the most common methods of brand growth. Under both the franchising and management contract business models, revenue generation is the key source of financial viability. As a result, revenue management has become critical for each stakeholder.

For hotel property owners who consider acquiring a brand through franchising, the main considerations are the advantages gained through brand recognition and the sales and marketing support a brand would deliver.

For property owners seeking a qualified manager to run the hotel, the main consideration is creating a management contract that aligns the interests of owners and managers. In the earlier days of management contracts, the contracts often favored the management company. By the 1990s, owners and their representatives (known as *asset managers*) began to effectively negotiate contracts in a way that better aligned the parties' interests. Some management companies (known as *first-tier* or *branded* management contract companies) offer a brand of their own, while others (known as *second-tier* or *unbranded* management contract companies) may manage properties under many flags. First-tier companies offer the power of their recognized brand, efficiencies on the cost side based on their supply chain management systems and volume discounts, and impressive revenue potential through multi-channel distribution systems. Second-tier companies can't provide the added benefit of a proven hotel brand, so hiring them will not produce any extra cachet that could translate into premium rates, but an owner may have more negotiating power and can exert more influence on balance. Owners who hire second-tier management contract companies may also decide to purchase a franchise or to use other branding options, such as referral organizations or marketing alliances (Best Western Hotels, Leading Hotels of the World, Relais & Chateaux, Small Luxury Hotels of the World, and so on).

Brand penetration in the hotel industry varies significantly on a global scale. In the United States, more than 70 percent of the hotels are branded. In Canada, the ratio is around 40 percent. France has the highest brand penetration in Europe, where about 25 percent of hotels are flagged.

Case Study: The Dropped Cake

Four Seasons Hotels and Resorts is one of the most successful global luxury brands in the hospitality industry. While Four Seasons hotels are luxuriously appointed, the company decided to focus its differentiation strategy chiefly on providing excellent personal guest service. The hotel company has a unique approach to hiring: its philosophy has always been to hire based on candidate personality and character. According to Four Seasons, new employees can learn the necessary job skills through training and mentoring, but if a candidate does not have the right attitude, he or she can't embrace the corporate culture and consequently can't become a brand ambassador.

In this case study, a high-profile Canadian computer hardware and software company held a two-day convention at the Four Seasons Inn on the Park in Toronto, Canada. The largest ballroom was rented for the duration of the event and hundreds of delegates rented a sizable room block. The hotel had to make sure it impressed the main event organizer, Ms. Sealy, the meeting manager in charge of all the details of the two-day event. She instructed the banquet housemen regarding the arrangement of chairs and tables in the ballroom; she oversaw the decorations, flower arrangements, and audiovisual setup. She made certain that the right welcome gifts got delivered to the assigned rooms and suites of key executives. She was somewhat exhausted as she approached the front desk carrying a white cardboard box at the end of the hectic first day of the convention.

Ms. Sealy said that a cake was in the box and asked if it could be kept refrigerated overnight. She said she would pick it up next day. The concierge courteously accepted the box and assured her that everything would be taken care of as requested. Mark, the night bellman, was called to take the box with the cake all the way to the bakeshop.

Two employees, a junior and a senior baker, staffed the night shift, which had just begun at midnight. The night bakers were responsible for all the wonderful baked goods offered at the breakfast buffet: crisp almond croissants, delicious Danishes, and a wide variety of bagels, among other delicacies. They were busy setting up for the shift. Leslie, the senior baker, was close to retirement and he disliked disruptions to his routine. Leslie finally stopped what he was doing and asked Mark what he wanted. Mark started to say that the meeting manager had asked that the hotel store the box in its fridge for the night when Leslie somewhat impatiently grabbed the box Mark was holding, in an obvious hurry to return to his work. He acted hastily and carelessly and the cake slipped out, landing smack in the middle of the bakeshop's floor tiles. Even in its ruined state, it was clear that the cake had been made in the shape of the computer company's famous corporate logo.

Leslie froze and swallowed hard. Mark was the first to react. He grabbed the house phone and dialed Gabe, the night manager.

"Hi boss, there is something I've got tell you. We dropped the cake."

Gabe was running the end-of-day reports, but he stopped and went to the bakeshop to assess the damage right away. It was clear that the cake was totally ruined and beyond repair. It was 12:30 A.M.

Gabe scratched his head and said simply that the cake had to be replaced. He ordered a new one from Leslie and said it must be completed by 7 A.M., when he would return to inspect it. But Leslie said, "Not so fast, boss. No cakes are baked overnight." They made the best hot-cross buns in the world but did not bake cakes, Leslie added. They were not trained to bake cakes.

Gabe asked Leslie to call Seetaram, the bakery chef, at home. Leslie initially resisted since he felt uncomfortable waking his supervisor in the middle of the night. Gabe promised that he would do the talking instead. He apologized to Seetaram for waking him, and described the problem and his proposed solution. Seetaram did not need persuading. He assured Gabe that the cake must have been an outside delivery, not made in the hotel's bakery. Nevertheless, he volunteered to come to work at 5 A.M. and make a replacement cake for the guest. It would be in the same shape, color, logo, and all, he promised.

Gabe returned to his office much relieved and confident that he had made the right call. Before he entered the event into the logbook, where all noteworthy events of a shift were recorded, he instructed the switchboard operator to activate the red-blinking message light on Ms. Sealy's room phone. The message was simple: "Call the night manager."

Much to his surprise, his phone rang at 4 A.M. It was Ms. Sealy, who asked what her message is about.

"Well, Ms. Sealy, I have good news and bad news," said Gabe. "The bad news first: We are so sorry, but we accidentally dropped your cake. It is damaged beyond repair. The good news is that we will replace it with a brand-new one."

Ms. Sealy must have expected worse news and didn't seem angry at all. "Don't worry about it," she said. "We had already presented it at the convention yesterday, so it's already played its part. We have no pressing need for a replica. Don't worry about that cake."

Gabe was immensely relieved to hear those words. However, Gabe had no intention of passing them along to Seetaram. Instead, he explained to Ms. Sealy that the new cake would look and taste even better than the original had and that he personally guaranteed that. And, of course, it would be on the house. What she planned to do with the new cake, he added, was entirely up to her.

"We sometimes make mistakes, Ms. Sealy, for which we apologize," Gabe added. "At this hotel, this is how we deal with it."

Gabe returned to the bakeshop at 7 A.M. as he had promised. A sleepy Seetaram proudly displayed the new cake. He explained that he hadn't been able to sleep after the telephone call in the middle of the night, so he had come to work even earlier than he'd promised.

Discussion Questions

1. Was Gabe right not to tell Bakery Chef Seetaram that Ms. Sealy had said the cake had already served its purpose and not to bother replacing it?
2. Why is it important to understand the hotel brand's differentiation and market-positioning strategy?
3. How is the solution to the service mishap grounded in the corporate culture of this given brand?
4. How can the night manager's approach to solving problems be related to revenue maximization?

Chapter 9 Outline

Market Segmentation Methods
    Mobile Commerce
Market Targeting
Market Positioning
    Repositioning/Rebranding
Promotion
Customer Relationship Management
Market Mix Management
Case Studies

Competency

1. Identify and describe several marketing concepts that play a significant role in strategic revenue management efforts. (pp. 117–126)

9

Marketing Strategies for Revenue Management

MARKETING IS CLOSELY RELATED to most facets of revenue management. Revenue management does not teach (or re-teach) the discipline of marketing, but it builds on most elements of marketing and discusses some of them from the perspective of revenue optimization.

Market Segmentation Methods

If a company believes that everyone is a potential customer, a mass marketing approach is reasonable. However, the hotel industry has realized that the market it serves is not homogeneous. To better understand the characteristics of different people, the market can be divided into groups that have common needs and distinct buying habits. Market segmentation is a necessary strategic measure for best results. Major traditional market segmentation variables are geographic, demographic, psychographic, and behavioral traits and price-sensitivity.

Geographic segmentation can be as broad or as narrow as necessary. There are geographic information systems (GISs) that contain significant amounts of information in databases that can be mined and layered based on numerous search criteria. Geographic areas can be identified by postal code or by geo-position (longitude and latitude), if that makes sense. It is frequently practical to use a location-based segmentation that considers driving distance to a destination. If one hotel defines a primary target market as one less than three hours' driving distance away, the boundaries of that geographic market can be identified on a map fairly simply.

Demographic segmentation includes age cohort, gender, nationality, marital status, family size, income bracket, and other similar information based on census data. One of the most frequently used terms in demographic segmentation is *Baby Boomers*. This age cohort comprises those born between 1946–1964 in the United States, Canada, the United Kingdom, and Australia, where a significant spike occurred in birth rates after World War II. This cohort has been large and affluent for many years and is the target of a great number of marketing appeals. This aging cohort is only one of several age cohorts that have arisen since over the years, with more recent cohorts including *Generation* (or *Gen*) *X*, *Generation Y*, and *Millennials*, among others.

Psychographic segmentation considers social class, lifestyle, and personality. The largest single group of customers (one third of the total) can be characterized as the mainstream group, made up of moderate-income families that value security, avoid taking risks, love team sports, like safety, and need social approval for the choices they make, whether it involves selecting a car, a vacation destination, or a clothing brand. The needs and preferences of a psychographic segment are important to consider when designing marketing communication to reach a given target segment. The newspapers the target segment members read, the television shows they watch, the colors that appeal to them, the faces they identify with in an ad, all are carefully selected for effective promotions.

Behavioral segmentation's typical breakdown includes buying habits, attitudes toward a product, and usage rate, among other criteria. For example, the psychographic segment known as mainstreamers prefers a simple and uncomplicated way in every aspect of booking, arrival, and staying (behavioral) at a hotel. Family holidays and the need to feel comfortable in a foreign environment are important to them. The Holiday Inn brand hit the right button for this segment with an ad campaign that used the tag line, "The best surprise is no surprise at all." This carefully targeted promotion appealed to a specific segment that became the message of the hotel chain. If a marketing appeal combined more than one segmentation method and targeted domestic mainstreamers of a certain age bracket, it would be classified as psycho-demographic plus geographic segmentation.

A market segment can be any size that makes business sense. The most important aspect is that the group members need enough characteristics in common that they will respond in a similar way to a marketing appeal.

Segmentation can start on a broad basis and then be further refined with additional criteria, if that makes sense. For example, we might start with the segment of corporate hotel guests that are domestic. If useful, we could further refine this segment to females who travel alone. Should there be a need for even further segmentation and reliable data is available, we might narrow the group to same state/province single female corporate travelers who have an annual income of $60,000–$99,000 and stay at least three times per year at a given hotel. This example combines geographic, demographic, and behavioral criteria.

Relatively new segmentation approaches go beyond the traditional segmentation approaches. Life-stage segmentation is a good illustration of this trend. The travel industry identifies *babymooners* as a segment comprising couples expecting their first child. Before the new baby arrives, the couple may want to take a vacation trip, just the two of them for the last time, creating memorable experiences.

Grandparents taking their grandchildren for vacation trips represent another emerging life-stage segment that cuts across the traditional boundaries of age, income, location, and buying method. This segment is targeted by travel companies that see more grandparents living in different cities from their children and who are delighted to bond with their grandkids by taking them on cruises, to theme parks, or to other child-friendly destinations.

A segment that deserves the attention of travel professionals is based on sexual preference and lifestyle: the LGBT market (Lesbian, Gay, Bisexual, Transgender). People in this cohort can belong to any demographic or geographic segment; however, they display a higher-than-average propensity for taking trips, are above-average spenders on those trips, and prefer gay-friendly destinations that are known for their diversity.

Another segmentation approach is based on a specific usage pattern: for example, those viewers of televised sports broadcasts who surf the Internet on their tablets or smartphones while watching games can be targeted regardless of age, income, or other demographic classification. These users can participate in real-time contests by predicting a game event (such as who scores the next touchdown, when a team will take its next time-out, what the final score will be, and so on) and can be targeted by QR (Quick Response) code coupons for instant purchases of meals, drinks, or other merchandise.

Revenue managers also are keenly interested in distinguishing price-sensitive guests from those who are not price-sensitive. These two basic groups call for different marketing and revenue management approaches. A widely used measure of price sensitivity is known as *elasticity*, sometimes called *demand elasticity* or *price elasticity*. Elasticity is a ratio that expresses how a change in the price of a product or service affects unit demand for that product or service. For hotel rooms, it is calculated as follows:

$$\text{Elasticity} = \frac{\text{Percent change in demand (unit occupancy)}}{\text{Percent change in room rate}}$$

The original unit demand and price are the bases from which the percentages are derived. That is, if a hotel changes an $80 room rate by $20 (to either $60 or $100), the percentage change is the dollar change divided by the original price, in this case, $20 ÷ $80, or 25 percent.

The concept of elasticity is based on the economic principle that, for a given level of demand in a market, a rise in price will cause unit sales to drop, while a drop in price will cause unit sales to rise. Elasticity tells us which change is larger. A value of less than 1.0 is interpreted as *inelastic* demand, while a value equal to or greater than 1.0 is interpreted as *elastic* demand. Since one change is almost always positive and the other is almost always negative, the calculation almost always results in a negative number, but by convention, the negative is ignored.

This is important information to calculate and track because revenue managers want to know how customers will react to price changes. If a 5 percent price increase produces only a 2 percent drop in unit demand, the elasticity is 2 percent divided by 5 percent, or 0.4, which is inelastic. In this case, demand is such that a price increase will not reduce unit sales disproportionately. Stated another way, the market will bear the increase and the hotel's room revenues will increase. On the other hand, if the same 5 percent price increase produced a 10 percent drop in unit sales, the elasticity would be 10 percent divided by 5 percent, or 2.0, which is elastic. In this case, the price increase caused an even larger drop in sales, meaning that the hotel's room revenues will suffer.

Managers should examine elasticity especially when considering room discounting. In 2003, research conducted on 480 hotels revealed that, on average, for every 10 percent drop in room rate, demand rose by only 1.3 percent.[1] When demand is inelastic, room rate decreases will reduce total room revenue.

Different market segments often display different levels of price elasticity. If a 5 percent room rate increase resulted in a 4 percent decrease from corporate bookings and a 12 percent decrease from leisure traveler bookings, the corporate segment was inelastic at 0.8, but the leisure segment's reaction was very elastic at 2.4.

Price sensitivity quantified with an elasticity index is a useful tool for tracking and benchmarking. Other frequently used elasticity indexes are *income elasticity* (which measures the change in income level compared with the change in quantity sold) and *cross elasticity* (which measures the price change of one product and compares it to the rate of change in sales of another product, such as the impact of a change in airfare on hotel bookings).

Mobile Commerce

Travelers are increasingly using mobile telecommunications technology for data access when traveling. Mobile users can easily get real-time price comparisons. Service providers use location-based triggers and global positioning system–based dynamic maps combined with access to online content regarding places of interest for travelers on the road. For example, Kootenay Rockies Tourism, a Canadian destination marketing organization, offers full online travel information services to mobile users. KootenayRockies.mobi provides travelers with hundreds of pages of information about accommodation options, attractions, events, and even restaurant menus, all of which is available through mobile phones or other handheld devices.[2]

The hotel industry is paying increasing attention to so-called *road warriors*—frequent guests who purchase a significant number of hotel room nights while traveling on business. For revenue management purposes, it is important to note that these guests want quick, easy access to booking and prefer to conduct transactions while on the go. They have extensive product knowledge and, by the time they dial in, they are already sold on their choice of hotel. This segment increasingly turns to mobile versions of distribution channels. Hotels that understand this segment provide booking options through mobile-friendly versions of their websites.

Some hotels also use the guest's mobile phone to page the guest or to forward instant messages. Mobile phones may even be used for direct one-to-one marketing opportunities. Smartphone users increasingly use their phones to pay for purchases at vending machines, to pay for parking at parking meters, for cab rides, and more. Lodging operators are tapping into this trend as well.

A few years ago, VingCard Elsafe, a manufacturer of electronic door locking entry systems, developed a mobile phone usage solution for guestroom access control using *near field communication (NFC)* technology. The hotel sends a text message to the guest's NFC-enabled mobile phone before the guest arrives; the text conveys the assigned room number and a code. The guest proceeds directly to the assigned room, where the mobile phone with the message revealing the code must be held close to the door lock. The door lock will pick up and verify the code, then grant access. That completes the check-in of a pre-registered guest.

Since the launches of the iPhone in June 2007 and the iPad in 2010, developments in mobile computing have changed our professional and personal lives. The capabilities of smartphones and tablets continue to rapidly evolve. Mobil-compatible and mobile-optimized websites can harness the possibilities of this new era. Websites made with responsive design that recognizes the user's technology platform, whether a laptop, a desktop, or a smartphone device, are proving to be effective. New apps are developed and launched regularly to cater to the interests of mobile users. Businesses in the travel and hospitality industries are paying attention to such new developments, regarding them as revenue tools to attract potential guests based on their location and geographical proximity, and also as communication tools (to, say, tweet and text guests when their table or room is ready).

Market Targeting

The objective of market targeting is to focus marketing efforts on a group that has the potential to respond to a marketing appeal and that the hotel is best able to serve. The process of evaluating different market segments for targeting should consider a segment's size and growth potential, as well as its structural attractiveness, which refers to such issues as age diversity, income brackets, geographic distribution, and whether it is easy to reach the segment through advertising channels. Analysis may show that, although the initial idea was not bad, a cluster of potential customers is too complicated to reach, too resource-intensive to locate, or not likely enough to respond to marketing efforts. A segment may look attractive, but the decision to select it for targeting must also consider the existing competition.

During the 1980s, companies were looking for the customer in each individual. That changed in the 1990s, when companies started to look for the individual in each customer. Today, a balanced approach that concurrently considers both the purchase intentions of customers and the customization capabilities of service providers seems to be more promising.

Quantifiable issues also must be considered even when a proposed booking comes from the target market. For example, if accepting a group booking is consistent with a chosen market mix strategy (in terms of transient/group capacity allocation), but the chosen group needs rooms only and it is unwilling to book meals, this factor must be addressed in the decision to accept or reject the business.

There are other concerns as well. Assume a hotel has a group room block of 100 units to sell on a given day four months out. The forecast suggests that, at the group rate of $100, it is probable that 80 percent will sell. That would generate $8,000 in room revenue and leave 20 units unsold from the room block. So far, there are only tentative bookings that need confirmation before the cutoff date, which is still one month away. What should a revenue manager decide if he receives a firm booking request for that date for 100 units at $60 per room? This offer would sell out the entire room block for a total of $6,000. Should the manager accept the firm offer of $60 because it is certain, or hold the rate at $100 in the hope that more lucrative bookings will arrive later as forecasted? The question is more important than the $2,000 revenue differential between the forecasted $8,000 and the firm booking for $6,000. This conundrum requires strategic thinking. The first question should be this: What is the hotel's target market? Is it the $100 per room guests or the $60 clientele? If the revenue manager is comfortable that the hotel's product can be successfully marketed at the $100 price, there should be no reason to undermine that price positioning just to lock up an early booking.

Market Positioning

Once a hotel differentiates its value proposition, the next step is choosing a positioning strategy. A successful positioning strategy will be based on a set of possible competitive advantages that the hotel identifies. The chosen positioning needs to be communicated to target markets that are defined through segmentation. Generally, positioning strategies can be built on product attributes, price, or the needs a product or service can meet and the benefits consumers gain from buying it.

There are also strategies to position against an existing competitor. For example, a hotel may choose to position itself as a child-friendly property. A competitive advantage can be its proximity to an indoor water park that has wave pools, slides, and lazy river rides. The hotel may also develop special amenities such as a supervised activity center for kids, enhanced safety and security, separate children's check-in station, games room, children's menu, and so forth. The needs for a safe and fun environment for kids are used for positioning. The benefit of a carefree vacation for parents is also emphasized.

Repositioning/Rebranding

Repositioning is one effective way to improve the revenue performance of an underperforming hotel. This effort frequently includes rebranding the property as well. The rebranding may involve branding a non-branded hotel or switching brands. Some owners drop their brands and become independent through repositioning, but that happens less frequently.

Repositioning a hotel down-market is often done when a hotel reaches a point in its life cycle when a major renovation becomes necessary to avoid functional obsolescence. Instead of a capital-intensive major overhaul, a hotel may choose a facelift only (new paint and furniture, but fixtures and building technology remain more or less the same) and a repositioning down-market. A struggling upscale hotel could become a competitive mid-tier one, or a mid-tier hotel could become a budget hotel. New brand affiliation is usually part of the repositioning to facilitate financing and entry into a new market.

Repositioning up-market is also done on occasion, when opportunistic investors identify an underperforming asset that can be acquired at a reasonably low price in markets where unmet demand is identified for the high-end segment. Through renovation and major upgrades, a hotel can meet new criteria required to become a higher-category hotel. The process may involve installing a new management team and rebranding to acquire an affiliation consistent with the new market positioning. Astute investors are often able to unlock hidden potential through repositioning a hotel.

Promotion

Promotion is a next logical step in the strategic revenue management process. Promotion includes a blend of advertising, sales promotion, public relations, and personal selling. It can begin after differentiation and a market positioning strategy have been devised and a target market is identified. A hotel needs to communicate what it has to offer to its target market. The different ways of promoting the product help to create awareness and suggest action. Successful promotion leads to increased bookings.

A classic adage about advertising says, "Half the money I spend on advertising is wasted, but I don't know which half."[3] Targeted ads that deliver the right message to a carefully chosen segment using the most appropriate media mix can significantly improve the efficiency of advertising. The spending on television ads in recent years has declined, while spending for online ads has increased. This trend is in response to the changing lifestyle and media consumption habits of the coveted higher-income, better-educated segment of consumers. With today's broadband infrastructure, mobile communication devices are increasingly used to deliver rich media content on top of voice and e-mail or texting to subscribers using high-speed connectivity. This trend opens promotional possibilities that many corporations are ready to exploit by shifting a growing proportion of their marketing budgets from offline to online media.

An important aspect of moving sales and marketing more and more into the digital realm is *measurability*, the significantly increased ability to track and benchmark. While it is possible to measure the impact of a roadside billboard, a newspaper ad, or a television spot, the measurement of a click-through rate or the analytics of a website provide a far more accurate measure of a promotional campaign or a marketing appeal. The return on digital advertising or digital couponing is easier to measure, which makes it easier to justify.

Customer Relationship Management

The theory and practice of *customer relationship management (CRM)* is a marketing field that has become more and more integrated with revenue maximization in recent years. The core concept of CRM is similar to the revenue management principle of identifying the highest-yield customers. It aims to generate more revenue through interacting with and retaining customers.

Any CRM system helps answer important questions of interest to a revenue manager:

- Who are my best customers?
- Why are they my best customers?
- How do I keep them?
- How do I find more like them?

The process starts with data analysis to help identify those guests that the hotel sees as having valuable revenue potential. By extracting information from the available data, revenue managers are able to differentiate those groups who appear to be the best prospects for targeting. The next step is pattern detection and identifying how services and products could best be customized to cater to those patterns. At the execution stage, the value proposition has to be communicated to guests through the best-suited channels.

The growth in data volume and data sources has created a demand for better business intelligence using CRM. Many companies try hard to assemble a coherent picture of the customer from scattered information located throughout the entire enterprise. Marketers cull demographic and behavioral data from various sources, but it has been a challenge to gain accurate attitudinal data. *Predictive analytics* has successfully taken on that challenge and contributed to an improvement in CRM in this regard.

Predictive analytics, a relatively new tool, can not only determine a customer's propensity to buy, it can also forecast whether a customer will respond to a specific marketing appeal within a given time frame. Despite exponential growth in the quantity of data available, businesses can still achieve insight by making strategic decisions based on the quality of analysis. Predictive analytics is a growing field that has already led to a more dynamic customer experience by building on CRM and helping to maximize revenue potential at customer touch points.

Market Mix Management

Each hotel can tell for itself which of the market segments it serves is the most profitable. The objective of *market mix management* is to maximize profitability by allocating sufficient inventory to the most important segment(s). Market mix management is a strategic approach that may result in higher profitability at comparable or equal occupancy levels. Revenue growth is supported by selecting and booking the most profitable market group instead of less profitable groups vying for the same rooms. If a hotel allocates too much of its inventory to a less profitable segment, its revenue potential may not be fully maximized.

Hotels are often tempted to accept bookings on a first-come, first-served basis. But by allowing less profitable early bookings to take up most of the capacity, the shorter lead-time but much more profitable corporate segment could be squeezed out. It requires accurate forecasting and continuous monitoring of demand to find the right capacity allocation strategy for each week to optimize revenue generated from the mix of available customers.

The targeted market mix will be determined based on the individual hotel's capacity, location, classification, market position, bed configuration, and other factors such as affiliation, rating, age, and so on.

Capacity. Smaller properties have to focus on a key segment of the market that they are best suited to target. Their market mix management can be a lot simpler than that of larger hotels. Midsize and large hotels are able to accommodate more travelers. These hotels need to develop room inventory allocation strategies. The larger the hotel, the stronger the need to seek business from the group market and the meetings and conventions market. The ideal market mix of a 100-room hotel is different from the ideal market mix of a 1,600-room hotel.

These considerations are also subject to seasonality. A hotel may more aggressively pursue the group segment in shoulder seasons or off-seasons than in the main season, when it prefers higher-paying transient guests.

Location. A hotel's location has a lot to do with the mix of potential guests it appeals to. There are geographic regions with special features (such as climate, scenic beauty, and historic sites) that influence both the seasonality and the nature of demand for accommodation. Business travelers favor locations considered major hubs of commerce. Some locations are known to be leisure getaway destinations, and some cities are major convention cities. Accessibility (for example, direct flights), facilities, and climate are key factors. Destination marketing can also make a difference. Destination branding builds on reputations and image to develop branding for a given destination (such as the Big Easy; the Big Apple; What Happens in Vegas Stays in Vegas; etc.). Hotels in urban locations and those in suburban locations will attract guests from different markets, just as warm winter resorts have a slightly different customer mix than cold winter resorts. Prime location helps price positioning and provides more leverage in managing the mix of market demand.

Classification. Hotels can be classified by a number of factors. A hotel classified as a suburban midsize full-service branded hotel that targets the corporate traveler will probably have a market mix that consists of mostly individual transient business on weekdays. The same hotel may have a different market mix strategy to allocate more inventory to leisure groups on weekends and during the off-season, when the corporate market is soft.

Classification can determine a hotel's market orientation and price range, leading to the identification of primary and secondary (and even tertiary) market segments that will make up the market mix. Different classifications result in different market mix strategies.

Market Position. The market position of a hotel affects how dominant the hotel can become within its comp set. If a hotel controls a significant portion of the room inventory, it has more clout regarding rates and targeted market segments. A hotel that has no significant influence within its comp set is like a small fish in a big pond; it has to be keenly aware of market forces.

A dominant player in a comp set has more leverage to set trends and drive rates or introduce a segment into the market mix. For example, if a hotel with a strong market position decides to pursue a health-conscious segment of the market through the addition of a spa, other hotels in the comp set will have to take note. Smaller hotels in the comp set may consider riding the same wave and introducing their own, less resource-intensive additions to cater to the needs of the new segment attracted to the market: alternative menus, upgraded gym equipment, and other wellness and fitness initiatives, for example.

A hotel's market position within its comp set will influence the decisions related to market mix strategy. Each comp set has leaders and followers.

Bed Configuration. The needs and wants of a market segment must be accommodated to earn the business of that segment. A hotel that decides to pursue family travelers has to be able to offer cribs, cots, extra beds, and adjoining rooms to cater to the needs of families traveling with any number of kids of all ages. If a hotel has only king-size beds, it will not appeal to travelers who want to share a room but not the bed.

Other. Some other factors may have a role in developing a market mix management strategy. A property's age is one. Older properties may have a better-established presence in a market. On the other hand, the physical shape of a property inevitably factors in the selection of a target market. Older buildings are a lot more challenging to keep up. Room size, amenities, building systems, and furniture, fixtures, and equipment can all show tell-tale signs of aging. Although there are great examples of old landmark hotels being well capitalized and kept current through renovation and refurbishment, the more usual occurrence is that, as a hotel starts losing its luster, the change in the mix of the clientele follows more or less in sync with the physical deterioration of a property.

Another important consideration to keep in mind when developing a market mix strategy is this: some customer segments mix together better than others. One of the most critical intangibles any hotel can possess is called *ambience*. It is a blend of smells, sounds, colors, objects, and the people that one encounters on the premises. Ambience can be carefully managed to provide guests with the feeling of being at a place where they are comfortable. Always keep in mind that other guests are part of the ambience. Therefore, a revenue manager should not allocate capacity to any segment that may potentially drive away members of a more important segment. The market mix on a given day must be balanced against strategic objectives.

For instance, one resort hotel that had successfully built a good family-friendly reputation learned a lesson the hard way. One weekend, to fill a gap, the hotel booked a convention of "swingers" known for their adult lifestyle. The hotel received numerous complaints and bad media when concerned parents staying that weekend with kids objected to scantily clad members of the convention openly displaying lewd behavior. The market mix that day became a source of trouble. The important lesson for revenue managers is to be mindful of who will share elevator rides. Some market mix solutions result in a perfect blend, while others do not. The market mix strategy should consider which segments and clusters can be blended without negative repercussions.

Endnotes

1. Linda Canina and Steven Carvell, "Lodging Demand for Urban Hotels in Major Metropolitan Markets," *CHR Reports* 3, no. 3 (2003). Available at www.hotelschool.cornell.edu/research/chr/pubs/reports/abstract-13608.html.
2. *Tourism Daily*, April 26, 2007.
3. John Wanamaker (1838–1922), U.S. department store magnate.

Case Studies

Case Study 1: The Last Two Rooms

The Hotel Empire is a 460-room full-service, branded, upscale hotel with a clientele that is 80 percent corporate transient and 20 percent affluent pleasure travelers. Larry Parks, the assistant front office manager of this downtown hotel, has had a very busy Friday evening. The activity in the lobby was winding down as he looked at the list of Expected Arrivals at 11 P.M. in the Front Office. All the names were checked off, meaning everybody on the list had arrived. The hotel picked up six walk-ins as well earlier in the evening. Three were walked from The Astor, a competing hotel a couple of blocks down the road, which is sold out and evidently overbooked due to a large convention. The downtown hotels were also filling up. Larry always liked the idea of picking up overflow from neighboring properties.

The Empire was practically full with 458 rooms occupied. Only two rooms were still vacant. The rack rate was holding up at $220; all walk-ins were paying just that. Everything looked pretty good for a Friday night. Later, Larry was in the back office finishing off some paperwork when the switchboard called.

"Larry, I've got two lines on hold for you, both outside calls. Where do you want me to transfer them?" asked the operator.

Larry took the calls there at his desk in the back office. The first one was from The Astor, the hotel that had walked three of its guests earlier.

"Hi Larry, this is Amy-Lou from the Astor. Thanks for picking up our walks earlier today. Our incoming traffic is winding down, but, before I finish my shift, I need to know if there is any chance you can pick up more walks if we need you to." Larry said he had two rooms left at $220, first-come, first-served. Amy-Lou took note and thanked him.

Then Larry took the second call. The caller was part of a family of four that had just arrived in town. The caller sounded a bit desperate. Larry thought he might have a chance to complete the perfect fill by selling the last two rooms.

The parents, Nigel and Janet Watson, were taking their two sons on a one-week vacation to explore the nearby lake district. Their plan was to find a budget hotel or motel for the night, then pick up their rental car the next morning and hit the road. Their sons were 10 and 12 years old. Nigel wanted to book two rooms: one for himself and the older boy, and one for Janet and the younger boy. Nigel hadn't anticipated any difficulty finding two rooms for around $100 per room for the night.

The Watsons had taken a cab from the airport upon landing and were surprised to see "No Vacancy" signs lit up all around the motels on the airport strip. They asked the cab driver to take them downtown, and soon learned that most hotels were sold out in the downtown core as well. Nigel was willing to pay up to $140 per room now, if push came to shove, but no more. When the second budget hotel turned them away, he had asked the driver to wait, grabbed his cell phone, and started to work the hotel directory he'd been given by a friendly guest service agent. The Empire was the third hotel he called.

Once Nigel had explained his reason for calling, Larry glanced at his watch, noted the time was 11:03, and quoted the rack rate of $220. Nigel asked if that was the best he could do. Larry replied that their rate for the Friday night was $220 and that satisfaction would be guaranteed. The rooms were on the top floor and included Wi-Fi access, a coffee maker, in-room safe deposit box, flat screen HD television set, super-soaker shower heads, fog-free make-up mirror, and more, but Larry hadn't finished describing all the room features when Mr. Watson abruptly apologized and put his wife on.

Janet Watson took over the conversation from her husband. She pointed out that their budget was $100 a room, but, as all the hotels in that price range were full, they realized that they would not find what they were looking for. Given the circumstances, they were prepared to pay up to $140 per room—but that was the highest they would pay. If the Empire agreed, the Watsons were ready with credit card in hand, would guarantee both rooms, and would arrive in mere minutes. Janet stressed that they would love to find a place for the night because the hour was getting late. "The kids should be in bed by now. Please, Mr. Parks, be considerate. I'm sure you have the authority to adjust that rate."

Discussion Question

What factors should Larry consider when deciding whether to accept the Watsons at $140 per room?

Case Study 2: Repositioning Strategy

The Hotel Citadel was a 411-room independent mid-tier hotel at a downtown location in Ottawa, Ontario, the national capital of Canada. The hotel offered 23,000 square feet of meeting space. Ottawa was considered a strong market at the time (the late 1990s). CHIP REIT (Canadian Hotel Income Properties Real Estate Investment Trust), the investor, had identified a promising opportunity to unlock the hotel's potential and had purchased it in April 1998.

The new owners decided to renovate and reposition the hotel to target an upscale market segment. CHIP successfully secured a franchise for the Crowne Plaza Hotel brand (owned today by InterContinental Hotels Group). The exterior of the property was upgraded and all meeting rooms, public areas, and guestrooms, including Club Floor and Club Lounge, were renovated in 1999. The changes involved management as well: a seasoned upscale management team was installed.

Total	Cost	Per Room
Purchase Price	$20M	$48,660
Investment	$11.5M	$28,000
Total Cost	$31.5M	$76,640

Following the re-opening, a targeted effort was made to secure business for higher-end social catering functions and events.

The following table provides data in Canadian dollars:

	8 months Before	8 months After	1999	2000	2001	2002
Occupancy	65%	74%	65%	74%	70%	71%
ADR	$86	$102	$100	$121	$120	$118
RevPAR	$56	$75	$65	$89	$85	$83
Total Revenue	$8.5M	$11.2M	$14.0M	$19.2M	$18.4M	$18.3M

Note that 2001 was the year of the 9/11 catastrophe. The entire travel industry declined in North America after the terrorist attacks of September 11, 2001. This hotel's performance metrics also reveal a minor decline.

The new owners and operators of Crowne Plaza claimed that their RevPAR market share increased from 77 percent in 1999 to 92 percent in 2002.

As a fine ending to the story of the acquisition and repositioning of the hotel, HVS (Hotel Valuation Services) Transactions published in its Canadian Market Report that in December 2007 the 411-room Ottawa Crowne Plaza sold for $63,638,829, or $154,839 per room.

Discussion Questions

1. What were the key reasons for the improvement in the hotel's performance?
2. What was CHIP REIT's return on the investment for the period of its ownership?

Chapter 10 Outline

Competing on Price
Rate Parity
Revenue Streams Management
Strategic Packaging
    The Package Development Process
    The Objective of Packaging
    Packaging and Segmentation
    Packaging and Revenue Streams
        Management
Case Studies
Chapter Appendix

Competencies

1. Outline critical considerations involved in strategic pricing decisions. (pp. 131–133)

2. Describe the nature of and need for revenue streams management. (pp. 133–134)

3. Explain the nature, process, and purposes of creating packaged value propositions. (pp. 134–139)

10

Strategic Pricing

MOST REVENUE MANAGERS AGREE that pricing is both tactical and strategic. Pricing tactics are applied when dealing with short-term issues. Same-day and same-week pricing decisions are tactical in nature. The hotel's objective in those cases is to generate cash flow. If a hotel believes that a room rate adjustment will increase its sales revenue for a given day or week, it will practice tactical rate management.

Strategic pricing has a different objective. It considers the long-term aspects of rate management to increase revenue by growing market share and improving market positioning. A hotel's strategy must be firmly grounded in market information and product quality. Inferior products will not earn a sustainable position in a competitive market. If a hotel has a poor product, no matter how well merchandised, it may not be able to build a loyal clientele of return guests over the years. Strategic positioning should align price point and product quality with target markets.

Competing on Price

The most important initial issue in strategic pricing is deciding whether a hotel will compete on price at all. The more a revenue manager knows, the less likely it is that he or she will recommend competing on price alone. The main problem is that any competitor can beat any low rate any time it wants to. The competitor may be desperate enough to do it or may simply want to create some buzz in the market. Most hotels have other ways to generate demand that are both more sustainable and financially more lucrative than trying to be the lowest-price operator in a market.

Some managers mistake the value perception of customers for price sensitivity. The customers' perception of value is created by a number of product attributes other than price.

Is price the most important driver of purchase decisions? Research that looked extensively at value drivers discovered that price was the third most important item for business travelers staying in economy and midrange hotels, behind property type/location and amenities. It was the main value driver for the same customer segment when booking upscale hotels. Price was second behind amenities for leisure guests selecting economy hotels, but the key factor for leisure guests when selecting upscale and midrange hotels.[1] Another interesting finding was the guests' willingness to pay up to 10 percent higher rates for enhanced safety and security. Another survey found that 38 percent of online bookers were willing to pay up to 20 percent higher room rates for customized services. These survey results indicate that low price alone is not necessarily the most important selection criterion for a significant portion of hotel guests.

If price is not always the most important decision driver at booking, the strategic choice to make price the primary competitive weapon must be considered with extreme care. Competing on price may work well for some hotels in certain markets, but it is definitely not for all hotels in all markets.

The objective of matching competitors' price points is to be on par with the competition. In most jurisdictions, a hotel cannot directly discuss product pricing with its peers and competitors because that would violate antitrust laws and regulations designed to protect consumers from price gouging. But it is legal for revenue managers to monitor the competitors' rates. Based on the price changes in a given comp set, a hotel may decide to adjust its own rates. A hotel might make the strategic choice to stay close to the rate levels of comparable products. There are pros and cons to such a strategy.

The first problem is control: who is in charge of a given hotel's rate management? If a hotel feels compelled to blindly follow its competitors' every price move up or down, the question is a valid one. Those who follow their competitors in this way often learn that they are just as smart as their dumbest competitor. Revenue managers should do their own thinking and strategy development, not just mirror others' actions. A second issue is the fact that the cash flow situation and the product costs of a competitor may be different, and those factors may provide the competitor's motivation for room rate changes. Revenue managers should know better than to change their own rates due to the operational challenges of competitors. If a hotel's revenue manager doesn't know why a hotel in the comp set is changing room rates and is not being pressured by operational issues, why would he or she be eager to meet price changes? Frequent price changes can also confuse customers.

On the positive side, the perception of the market needs to be considered. Guests shopping for accommodations at a destination may need to see comparable prices in order to encourage them to look further into other product attributes. To prevent a booking decision made on rates, take the rate difference out of the picture. Then let the location, service quality, brand power, or other differentiators become decision drivers. If preserving market share is a concern, a hotel may need to match discounted rates. If a competitor raises rates, these increases might be matched as well so the market will not perceive one hotel's product as inferior simply because it's cheaper.

A hotel may or may not choose to set competitive rates. Nonetheless, revenue managers should always monitor rates in their comp set and act on rate changes if a justifiable reason that is consistent with a chosen pricing strategy compels them.

Pricing Strategy and Market Share. Research has shown that hotels that hold their rates and do not pursue a strategy of underpricing competitors achieve higher RevPARs. If a hotel's strategic objective is to do anything to increase market share, strategically positioning its room rates lower than those of the comp set will provide results (at the cost of financial performance). The gain in market share is not likely to be solid, though. Guests who are price-loyal will always base their booking decisions on price and go wherever they get a lower rate. Should there be another hotel in the market one day with a steeper discount or a better deal, the price-driven clientele will probably switch without hesitation. This game of "price limbo" cannot be won with certainty.

Physical Rate Fences. Room rate management may use physical rate fences to differentiate similar value propositions. Examples include the size and location of a room, the view, bed configuration, and the presence or absence of amenities (such as hair dryer, robe, separate check-in counter, Wi-Fi, iPod docking station, HD television, fruit plate, etc.).

Non-Physical Rate Fences. Non-physical rate fences can also affect price points. Examples include the season of the year, time of booking (same-day or advanced booking), membership (loyalty program, associations), form of payment (non-refundable, full advance payment in exchange for a lower rate), booking channel (lower rates for hotel-direct Internet bookings), volume discounts (group rate), and so forth.

Rate Parity

Competitive pricing is based on keeping up with competitors. In contrast, *rate parity* is focused on a given hotel's own rate management practice. Rate parity means offering the same room rate for the same room night, regardless of distribution channel (e.g., voice or Internet) or booking mechanism (e.g., direct or third-party).

While hotels may strive for rate parity, it has often been difficult to achieve. When there is rate *dis*parity, bookers will find different rates for the same room night based on distribution channels. The chances are good that they will exploit the differences. If they can find a rate lower than the hotel-direct rate, they will take it.

As an unspoken acknowledgment of rate disparity, many hotels have initiated highly successful *best-rate guarantees* that promise to meet or beat the rates of third-party resellers. These guarantees have driven the majority of room bookings back to a business-to-customer model, thus taking the bulk of room bookings back from third parties. It is a key issue for hotels because there are cost differentials between bookings. Even when the same rate is offered to guests, the hotel's *net* rate may be different depending on the unit cost per booking associated with non-hotel-direct bookings. Revenue managers should remember to consider the net rate for decision-making purposes.

Customers prefer transparent pricing. If the same product is available at different price points, customers may begin to wonder what it is they are actually paying for. Too many price points and complex pricing tend to lead to confusion (although customers will remain clear-headed enough to book the lowest price). The simpler a pricing strategy is, the more manageable it becomes both for hotels and their customers.

Revenue Streams Management

Most hotels have several revenue centers providing revenue streams. Different revenue streams typically have different contribution margins, so sales in one department can be more or less profitable than equal sales in another department. Even within a single department, different items can have different contribution margins. In the food department, for example, steak dinners usually have a higher margin than chicken dinners. Premium beverage brands have higher margins than the hotel's well brands. A failure to understand the importance of revenue stream margins can lead a manager to increase gross sales in a way that actually has a very small effect on net revenue.

As a simple example at the departmental level, consider a hotel that has $10 million in sales revenue derived from rooms, food, and beverage sales. In hotels having these three revenue centers, room sales almost always produce the highest contribution margin, followed by beverage sales, and then food sales. Assume this sample hotel has a revenue breakdown and contribution margins as follows:

	Gross Revenue	Percent of Gross Revenue	Contribution Margin	Net Revenue	Percent of Net Revenue
Rooms	$7,000,000	70%	85%	$5,950,000	74.4%
Food	2,000,000	20%	65%	1,300,000	16.2%
Beverage	1,000,000	10%	75%	750,000	9.4%
Total	$10,000,000			$8,000,000	

Note that room revenue is 70 percent of gross revenue, but that it accounts for more than 74 percent of the hotel's net revenue. The net revenue percentages for food and beverages are smaller than their gross revenue percentages.

Revenue streams management, also called *revenue mix management*, involves making decisions on the basis of contribution margin information. Revenue managers need to know what the margins are for the various revenue streams in order to know which streams to focus on for better financial results. The fundamental purpose of revenue streams management is to maximize profitability by focusing on the most profitable revenue streams and increasing their volume within the total. A conscious effort is made to increase revenue from the more profitable (higher margin) revenue streams. For example, it is more desirable to generate rooms revenue than function space revenue. When negotiating a group contract, a hotel should focus more on food and beverage revenue than on audiovisual equipment rental or meeting room decoration upgrades. Efforts spent on negotiating for (low margin) ice carvings should rather be spent on negotiating for premium beverage brands. Revenue streams management decisions may also affect the allocation of marketing and other resources.

Strategic Packaging

If a hotel is happy with its revenue performance, it has no pressing financial need to develop packages. However, if a hotel would like to generate more revenue through higher occupancy and/or higher per capita spending, it may consider strategically packaging a variety of products and services. A complex product can at times be more appealing to guests than offering rooms only. This strategy is somewhat underrated and underused because effective packaging takes work.

When created and marketed well, however, packaging can increase both occupancy and overall revenue.

When a hotel offers products and services bundled with room nights, it is called a *package*. Although there are no rules about how many components a package should have, the traditional notion is that it will have at least two items in addition to the room accommodation. The addition of only one item (say, a breakfast) is not widely considered a package in marketing terms. A simple package with room, meal, and transportation is often an appealing one. The most frequently offered packages include food and beverage, transportation, entertainment, and/or wellness and fitness components.

A hotel may choose to apply discounted rates to a package, making the package cost less than the components would cost if purchased separately, *but it doesn't have to*. Discounting any or all components is at the discretion of the service providers. Hotels may believe that discounting will help sell the package, but they may also create packages that are so attractive they don't need to be discounted. Customers may perceive value even at full rates if a package is well composed and creative and meets the needs and wants of carefully targeted customers.

To make the right decision regarding the delicate issue of pricing and discounting, a hotel needs to consider the price sensitivity of the targeted market segment, as well as how its package measures up to its competitors' packages. Is there a special element in the package? The more unique a package is, the better its chances to generate interest without discounting. The most challenging and resource-intensive aspects of package development are finding the concept, the theme, and the targeted market segment. Pricing comes well after that homework is done.

The Package Development Process

The package development process must always begin with a careful look at data. If package development is based on supposition instead of solid data, it becomes a gamble. Responsible managers prefer not to gamble. Data (independent facts) can be trusted. Data won't lie and it doesn't have an agenda.

What data should be considered? First we analyze what we already know about our own business need. A CRM system is a great source of information. A hotel will want to identify:

- The guests' reason for staying at a hotel (business, pleasure, or both).
- The average length of stay.
- The average dollar amount spent per guest (broken down to room and others).
- The average lead time and method or channel of booking.
- Rate and occupancy data by season to identify high, low, and shoulder season.
- High and low RevPAR days of the week.

Interpreting this data can lead to a better understanding of a hotel's clientele.

If it makes business sense to fine-tune the market segmentation, a revenue manager may want to collect information (using observation, survey questionnaires, outside consulting firms, etc.) regarding the geographical market served. (Where do most of our guests come from? What is their preferred means of transportation?) Demographic information can also be meaningful. (What age brackets do they belong to? What income brackets? What is the gender breakdown?)

Weekday and weekend packages may target different segments and offer different package elements based on the data mined and analyzed. Smart packaging shouldn't be based on guesswork. Sound research may allow the hotel to create packages that work for guests the hotel knows. Some packages can be developed to increase revenue from a dominant market segment, and other packages can be designed to generate greater demand from a smaller segment that has latent potential (the latter being an example of supply-induced demand).

The perception of value is the most critical aspect of package design. Packaging just for the sake of packaging is unnecessary and mistaken. The targeted customers need to perceive the value of packages. Each bundle has a chance to become successful only if it appeals to its audience. Suppose a hotel offers the choice of special dietary meal selections (organic, vegetarian, low carb, etc.) and babysitting services to go with a show featuring a superstar. It may get the attention of a health-conscious market segment that travels with underage kids and appreciates world-class entertainment. In this case, a discounted price is not likely to be the element that creates a perception of value: it would be the combination of carefully chosen elements hitting the right buttons for its intended target segment. We may have a winning package even at full rates.

Packages with Internal Components. One way to bundle items is to use only components that the hotel itself produces and controls. For example, a hotel might offer a "Weekend Getaway" package that includes transportation from the airport to the hotel, a welcome cocktail, a Saturday room night in a junior suite, and a dinner for two. In this case, the hotel offers its own shuttle bus for the transportation, its own lobby bar for the drink, and its own restaurant for the meal. This way, the hotel has the highest level of control over the total package in terms of quality, price, and other product attributes (menu selection, room location, etc.).

Internal packages are easier to develop because they require less coordination, and they are less labor-intensive to develop because the developing department doesn't have to scout, rank, and qualify external service providers. The risk of anything going wrong or of being forced to troubleshoot is also significantly smaller. The hotel that offers only its own products in a bundle would know if a vehicle were being serviced at the shop, an employee calls in sick, or a suite is out of order. Corrective measures can be taken, and guests may not even notice if a minor change becomes necessary.

There is, however, a downside to internal bundles. A hotel has a finite number of items it can package, which will limit the possibilities if can offer. It is extremely difficult to offer a meaningful differentiation and to generate excitement if a hotel lacks unique attributes. Sometimes the missing piece of the puzzle is not available inside one's hotel.

Packages with External Components. Given the limitations of packages containing only internal components, some hotels take on the challenges of teaming up with external service providers to create that spark that they hope will light up the switchboard. For example, a "Night on the Town" package might offer a room night, a drink, an event ticket, and a sightseeing tour. In this case, the hotel controls only the room and the drink. The event (a show or a sporting event) and the sightseeing tour are offered by outside operators. The hotel may negotiate favorable rates with a theater, convention center, arena, or major league sports franchise and a tour operator, but it has no control over those components.

A hotel may not have legal liability for a third-party mishap, but the hotel that is developing a package is responsible for screening and qualifying those businesses it partners with. A hotel that trusts its guests to another company's limousines, buses, eateries, or entertainment must know the product it offers in its bundle. Knowing does not come from phone conversations, websites, or hearsay. Testing, shopping, and experiencing the product is fundamental. We have to taste it, smell it, see it, and touch it in order to evaluate it and, if it is acceptable, to properly promote it to guests.

Some managers question the rationale of bundling external items with a hotel's room nights. They ask, "Why discount my rate to sell someone else's product?" There are various possible answers. A show or game ticket may help sell a room night that would otherwise remain unsold. In some packages, the external component may be the main demand driver. Just consider what a Super Bowl, a Grand Prix, or a Mardi Gras can do for a region's hotels. In these cases, hotels may benefit from the cross-marketing exposure and generate business as a result of their associations with key external events, attractions, or shows.

The Objective of Packaging

Hotels in different markets use packaging for different purposes, but all packaging has one common element. The fundamental purpose of packaging is to create *the perception of value*. If a hotel successfully creates an appealing value proposition at full rates that guests perceive as a good deal, discounts may be unnecessary. The temptation to discount can be significant, as dropping rates is a lot easier than going through the trouble of developing creative packages. But great packages can distinguish hotels and help them earn business.

A significant difference exists between the objectives of urban commercial properties and resort hotels. The author and Hoffer Lee, an MBA student at the University of Guelph, conducted research which showed that the primary purpose for packaging in urban hotels was to boost occupancy, while resort properties offered packages to boost revenue in the first place. If a hotel has to compete in a fragmented metropolitan market, every meaningful point of differentiation matters. Attractive packages may become demand drivers if all other factors (location, quality of service, rate, amenities, loyalty programs) are comparable.

The resort business is different. Even in a fragmented resort market, the packages offered by a resort hotel may not become critical factors at the point of purchase. Guests will consider prices, service quality, brand familiarity, amenities, and proximity to attractions (or the airport) before they consider the hotel's packages.

Note that vacation packages offered by tour operators show different dynamics. In those cases, consumers are dealing with a value proposition of a third party, not a service provider. Tour operators also benefit from revenue management strategies and tactics, but their primary source of income is the margin they realize by marketing a variety of service providers' products. In a vacation package, the transportation and the hotel are the key components; location, price, and the convenience of the schedule are also key decision drivers. For example, a guest may prefer an all-inclusive one-week vacation package that offers a Saturday departure over a similar package with a midweek departure date. In this case, the package differences offered by the competing hotels didn't even come into play. Regardless of each package's other components, the traveler's decision may be based on the practicality of the departure date.

Our research identified another difference: resort hotels seem to favor a high variety of different packages, while urban properties favor a smaller selection of high-content packages instead. Once a resort hotel got selected for a vacation that is sold in weekly blocks (for the most part), the arrangement includes a given meal plan. After the guest books the vacation, the best way for the hotel to maximize revenue is to offer appealing packages of activities to guests after they arrive. Whether it is golf, sailing, scuba diving, salsa dancing, or helicopter-skiing depends on the location and type of resort. Some destinations are rich in sights; day trips can be offered to visit historic sites and museums and to experience native culture. Other destinations have spa packages or can capitalize on their close proximity to cities with great shopping or cultural points of interest. A high variety of packages can be effectively marketed to a captive audience at resort hotels, as the average length of stay is longer than that of urban commercial hotel guests.

City center hotels have to consider the shorter duration of stay and make the most of their amenities. That explains the rationale of smaller selection: a hotel may sell only one package per stay at best. The high content is necessary to compete with the destination's sightseeing offerings and to include as many of the hotel's own services as possible to maximize revenue opportunities. A good blend of internal and external components can get the attention of guests if promoted at the time of booking and/or at arrival. The higher the content of internal items in a package, the more profitable it can become for the hotel.

Packaging and Segmentation

The importance of market segmentation was discussed earlier. Different market segments have varying needs and wants. The packages that attract leisure travelers differ from the packages that attract business travelers. If a hotel has a well-defined approach to segmentation, customized packaging can be most effective. A corporate traveler may not be enticed by free parking or a coupon to the local zoo. However, leisure guests driving their own cars and traveling with kids may welcome packages that include an entrance to a theme park, free valet parking, breakfast, and unlimited video games played in the convenience of the guestroom using interactive television.

A business traveler may be more interested in high-speed Wi-Fi and access to a boardroom or hospitality suite bundled with no-charge pay-per-view movies. The point is that each hotel must determine for itself the needs and wants of its clientele. It must also know intimately what its competitors offer. This way, management can successfully manage differentiation and demand drivers.

A segmentation challenge has emerged since the mid-1990s: the combo package. Many commercial hotels have noticed that a growing segment of corporate guests tends to blend a day or two of leisure time with a business trip. For the first two nights, the guest may attend a conference, but on the third day, she becomes a tourist. The same guest in the same room at the same rate exhibits different buying behavior on the third night. Some brands are successful with pre- and post-event packages, custom packages, or dynamic packages in which guests select from a number of options to build their own package. This may involve air, car rental, local attractions, entertainment, gambling, or spa visits.

Packaging and Revenue Streams Management

It is important that hotels identify the profitability of each component in a given package. Food and beverage products have different margins than room nights, and guided sightseeing tours or car rental margins differ from spa treatments. High and low margin items may be bundled together, but the overall revenue impact and profitability implications need to be clearly identified and aligned with the hotel's strategic marketing purposes.

There is tremendous potential in value-added packaging. Guests prefer one-stop shopping. Convenience is the driver, and good packages offer that. Sometimes, guests design their own packages and cherry-pick what they need. The hotel that offers both the technology and well-trained guest service agents (or a concierge) to take care of all guest requests can generate more revenue than hotels that can't or won't meet their guests' unique needs. If a guest needs to make only one call to arrange for a table in the hotel's restaurant, for a pickup of items that need dry cleaning, for a massage in the hotel's spa, and for a limousine, the hotel is much more likely to maximize its revenues.

Another demonstrated guest preference since the 1990s is inclusiveness. The drivers in this case are both value and convenience. Guests don't like to be nickeled-and-dimed. They find it annoying to be charged separately for Internet access, a coffee and muffin breakfast, or the use of fitness facilities. More and more guests expect more and more services to be included in the room rate. All-inclusive resorts and cruises have been gaining popularity steadily.

From the service providers' perspective, value-added packaging is a well-invested effort that helps generate more revenue, boost occupancy, and maximize profitability.

Endnote

1. R. Verma, G. Plaschka, C. Dev, and A. Verma, "What Today's Travelers Want When They Select a Hotel," *HSMAI Marketing Review* (Fall 2002).

Case Studies

Case Study 1: Package Deal at Hotel Progeny

Hotel Progeny is a 420-room, full-service, upscale downtown hotel in the heart of a major metropolitan area in North America. The hotel offers meeting and convention facilities, a spa, and an underground parking garage. The hotel also has a steak house, an Irish pub, a café, and a business center. Each well-appointed guestroom is equipped with in-room safety deposit box, flat screen HD TV, coffee maker, hair dryer, and iron and ironing board. High-speed wireless Internet access is also provided throughout the hotel. The best available rate (BAR) on weekends is $160.

About 80 percent of the hotel's clientele is made up of business travelers, who spend on average 1.8 nights per stay. The remaining 20 percent comprises leisure travelers, who stay 1.2 nights on average at the Progeny. The hotel has experienced somewhat softer demand this year compared to the previous year, as did all hotels in town, although a rate increase did not encounter measurable resistance.

At a weekly revenue meeting, the discussion focused on generating demand through package offerings. There was consensus around the table that a creative, appealing, and well-targeted bundle could help increase demand. Teams of sales and marketing, front office, and revenue management employees cooperated to develop the following two package proposals. The Director of Rooms is convinced that only one of the two proposed packages can be introduced at this time.

Package A:
Target: Pleasure travelers.
Pitch: Getaway weekend for the family.
Two-night package at the Progeny: Arrival Friday any time after 3 P.M., departure Sunday with guaranteed late check-out time up to 4 P.M. at no charge.
Room rate: 40 percent discount off BAR, complimentary breakfasts on both Saturday and Sunday. Kids under 12 stay for free in their parents' room. The offer includes complimentary parking and one complimentary in-room pay-per-view movie, plus a 50 percent discount coupon for one spa treatment over $80. Free local calls, unlimited Internet for $9.95/day.

Package B:
Target: Business travelers.
Pitch: Extend your stay with a fun weekend.
The package: Add a Friday and a Saturday night to your business trip and get 30 percent off BAR. Offer includes complimentary breakfast for each night, free parking, free unlimited Internet and free unlimited in-room pay-per-view movies. Buy any spa treatment over $80 and get the next one free.

Discussion Questions

1. Which package has more revenue potential?
2. Which target customer generates higher room revenue?
3. Which package has the potential to generate higher food and beverage revenue? Higher spa revenue?
4. Which offer creates higher value perception?

Case Study 2: Differentiation, Positioning, Packaging Strategy

The Puntareno is a resort in Central America, where the warm climate has a dry season (winter) and a rainy season (summer). The region is most attractive to North American travelers during the winter and spring months. Its busy season is from January to May. The lodge's unique jungle location is a major strength of the small resort. Its capacity of 60 suites and a restaurant with a bar makes it one of the largest capacity food and beverage establishments in the small coastal resort town. The Puntareno is situated on a hill above the Rio Verde River that flows through the rainforest in curves and loops and reaches the sea a couple of miles away.

Lush rainforest vegetation, rich forest canopy, and warm climate coupled with a refined service culture are the main ingredients behind the success of this resort. The Puntareno is visited by tourists and nature lovers mostly from North America. The bulk of its clientele is made up of U.S. and Canadian travelers, including fly-fishers, who can choose between fishing the Rio Verde and the shallow waters of the Caribbean Sea. They enjoy the excitement of catch and release during the fishing season. This market segment has proven to be affluent and above-average spenders in terms of vacation spending per trip. The fly-fishers appreciate the skills of the resort's local bartenders, who create cocktails infusing special local flavors with premium ingredients. The fishers also enjoy the international fusion cuisine menu created by the chef, who uses mostly local ingredients. The fly-fishers take advantage of the resort's speed-boat flotilla that takes them to the best fishing spots both upstream on the Rio Verde and downstream to the best coral reefs close to shore in the open waters of the sea, relying on the expertise of local guides.

A fast-growing new market has also discovered the Puntareno: the bird watchers or "birders" as they call themselves. They come to see the abundant selection of bird species living in the rainforest in their natural habitat. They get up early as they are very task-focused. The birders are not too price sensitive, and they too appreciate the cuisine and the amenities that the resort has to offer. They tend to arrive in small groups of 6 to 20 per booking.

The resort has a significant portion of land that stretches across thousands of hectares of forest and fields, where they plant and grow mango, papaya, orange, banana, herbs, and vegetable crops. The Puntareno raises chickens and pigs as well. The Puntareno's chef has successfully achieved an ambitious objective: two-thirds of the food prepared in the kitchen is grown on the estate by resort employees. On top of being self-sufficient, the resort caters to the eco-conscientious clientele that likes the idea of farm-to-table cuisine. Local foods, produced in an environmentally responsible way (organic where possible), appeal to a growing segment of travelers.

The resort employs local residents for line and supervisory positions. The General Manager, appointed by the owner, is an experienced industry veteran from Canada. The sales and marketing area is under development; the initial concept has been to rely on travel agencies and tour operators to sell their room inventory. The resort has relied on Hotels.com, Travelocity, Expedia, and other agency partners to sell rooms. Puntareno has favorable reviews on TripAdvisor and has created a Facebook page to engage with past and future guests. With the barriers of selling online to a global marketplace coming down, it became affordable to beef up the resort's online capabilities. The owner instructed the General Manager to explore the idea of self-reliance with regard to harnessing the power of electronic distribution channels, investing in improving the resort's website, and learning the tools of revenue maximization instead of dishing out discounts only.

The resort owner has decided to hire a company specializing in asset management. A dedicated asset manager has visited the Puntareno. She conducted a site inspection, met with the management, and asked for access to all reports and statistics. She promised to come back on a quarterly basis. On her second visit, she sat down with the General Manager only and had a discussion with her about revenue targets. She suggested that the Puntareno develop a more focused marketing strategy and asked for a revised strategic revenue management plan that would provide the fundamentals of revenue growth.

Discussion Questions

1. What are some targeting and positioning options available to the Puntareno?
2. How can the Puntareno develop packages to take advantage of its strategic opportunities?

Chapter Appendix

The Emerging Trend of Hotel Total Revenue Management

By Chuyi Zheng and Dr. Gabor Forgacs

Abstract

Total hotel revenue management has emerged in the hotel industry as a next stage in the evolution of revenue management. By integrating several revenue streams including food and beverage, function space, catering, spa, retail, golf, and others with room revenue management, total revenue management enables hotels to achieve their goal in maximizing revenue in highly competitive markets.

This study investigates the practices of hotel revenue management and discusses several future trends of total revenue management. In-depth interviews were conducted with 12 revenue professionals. Current issues and challenges in hotel revenue management are discussed and recommendations are offered.

Introduction

The hotel industry is one of the numerous sectors that apply revenue management to maximize their revenue potential. With decades of growth and development, the approach of total revenue management has emerged as an improvement of traditional revenue management (Buckhiester, 2012).

The concept of total revenue management is not a new notion since hoteliers are always focused on discovering a way to maximize revenue from the entire hotel asset (Buckhiester, 2012). This is an approach that integrates all the revenue streams within a hotel property to optimize revenue. Total revenue management enables revenue professionals to explore revenue opportunities from food and beverage, function space, spa, retail, golf, and other revenue streams.

Revenue management seems to evolve toward total revenue management and hotels have begun to execute strategies using this concept. However, even though many hoteliers understand the importance of utilizing the total revenue management approach, in reality, few are making meaningful progress following this direction. This study discusses the current practices of total revenue management in hotels, its relevant challenges, and future trends through in-depth interviews with industry experts.

Source: Zheng, C,. and Forgacs, G. J. *Revenue Pricing Manag* (2016). doi:10.1057/s41272-016-0057-x. Reprinted with permission.

Literature Review

Pricing Strategies

In the past few decades, hoteliers have focused on designing their revenue management strategies based on room revenue. There were three main traditional pricing strategies, including cost-based, competition driven (price matching), and customer driven (demand-based) pricing strategies (Gu & Caneen, 1998; Collins & Parsa, 2006), deployed by hoteliers. However, these traditional approaches need to be refined to optimize revenue for hotels. They all encounter certain deficiencies when it comes to anticipating customer demand and considering current market conditions (Collins & Parsa; Steed & Gu, 2005), exerting negative influences on the overall market pricing (Enz, Canina, & Lomanno, 2009) and, on occasion, practicing false positioning (Hung, Shang, & Wang, 2010).

To thrive in a competitive environment, hotels need to reevaluate and improve their revenue management strategies. Demand-based dynamic pricing strategy became one of the most prevalent and frequently utilized tactics in hotels (Palamar & Edwards, 2007; Abrate, Fraquelli, & Viglia, 2012). This is a strategy that requires a hotel to continually adjust its price according to the actual demand and market conditions of different segments. As a result, its flexibility and adaptability benefits hotels in highly competitive markets (Palamar & Edwards).

While revenue optimization is momentous for hotels, room-centric revenue management is not sufficient to achieve financial goals (Freed, 2012). Competition coupled with cyclical and seasonal changes in demand become the motivating factors for hotels to embrace total revenue management practices, which integrate different revenue generators within the hotel and achieve the objective of maximizing revenue.

Revenue Management Implementation

The concept of implementing revenue management in departments other than rooms within the hotel has been discussed in previous studies. For example, food and beverage is one of the most frequently discussed areas in implementing revenue management practices (Thompson, 2003; Kimes, 2008). Analysis by consulting company PKF shows that the combination of catering revenue, function room rental revenue, audiovisual fees, and banquet service charges accounted for 55.5 percent of total food and beverage department revenue, followed by 30.2 percent from restaurants, 5.6 percent from lounges, and 4.4 percent from room service in 2010 (Mandelbaum, 2011). Hoteliers begin to incorporate food and beverage revenue in measuring the hotel performance (Kim, Cho, & Brymer, 2013). This is in line with the theory of total revenue management, which focuses on integrating the ancillary revenues into a whole system. The implementation of revenue per available seat hour (RevPASH) is recommended to measure the restaurant operation using revenue management (Kimes, 1999). This RevPASH system evaluates both revenue generated and meal duration, two major concerns in restaurant revenue optimization. Another concept for restaurant revenue generation is the contribution margin per available seat hour (CMPASH) that focuses on profit rather than revenue (Thompson). This concept requires the restaurant to achieve combinability, which means having flexible table mix options to utilize the same tables in serving parties of two or four and even six at different periods.

Cornell University professor Sherry Kimes conducted research (2010) regarding the future of revenue management in hotels that identified key challenges and future trends of revenue management. Besides food and beverage department, the paper indicated that function space revenue could be considered another key component with a high potential to increase revenue for an operation. Contract customers who book hotel function space for meeting and training tend to need food and beverage services as well (Quain, 1992; Choi, 2006; Kim, Cho, & Brymer, 2013). It is a frequent tactic of hotel revenue professionals to bundle function space with MLOS (minimum length of stay) for hotel rooms and required meals to maximize the total revenue of a group block.

Besides the main revenue streams that generate most of the revenue for hotels, there are other resources within hotels that can increase the overall profit. From the operation side, there are spas, gift shops, and convenience stores; from the service perspective, movie rental, in-room refreshments, Internet access, laundry, and parking are options for hotels to generate revenue. If hotels can capture revenue from these amenities applying integrated revenue management practices, profitability can be maximized.

Methodology

Research Design

This study was designed as a qualitative study utilizing a combination of both primary and secondary research. The rationale for the qualitative approach was that the topic of the paper seemed better suited for a discussion in a strategic context that focused on some of the issues related to the evolution of revenue management entering a new phase, versus a quantitative work that would have focused on data analysis. Another contributing factor was that securing access to reliable industry data proved to be too much of a challenge with the available resources and time constraints.

One-on-one in-depth interviews were conducted with a representative sample of 12 industry experts that offered a cross-section of revenue professionals including practicing hoteliers working in revenue management–related positions, revenue management consultants, and academics teaching courses in pricing and revenue management. The duration of the interviews varied between forty minutes and one hour. Five interviews were conducted face-to-face and seven were by phone. These experts are very knowledgeable, with years of experience in revenue management and related fields. Interview questions were formulated based on previous secondary research studying recent trends in hospitality revenue management.

Based on the current revenue management practices in the hotel industry, several key issues were raised and addressed during the interviews. The content of the interviews was analyzed to identify whether different responses for same questions had discussed similar issues, challenges, and concerns. Shared viewpoints by these industry leaders were noted. The study also examined those recurring topics and discussed solutions or suggestions. The study has integrated the responses by the interviewees with regard to the emerging future trend of total revenue management and provided recommendations. (The questions are listed in the sidebar.)

> ### Interview Questions for MRP
>
> New Trends in Hotel Total Revenue Management
> 1. How is revenue management practiced currently in your hotel?
> 2. What are the most important issues in revenue management?
> 3. Do you envision any tactical or strategic changes in your revenue management practices in the future?
> 4. What other revenue streams beyond rooms could be considered for revenue managers to work with?
> 5. What KPIs (key performance indicators) do you track on a regular basis?
> 6. How do you think total revenue management can be implemented?
> 7. What are the challenges for revenue management practitioners in introducing total revenue management?
> 8. Do you anticipate changes in pricing strategy in the future?

Discussion

Issues and Challenges in Total Revenue Management

The concept of total revenue management has been discussed for more than a decade; however, few hotels have implemented this strategy. A number of issues and challenges were identified that limit the application of total revenue management.

Lack of Talented Personnel to Manage Different Revenue Streams. Revenue management has already been implemented for more than 20 years; however, there is still a lack of a sufficient pool of talented people in this area. Five years ago, qualified revenue managers were identified as a top concern for revenue management (Kimes, 2010). Mr. Stuart-Hill, president and founder of Revenue Matters, also rated "the talent gap" as the top revenue management issue (Stuart-Hill, 2014). Today, this is still a concern for the industry. Most of the interviewees mentioned this issue and discussed several reasons why the talent gap still exists. An important reason would be that the compensation offered for revenue managers is still not attractive enough. A good revenue manager should be able to monitor and analyze the internal operation of the hotel and be able to sense the changes in the external market, including economic environment, competition, technology evolution, and new trends in social media. Currently, there are few incentives for qualified revenue managers to stay at a hotel for a long period of time. Once those talented people have gained enough experience in hotels, they are more likely to move on to consulting or technology companies, which may pay them about twice the salary they received at the hotel.

Since hotel revenue managers tend to be underpaid, quite a few of them do not fully grasp the theory of revenue management, not to mention the concept of total revenue management. In addition, it costs a lot to hire qualified and experienced professionals who understand how different departments work. It creates a barrier for great talented people to work in a hotel property. Given the current circumstances, most interviewees are concerned whether there will be sufficient qualified revenue managers to practice total revenue management in the future.

Technology for Seamless Management of Multiple Revenue Streams. Based on the interviews, it is safe to conclude that talented personnel combined with the right technology are the keys to success for total hotel revenue management. A most pivotal issue for total revenue management is the lack of advanced systems to support the function of seamlessly interfacing all revenue streams for each department. Obviously, hotels utilize several different systems and sub-systems for different departments. A technical challenge was also pointed out in some of the interviews: interdepartmental flow of data. It was mentioned that in some hotels, the PMS (property management system) used by the room department is not necessarily interfaced with the POS (point-of-sale) system used in the food and beverage department. These systems were either inherited from the previous management or acquired in different times from different vendors.

When a hotel is using a variety of systems, it may pose a challenge to seamlessly interface the flow of data for revenue managers to work with different departments for the implementation of optimization measures based on real-time access to data. It was pointed out more than once during the interviews that "System communication is just as important as personal communication."

On the one hand, there are few hotel property management systems that can achieve smooth, fluent communication with each disparate revenue center. On the other hand, it can be a significant investment for a hotel to replace or upgrade whole systems and provide necessary employee training. Thus the implementation of total hotel revenue management is still challenged for the cost and integration issues of related technology.

Conflicts Between Different Departments. The conflicts between the sales and revenue departments have existed for a long time. Previously, the goals of sales and marketing plus the way their managers were incentivized were different from Revenue Management. However, sometimes a 95 percent occupancy rate may yield better revenues than a 100 percent occupancy rate. With disparate objectives, the sales unit may sacrifice room rate on occasion in order to achieve high occupancy for meeting a unit sales target. It would require an integrated approach to analyze the decisions of a sales department and align them with revenue and profit objectives. According to the interviewees, the final decision maker on pricing and group sales should be the Revenue Manager, the Director of Revenue, or the General Manager who embraces revenue management. Furthermore, all interviewees agreed that a Revenue Manager should have more authority than a Sales Manager. However, there are still hotels where the revenue management department reports to the sales and marketing department as per the chain of command.

The importance of communication skills for Revenue Managers has been identified as well for sharing information and building teams for a common purpose. One of the interviewees mentioned, "It's important for revenue managers to visualize the data, not just show a spreadsheet." It was also pointed out that Revenue Managers need to communicate decisions to every related department in an easily understandable way "since not everyone is comfortable reading 10 pages of Excel data." Total revenue management requires a team approach to make it work.

Organizational Culture and Employee Education. One of the keys to practicing total revenue management is to have it embedded in organizational culture. Most interviewees believe that it is critical to have employee buy-in to embrace this concept. It was also mentioned that "Hotels need employees to chase aggressively every revenue opportunity." For example, front office employees can leverage their familiarity with guest history and customer profile to upsell and promote other hotel revenue centers. On the one hand, it requires a certain level of employee training to operationalize the promotion of revenue opportunities from every facet of a hotel's operation; on the other hand, accepting and embracing cross-departmental thinking for total hotel revenue optimization needs to be firmly grounded in organizational culture to achieve success.

Revenue Streams Beyond Rooms

When it comes to the discussion of total hotel revenue management, the interviewees shared their opinions of other profitable revenue streams beyond rooms. Hotels may not attribute equal importance to their own various revenue streams. Hotels with gambling and spa operations differ in their approach from focused-service operations. All the respondents agreed that currently they would mainly focus on the most profitable departments when trying to implement the total hotel revenue management concept.

Function Space. Function space was the most frequently mentioned area to introduce to total revenue management. The most common practice is bundling or packaging function space rental with catered events to optimize revenue. Most revenue managers will attempt to combine food and beverage services along with the meeting rooms and guestrooms under constrained demand conditions. If market conditions indicate a softening in demand, function space rental may be offered unbundled as requested by customers and this way an additional revenue stream is generated for a given operation.

Restaurants. Restaurant revenue streams may or may not be profitable for full-service hotels. The location of a hotel can be a significant factor in securing a sufficient volume of demand for each meal period. It was indicated that the hotel restaurants that are profitable tend to utilize strategies such as packaging, incentives, and advertisement for promoting the outlet. Since not all the interviewed hotels have their own onsite restaurant and not every restaurant is highly profitable, few interviewees considered a hotel restaurant to be a revenue stream with a strong potential.

It is widely accepted that function space and restaurant are two main revenue streams besides rooms in a hotel that can utilize revenue management techniques

(Kimes, 2010). In order to capture and manage the extra revenue from these two departments, hotels work with different key indicators and performance measurements. For function space, some hotels are using revenue per square foot to measure profitability, while others are using revenue per rental. On the restaurant side, revenue per available seat hour (RevPASH) was a frequently suggested measure for hotel restaurants besides table turnover, average check, and other commonly used metrics.

Other Amenities. Spa, retail, and parking were in the top six revenue streams in hotels (Kimes, 2010). However, in downtown locations, most of these amenities can be outsourced to third parties. As a result, these amenities may only yield rental or lease revenue for a hotel.

An Internet usage charge is a revenue stream that most managers paid less attention to. A point was brought up that the revenue from providing Internet access is insignificant compared to other revenue streams like restaurant, function space, and retail. The portion of Internet revenue is less than one percent of the total revenue for most hotel operators. Some interviewees pointed out that the possible return is not worth the input of time and effort dedicated to this particular revenue stream. However, others believed that the Internet could be a good resource that helps generate more profit for the hotel. A growing portion of travelers are multi-device users and need Wi-Fi connectivity. Internet connectivity has become an indispensable part of both business and leisure travel. Therefore, if a hotel can include the usage fee of the Internet in the room rates, that can be appealing for guests.

For example, one of the interviewees mentioned that if the customer is booking through the loyalty program, he or she gets free Wi-Fi. This value-added feature can also be an incentive for guests to book directly through hotel websites versus third parties. Nowadays, complimentary Internet has become an expectation for guests and even some of the luxury brands offer free Wi-Fi. In order to generate extra revenue from it, there are different strategies that can be utilized. Some hotels may set up a two-tiered Internet access based on data usage and bandwidth. A low-usage (e.g., checking e-mail only) can be complimentary, while high-usage that requires significantly more data transfer (e.g., downloading full feature movie) can be offered for a usage fee.

Recommendations

The views shared by 12 industry experts were insightful and valuable to understanding the current practice of total revenue management in today's hotel industry. The discussion part revealed the current challenges and concerns in hotel revenue management. Based on the analysis of these emerging issues, this paper offers several recommendations for hoteliers.

Value of Qualified Revenue Management Personnel

It was commonly pointed out that there is a talent gap in the field of revenue management. More and more experienced revenue managers choose to pursue their career in consultant companies and at technology companies. If hotels do not value their talented personnel, they may easily leave and move on. It is important to note that good revenue managers add significant value to the business, which should be reflected in their compensation. On the other hand, it was suggested that hotels should pay attention to educating and developing strong revenue managers. Many hotels are hesitant to invest in cultivating future revenue specialists. They would rather hire experienced people than accept and groom junior candidates. If this trend continues, there will be a scarcity of qualified revenue managers in the hotel industry.

It is suggested that in order to help develop total revenue management, each integrated department could appoint a revenue specialist to assist the revenue manager, besides their daily job function. This will not only support the revenue manager but also cultivate potential revenue talent for the future.

Integrate Digital Marketing and Chase Every Possible Revenue

Digital marketing is a relatively novel approach, while innovative ideas in day-to-day operation are also effective to optimize revenue. For example, in one case, a hotel offered both complimentary coffee and Starbucks coffee. The Starbucks coffee was valued at about five to six dollars at Starbucks stores, but hotel guests were only charged three dollars to their account for it. It was surprising to see that many customers chose to purchase the Starbucks coffee over the complimentary coffee. It became evident that if customers see the value and recognize it, they may opt to pay for a priced product instead of choosing a complimentary one. This extra revenue resulted in a profitable stream for the hotel. This was also an illustration of price elasticity, which reinforces the importance of understanding guest preferences and meeting their needs. Similar strategies can be considered for other revenue centers.

Location-based mobile applications are a recent trend in digital marketing. For example, Starwood SPG mobile App and Hilton HHonor App offer numerous functions including booking capability, hotel amenities listing, link to local attractions, guest reviews and comments, self-check-in, and mobile keys. Besides mobile room key codes, one of the interviewees mentioned that some hotels offer a mobile application that can customize their mobile platform for guests who accept an invitation to opt in for location-based, beacon-transmitted advertising pushed to the guest's smartphone. Once a guest is in close proximity to a participating outlet (point of sale like a bar, restaurant, or spa), a digital coupon can be sent to the guest's mobile device. If the guest is interested, he or she can convert the coupon right away. Using this method creates value incentives for the customer and increases overall spend per visit through incremental revenue for a hotel. Revenue managers who leverage the power of location can harness the revenue potential of real-time digital marketing in the future.

Development of Property-Specific Tactics

It is important that hotel revenue professionals base their tactics and strategies on a solid understanding of the local market conditions and customer demands. It was suggested that every hotel should establish its own method of increasing revenue after analyzing the economic conditions and the competitors. There is no ready-made best solution for maximizing revenue for every hotel; therefore, the beauty of the challenge for revenue managers lies in discovering and developing the most useful practice that suits best their given hotels.

Conclusion

Revenue management is central to optimize revenue for hotels and the approach of total hotel revenue management is an emerging trend within this field. There are various options to achieve revenue maximization using different tactics and strategies. Some of the main issues and challenges were discussed with 12 industry experts demonstrating a qualitative research method that has an important role to play in identifying key areas of concern. The following areas were identified:

- Lack of talented personnel to manage different revenue streams;
- Technology for seamless management of multiple revenue streams;
- Conflicts between different departments; and
- Organizational culture and employee education.

Hotel revenue professionals will have to find meaningful solutions to the above in order to unlock the full potential of total hotel revenue management.

References

Abrate, G., Fraquelli, G., & Viglia, G. (2012). Dynamic pricing strategies: Evidence from European hotels. *International Journal of Hospitality Management, 31*(1), 160–168.

Buckhiester. B. (2012). Optimizing total revenue management. *Hotel News Now*. Retrieved from http://www.hotelnewsnow.com/Article/8251/Optimizing-total-revenue-management

Choi, S. (2006). Group revenue management: A model for evaluating group profitability. *Cornell Hotel and Restaurant Administration Quarterly, 47*(3), 260–271.

Collins, M., & Parsa, H. G. (2006). Pricing strategies to maximize revenues in the lodging industry. *International Journal of Hospitality Management, 25*(1), 91–107.

Enz, C. A., Canina, L., & Lomanno, M. (2009). Competitive hotel pricing in uncertain times. *The Center for Hospitality Research, Cornell University. 9*(10), 1–17.

Freed, J. Q. (2012). Total revenue management is the future. *Hotel News Now*. Retrieved from http://www.hotelnewsnow.com/Article/8494/Total-revenue-management-is-the-future

Gu, Z., & Caneen, J. M. (1998). Quadratic models for yield management in hotel rooms operation. *Progress in Tourism and Hospitality Research, 4*(3), 245–253.

Hung, W. T., Shang, J. K., & Wang, F. C. (2010). Pricing determinants in the hotel industry: Quantile regression analysis. *International Journal of Hospitality Management, 29*(3), 378–384.

Kim, W. G., Cho, M., & Brymer, R. A. (2013). Determinants affecting comprehensive property-level hotel performance: The moderating role of hotel type. *International Journal of Hospitality Management, 34,* 404–412.

Kimes, S. E. (1999). Implementing restaurant revenue management: A five-step approach. *Cornell Hospitality Quarterly, 40*(3), 16–21.

Kimes, S. E. (2008). The role of technology in restaurant revenue management. *Cornell Hospitality Quarterly, 49*(3), 297–309.

Kimes, S. E. (2010). The future of hotel revenue management. *Journal of Revenue & Pricing Management, 10*(1), 62–72.

Mandelbaum, R. (2011). Hotel food and beverage. *Hotel, Travel and Hospitality News.* Retrieved from: http://www.4hoteliers.com/features/article/6106

Palamar, L. A., & Edwards, V. (2007). Dynamic pricing: Friend or foe. *BTE Tourism Training and Consulting, Buckhiester Management,* 1–14.

Quain, W. J. (1992). Analyzing sales-mix profitability. *Cornell Hotel and Restaurant Administration Quarterly, 33*(2), 57–62.

Steed, E., & Gu, Z. (2005). An examination of hotel room pricing methods: Practised and proposed. *Journal of Revenue and Pricing Management, 3*(4), 369–379.

Stuart-Hill, T. (2014). Top 10 revenue management issues for 2014 and beyond. *HotelExecutive.com.* Retrieved from: http://hotelexecutive.com/business_review/3721/top-10-revenue-management-issues-for-2014-and-beyond

Thompson, G. M. (2003). Optimizing restaurant-table configurations: Specifying combinable tables. *Cornell Hotel and Restaurant Administration Quarterly, 44*(1), 53–60.

Chapter 11 Outline

Distribution Channels
    Voice Channels
    GDS Channel
    Internet Channels
Social Media
Mobility and Mobile Users
Responsive Design
Case Study

Competencies

1. Identify and describe various distribution methods and channels and explain why distribution channel management is important to a hotel's success. (pp. 155–161)

2. Outline the business reasons for following and using social media for revenue. (pp. 161–164)

3. Explain how mobile devices and responsive design have changed sales and marketing efforts. (pp. 164–166)

11

Distribution Channel Management

THIS CHAPTER PROVIDES a framework and the theoretical underpinnings for the exciting, quickly evolving topic of distribution channel management. The chapter discussion goes somewhat beyond the profiling of current distribution models as it also offers some context for understanding and harnessing the potential of social media from the perspective of revenue management.

Distribution Channels

Revenue managers work with a variety of distribution channels concurrently. The strategic objective of distribution channel management is threefold. Managers try to obtain most of the hotel's revenue through those channels that are (1) the highest revenue producers, (2) the most cost-effective, and (3) the most easily controlled. The challenge of balancing these criteria should not be underestimated.

It is important to identify which distribution methods and channels are able to reach a hotel's target market. The cost per booking also must be factored in when the net revenue is affected by the distribution channel.

Hotels can obtain reservations directly or indirectly. Both methods use a variety of distribution channels. In the direct-to-guest approach, a hotel can accept bookings directly from the guest in person; on the hotel's website; on the telephone; and in written communication using e-mail or text messaging, faxes (which are being used less and less frequently), and mail (which is fast becoming obsolete). The days of the telex or tele-writer, which combined an electric typewriter and a phone-line to establish real-time connection in order to produce a written record, are long gone. It is a safe prediction that, in the not too distant future, the fax machine will follow the fate of the telex. Written communication is increasingly generated through keyboards or keypads.

When there is an intermediary between a guest and a hotel in the process of booking, the method is indirect. The most common intermediaries are travel agents, tour operators, demand collectors (web portals), *central reservation services (CRSs), destination management services (DMSs), global distribution systems (GDSs),* and call centers of representation agencies, referral services, and marketing alliances. Each intermediary can drive revenue to a given hotel. Revenue managers need to maintain good working relationships with all of them. The source analysis of revenues will identify which partners are main revenue producers. The ratio of revenue production per intermediary might vary depending on the season, the target market, or other circumstances. There are hotels that get most of their off-season revenue from travel agents, but directly book their own transient guests in the main season.

All of these methods of booking use voice, the GDS, or the Internet for communication and actual transaction purposes. The methods of distribution and the channels available can be combined in any way.[1]

Voice Channels

Hotels can use direct lines connected to their reservation office, front office, or PBX to take bookings. The number of hotel guests who are comfortable booking their stay without intermediaries is growing, but the growth is not on the voice channels. Call volume on voice channels has been decreasing since the turn of the century. At the same time, the conversion rate is up, meaning that a higher percentage of calls end up with closing a sale. That can be attributed to better training of the reservation agents and the efficient use of guest history files that can speed up the booking process. Another contributing factor is the fact that a growing percentage of potential guests conduct their search for accommodation online before they place a call. While many customers are comfortable using the Internet to search for destination information, look up accommodation options, comparison shop, and even sift through guest reviews to see what past guests have to say about a specific operation, some still prefer to make the actual reservation by speaking with the chosen service provider.

There are various reasons for this phenomenon. One is the doubt some guests have in the security of online payment methods, which leads them to switch to the telephone to complete their transactions. Another is the need to talk to a live agent who can answer relevant questions on product information and local particularities not found on the Internet. The point for revenue managers is to pay attention to customer preferences.

Hotel operators serving the upscale market have learned the importance of personal interaction for their high-touch clientele. They may hesitate even to introduce automated voice systems that could replace reservation agents. Individual attention can be extremely important from the outset. A familiar adage says, "You never have a second chance to make a good first impression." For hotels, the first impression may happen long before the guest arrives, when the first call is placed to book the reservation.

Call centers of hotel chains or referral services offer an effective solution for handling high call volumes. However, the cost per booking may increase and the service quality may be lower. Reservation agents employed at the property level may have better product knowledge and more motivation to upsell. The importance of inside information should not be underestimated. Knowing about the renovation date of the pool, the channel selection of the cable package in guestrooms, a new chef being hired, and the trendy new curved shower curtain rods can help close a sale.

Revenue maximization strategies will have to include voice channels for the foreseeable future.

GDS Channel

The *global distribution system (GDS)* was *the* electronic channel before the Internet emerged. The GDS offers an important channel that hotel revenue managers use to connect with travel agencies and other demand collectors. It started out as the central reservation system for the airline industry in the late 1970s. It became necessary because travel volume had increased so much that manual systems were too slow and labor-intensive. It was made possible by new electronic data processing that emerged as a result of the evolution in microprocessors. Travel agents found that booking air travel through the GDS was cost effective. Hotel and car rental bookings became add-ons in the 1980s.

Some operators of high-end hotel chains were reluctant to offer online booking engines on their websites in the late 1990s, at a time when most other hotel chains had started doing so. Their reasoning was that most of their clients were already online with them through the GDS and that the senior executives, wealthy individuals, and group guests who made up their critical volume were not expected to start booking their stays themselves. These guests still entrusted their office or travel agent to book their trips, and those bookings were done online already through the GDS. Times have changed. It is unusual today to find a hotel website that does not feature booking capability.

The major players are Sabre, Galileo, Worldspan, and Amadeus. The reservations processed through their networks have to go through switching companies to interface with the service providers. Although the GDS has traditionally been a business-to-business (B2B) model, the evolution of electronic travel transactions facilitated by the Internet has offered new opportunities to GDS businesses that were too good to pass up. A number of GDS companies extended their business by launching consumer websites and offering hotel inventory to online agencies as well. The traditional role of managing the traffic between suppliers and distributors has evolved into something more complex. The volume booked through the GDS will keep it relevant to revenue managers for years to come.

Internet Channels

The Internet has changed the way business is conducted. It took a number of years for the hotel industry to unlock the potential of the Internet, and the learning curve was steep. In the late 1990s, when businesses started to establish their presences online, it was mostly considered a promotional opportunity with little direct revenue impact. However, as the household penetration of the Internet started to grow exponentially, the software applications used to get online became a lot more user-friendly. As a consequence, more and more businesses seized the chance to realize first-mover advantage in the new field of e-commerce.

The early years of the tech bubble were exciting and turbulent times, when the emergence of Internet-based businesses resulted in a lot of start-ups. After the dust settled, it became evident that choosing the Internet as a platform would add the most value to those businesses that could not do what they were doing without the Internet. Some of those online businesses allowed customers to search travel information, book a travel service or product quickly and easily, process payment, and issue confirmation around the clock, and these sites became very popular.

Around the turn of the century, the hotel industry allowed third parties to collect demand and act as intermediaries between hotels and guests. Hotels initially regarded online resellers as a convenient additional distribution channel generating new revenue: the agencies did all the work of investing in the technology; building the online businesses, web portals, and booking engines; and finding customers and selling the product to them. It took a few years before the industry realized the magnitude of revenue leakage (measured in billions of dollars) that this approach allowed.

The industry finally responded, and the B2C direct distribution model emerged as the most important Internet distribution model as a result. That said, the external online travel agency (OTA) providers continue to exist under a variety of business models.

B2C Model (Hotel Direct). A *B2C (business-to-customer)* model allows guests to book their stay with a hotel or hotel brand without an intermediary. This Internet-based direct distribution model is the most profitable because it is the most cost-effective. Hotels have the highest level of control over this model.

The hotel industry started to get seriously interested in taking back control over product distribution when, after 2000, a record year for the tourism industry, demand started to dwindle. The events of September 11, 2001, accelerated and worsened the decline in travel and tourism, and the hotel industry went through cost cutbacks and deep discounting. It became obvious that revenue generation was the only way forward, and interest in revenue management strategies and tactics grew. The analytical approach highlighted the importance of profits taken by online resellers (revenue leakage). This became a point of contention by 2003, when hoteliers realized that instead of tapping into new revenue sources, the online booking intermediaries were tapping into existing customers who simply had new buying behaviors.

The strategic response needed was evident: hotels had to try to take back control and sell most of their capacity themselves, directly to the customers, bypassing intermediaries. The keys to success were in understanding the online distribution channels and their dynamics. This understanding was then coupled with improvements both in the technology (transaction speed, real-time dynamic pricing, availability controls, search engine optimization, etc.) and the appearance and design of the hotels' websites. Websites were redesigned to offer faster downloads and clarity to help users find what they wanted within a couple of clicks. The sites began to offer booking capability and relevant links (to maps, local weather, events, attractions, etc.) on the landing page.

In addition to user-friendly websites and cutting-edge technology, the direct distribution model needed to make it worthwhile for the guest. Best-rate guaranties were offered and guests voted with their mouse clicks. Direct bookings through the Internet started to grow significantly. By the second half of the decade, the hotel industry successfully took back control over the sales of the majority of room nights sold over the Internet. The direct B2C model has proved to be the best contributor to hotel revenue growth and profitability.

Harnessing the Internet and exploiting its opportunities are absolutely critical in today's business environment. The most popular online activity after checking and sending e-mails is using a search engine.

About search, Google, and revenue management. Search engines want to see content when they visit a website. Content-rich pages appeal to both website visitors and to search engine spiders, and creating such pages can help a hotel achieve higher visibility. The use of relevant keywords can drive both online and offline sales. The number of keywords used per page and the frequency of website updates containing fresh content affect search engine visibility.

Having an online presence is no longer an option for businesses wishing to connect with customers in the twenty-first century. Hospitality business websites have become integral parts of revenue generation and strategic marketing efforts. An effective website needs to achieve at least the following objectives:

- Attract/connect (through search engine optimization);
- Capture/retain (through engagement to keep traffic coming to the website); and
- Convert/take desired action (e.g., book, buy, sign up, post something).

The first of these objectives is based on the realization that, to maximize revenue, a business's website needs to be easy for customers to find. Search marketing, if mastered well, can help a business to rank high on organic searches. Organic or non-paid search results are determined by search engine algorithms. *Search engine optimization (SEO)* is building on one of the most important algorithms that the major search engines use: determining search term relevance and link popularity (i.e., who is linking to a given website?). Websites can rank higher on search engines based on the quality and relevancy of links to the website.

People use search engines to find information online. Google is indisputably the largest search engine. Any business can benefit from using Google as a way to generate more/new business. Users turn to this search engine to find answers to their questions. Google then tries to deliver the best results possible. These results can include links to websites, maps, images, translations, or information about a location, person, or business. Most of the resulting listings are organic and free, but sometimes an ad delivers the best or most direct result to a user query. A business can benefit from these results by adding relevant content to its website, connecting a given business to Google maps, creating a Google+ account for the business, or bidding on relevant search terms.

A Google search generates two types of results: *organic* or *natural search results* as well as *paid search results* (ads). Organic search results are derived by an algorithm ranking webpages according to relevance to the search query. Paid search results are ranked in a similar way. The difference is that advertisers decide which search terms they want their ads to feature. The order the search results are listed in is determined by a variety of factors, including the relevancy of the ad in relation to the search term and the amount advertisers are willing to pay Google for each user click on their ads.

Revenue professionals can consult Google's free Webmaster Tools at google.com/webmasters for perhaps the best explanations of how Google crawls and indexes a site, as well as how revenue professionals can improve the visibility of their websites in Google searches. Revenue professionals can explore a great variety of ever-evolving tools and gadgets to track and benchmark how their websites live up to their business's expectations. Google Analytics can reveal traffic sources, bounce rates, click-through rates, average time spent, pages viewed, and much more to revenue managers and other hospitality users.

A *meta-search engine* sends queries to various other search engines and combines the results into one list. Travel-specific meta-search engines are exemplified by Kayak, Orbitz, Google Hotel Finder, TripAdvisor, Hipmunk, and Trivago, among others. Consumers go to these sites and input their trip variables, and the sites display results with names, images, rates, links to various *online travel agencies (OTAs)* like Expedia and Travelocity, and even direct links to websites. This capability offers convenience to travel shoppers for researching, rate shopping, and booking trips. Meta-search sites also offer independent hotels and resorts a chance to directly compete with branded properties whose access to greater resources would otherwise allow them to easily out-market independent properties.

Hotel brands that succeed in their efforts to stay relevant and connected to their customers go beyond search engine marketing and embrace the social Internet and new media formats such as *consumer-generated media (CGM)*, sometimes also called *user-generated content (UGC)*—exemplified by Facebook, YouTube, and TripAdvisor—blogs, wikis, and other fast-evolving forums and channels. Mobile Internet usage patterns also show a significant growth in data access.

Agency Model (Retail Model). The *agency model* is based on simple straight commissions. There is no commitment for any of the parties in terms of capacity allotment or rate, and if an Internet travel agency can find a guest for a room night, based on availability, the hotel pays a commission, often around 10 percent of the room rate, in recognition of the business. This model gives the hotel a high level of control over price and availability. However, the volume driven through this Internet distribution model is not significant compared with the other models.

Merchant Model. For online merchants, the *merchant model* became the most successful Internet business model for selling hotel capacity and related products. Internet-based businesses serving the travelers' every need became highly successful investments as the traveling public began to use the Internet.

The concept of the merchant model is not new to the hotel industry. Hotels have used a similar deal structure for many years when dealing with wholesalers. This model is based on an agreement between the hotel and the e-merchant or OTA that allows the online agency to take a hotel's negotiated capacity allotment with a cut-off date at the best available rate and mark it up to resell it to customers. The usual mark-ups are in the 20–30 percent range, and the sell rate is controlled by the online agency.

Revenue managers cannot afford to ignore online agencies, regardless of the business model they follow. However, it was important for the industry to know that in the period between 2000 and 2004, the merchant model eroded price parity. Hotels gave up control over the prices of their rooms and in some cases ended up competing with themselves when online agencies decided to undercut the hotel's rates for last-minute customers. It is also important to point out that the listing of hotels on a merchant's website follows one significant criterion: hotels are ranked by their production for the merchant. That is an astute approach by the merchant, as it provides an incentive for business partners to be high producers and appear on the top of a list, because half of customers on average choose from the first screen; they do not proceed to the second screen of a lengthy listing of available hotels. Half of the viewers who go to the second page do not look at a third. The hotel's ranking in a search result clearly can significantly affect the probability of getting a booking. According to Expedia, 95 percent of bookings originate from first-page rankings on its site. Online merchants have an interest in promoting those hotels that are proven sources of revenue for them. When working with online merchants, hotel revenue managers need to see the facts and base their strategy on a lucid understanding of the business model.

Hybrid Model. The *hybrid model* is a combination of the merchant and agency models. Online agencies may choose to offer a package of products with somewhat lower mark-ups and certain strings attached for consumers: non-refundable payment on booking; minimum three-day advance purchase, after which no changes are allowed; etc. A frequently offered bundle includes air transportation, a room selection from among participating hotels, and a car rental.

The sales tactics of online agencies include bundled and unbundled (hotel-only) product offerings. If that's the case, the ranking offers the merchant model items first, followed by agency model constructs.

Opaque Model. The *opaque model*, also called a *reverse auction*, has been quite successful on the customer side with brand-neutral hotel guests who book at the last moment. An opaque site (such as priceline.com and hotwire.com) lets the customer describe his or her needs and name a price that he or she is willing to pay. If a hotel meets the criteria (location, service level, and price), the customer must prepay before learning which hotel he or she just booked with. Because of the initial anonymity, hotels can dump distressed inventory on opaque sites to pick up incremental business without damaging their rate integrity.

The opaque model is a good example of a business solution that could not exist without the Internet. Under this model, the hotel offers rooms to the site at a net rate that the customer will not see. The opaque site matches customers to hotels that meet their criteria. The opaque site will take the payment from the customer and will keep the difference between the hotel's net rate and the rate paid by the customer.

Social Media

Social media is an umbrella term that refers to the tools and platforms used to publish, discuss, and share content online. The tools include Twitter, blogs, wikis, and webcasts, as well as sites designed to stimulate interaction among users through the sharing of opinions, experiences, photos, videos, and bookmarks, among other items.

It is a significant challenge for hospitality operators to conclusively measure their return on investment in social media. However, the logical approach is that if your business is discussed on social media forums, whether you like it or not, it

Industry Insight: Social Media Fundamentals— Social Media for Hospitality and Tourism

By Wendy Freeman and Janice Fung,
School of Professional Communication, Ryerson University, Toronto, Ontario, Canada

Most individuals are familiar with social media. A recent study* of Internet users estimated that 83 percent of adults aged 18 to 29 use Facebook regularly to communicate with friends and family. Just as individuals have moved online, companies are participating in this fast-paced virtual space made up of a rich variety of social media. Marketing and advertising is now a two-way interactive conversation between customer and company.

Social media is used widely by customers and potential customers to search and share hospitality and travel experiences. Through social media platforms, individuals and companies can share information quickly to a wide audience. In this way, companies no longer completely control their brand messages.

The social media landscape is made up of a wide range of platforms that allow people to share and discuss video, text, image, sound, location, and relationships. Although new applications appear and disappear, many of the social media applications listed here are well established with millions of users.

Type	Use	Examples
Social networking	Build networks based on interests, relationships, affiliations	Facebook, Google+, LinkedIn
Blogging	Share content (images, links, stories, news) in chronological posts	Wordpress, Tumblr
Micro-blogging	Send brief posts shared with followers	Twitter
Media sharing	Post video, images, audio organized in channels or through tags	YouTube, Flickr, Pinterest
Location sharing	Engage individuals based on location through comments, reviews, and incentives using geo-tagging	FourSquare

There are several risks and rewards that organizations in the hospitality and tourism sector should first consider before incorporating social media into their communication strategy. These risks and rewards include the following: trial and error, privacy and identity, copyright and piracy, and quality and relevancy.

The use of social media in the hospitality and travel industry is still in its infancy. Part of the process in establishing your online rapport with prospective

---

* Brenner, J. (2013). Pew Internet: Social Networking. Pew Internet & American Life Project. Retrieved from: http://pewinternet.org/Commentary/2012/March/Pew-Internet-Social-Networking-full-detail.aspx

Industry Insight *(continued)*

or existing clients is through **trial and error**. Although not all media and methods are proven to work for each organization's purposes, consider your social media venture as a chance to expand your existing communication strategy—one method that can generate a stronger and wider outreach on a global scale. Decide on the right platform(s) for your organization and creatively establish and regularly maintain your online presence.

The **quality and relevancy** of the content posted on social media platforms can improve or diminish your organization's reputation. First, consider the type of information that your audience is most interested in and seeks to locate online. Write for your audience rather than at them. Part of online social engagement is maintaining a personable experience for your followers; catering your company's online content to the interests of your audience can strengthen your client relationships. Second, the timeliness of your response to queries, compliments, or even complaints can demonstrate the service-oriented nature of your organization. Maintaining a professional and objective tone without being evasive, particularly when addressing negative comments, can boost your organization's online (and offline) credibility.

Privacy and identity extend to both the company and its clients. Companies in the hospitality and tourism sector should initially consider the type of content they want accessible to the public. Filtering the information you release online not only protects your company, but also enforces key messages to your main target audience. Another aspect to consider is the privacy and identity of your potential or existing clients. Not all visitors are comfortable with releasing their online identity through posts or comments; providing the option to privately contact the company or log into a client account can provide a greater sense of safety and security.

Copyright and piracy are growing concerns for organizations that choose to use social media platforms. Any original content you release such as written content, photographs, audio or video files, can be copied or replicated without your permission; the policing of illegal use of these materials is minimal, if at all present. Companies can try to track the usage of their material by others, but this can be time-consuming and costly. Consider that reposting or duplication of online material has its rewards and intentionally posting content that you want others to share and source can generate a stronger connection and following from your audience.

Useful resources for learning more about social media

Brian Solis: Defining the Impact of Technology, Culture and Business
http://www.briansolis.com/

Creative Commons
http://creativecommons.org/

Seth Godin's Blog
http://sethgodin.typepad.com/

Social Technographics Profile of Your Customers
http://empowered.forrester.com/tool_consumer.html

is better to be part of that discussion than outside of it. In addition, search engine rankings are influenced by social media mentions.

Another line of thinking suggests that active participation in social media is good for more than just getting higher rankings on organic Google searches. This line of thinking suggests that the old paradigm for marketing merits new consideration. According to the old approach, marketing strategies attempted to create a high level of product awareness in the minds of consumers in order to positively influence purchase intentions at the moment of truth (the act of buying). The new thinking suggests a shift and proposes that marketing efforts use social media to create a presence for businesses at every stage of the consumer journey to gain a "mindshare" of consumers' considerations earlier in the process. This way, businesses have better chances at the purchase point to get into consumers' wallet-share as well. This thinking of "get them early and stay with them throughout" has its merits, as the consumer journey (also described as a purchase funnel) begins with the consumer's initial interest and inspiration for purchasing a given item, where consumers consider many brands and product options at the outset. During the journey, consumers narrow these choices to a few, before deciding to actually pick one option and make the purchase. The process involves social media participation at each stage. The sharing and exchanging through social media does not necessarily end with the purchase, especially for experience-based hospitality products like a meal or a vacation: the validation phase or post-consumption stage frequently involves social media in the form of posted and shared reviews, pictures, experiences, stories, and tweets about what happened.

Hospitality managers should be aware of the new reality that a guest's experience, good or bad, is no longer kept between a hotel/resort/restaurant and that one guest only; guests can instantly share experiences with hundreds on their contact lists. They can take pictures or videos and, in a heartbeat, upload them on social media sites. A video or an image on occasion can go viral and be viewed by millions in one day.

The traditional rating agencies are gradually getting bypassed by review sites and customer ratings. Google says the average guest visits 22 websites before booking accommodations, and it is proven that ratings and reviews drive purchase intent. The potential exposure to all social contacts of customers can have both positive and negative results, but also presents a tremendous revenue opportunity for a business.

Mobility and Mobile Users

Mobility is the key word in new consumer trends in accessing information, in socializing, and even in making transactions. Over the past several years, rapid growth in mobile device adoption has dramatically affected daily life worldwide. Smartphone ownership is soaring, and a growing number of travelers are adding a tablet to the mix, making multi-device ownership more and more commonplace. Travel companies continue to innovate and adapt to a new breed of hyperconnected, always-on mobile travelers. While travelers' mobile expectations continue to rise worldwide, the specific ways in which consumers use mobile devices to search, shop, buy, experience, and share travel vary by region and market.

Mobile devices are able to access real-time inventory availability, and revenue professionals can take advantage of dynamic pricing tactics to capture mobile users who display booking intent.

A significant distinction must be made between tablets and smartphones. Tablets are getting smaller, while smartphones are getting larger and offering more and more functionality. The significant distinction is the technology platform for getting online: all a smartphone needs is a wireless signal, but a tablet may need Wi-Fi for connectivity. Interestingly, research by device category has revealed differences by time of day for searches by platform: more desktops are used than mobile devices for searches during the day; however, in the evening hours, tablet use spikes and desktop use dwindles. Market research has also noted that bookings made via tablets generate almost three times more room nights and five times more revenue than bookings made via smartphones. Hospitality industry revenue professionals are keenly aware of these nuances as smartphones are rapidly becoming the source of instant purchases for consumer goods and travel-related products and services.

Provided that revenue managers understand the importance of proper targeting, the technology consequences of platform differences for online distribution channel management merit a brief discussion on website design variances among the four screens: TV, PC, tablet, and smartphone, in the next section.

Responsive Design

In simple terms, *responsive design* means that a website responds to the device or screen on which it is being viewed. The website morphs to better accommodate the resolution and size (pixel count and configuration) of the screen—from site layout to size of imagery, sometimes even to the amount of copy. So whichever of the four screens—PC/laptop, tablet, smartphone, or Internet TV—a travel shopper uses, the website will look customized for that screen. With more smartphones in the world than ever, websites must provide a mobile experience that truly speaks to their users. By creating sites that offer a seamless, engaging experience no matter which platform or device a user is on, revenue professionals can help build their brand, improve customer mobile shopping experiences, and optimize their entire distribution channel management strategy.

We have entered the era of multi-device users. A potential guest might use a laptop PC during office hours to begin a search for a resort vacation. Later in the day, the guest might use a smartphone to review sites and friends' postings, and exchange text messages about possible top choices. Finally, the potential guest will reserve an actual booking via a tablet device before the night is over. In this scenario, one user searches for and completes one booking on one day using three different devices. Today's guests find nothing unusual about this.

The combination of driving traffic to a website and communicating with clients is very important, and these should be synchronous efforts. User behavior is changing swiftly, and revenue managers must understand the user journey. Therefore, to reach consumers, a revenue professional needs to follow user behavior and offer the information users seek when they seek it, via the channel they use to search for it. An Internet presence is an essential starting point, and a business's website should be accessible through different devices.

Endnote

1. For a detailed overview of distribution channel management, see Cindy Estis Green and Mark V. Lomanno, *Distribution Channel Analysis: A Guide for Hotels*, an American Hotel & Lodging Association (AH&LA) and STR Special Report, published by the Hospitality Sales & Marketing Association International (HSMAI) Foundation. 2012.

Case Study: Capacity Allocation at the Sunrise

Mindy Lee is a software engineer who works for a company that is known for its inventory management software suite. She specializes in designing interfaces that help a business migrate its inventory data to cloud computing. Mindy has loved the Internet since her school years; she used e-mail services and browsers before any other kid in her class. She books all her travel arrangements online, including flight tickets, car rentals, and hotel rooms.

After an unexpected loss in her family, Mindy has inherited some money that she thinks is enough to invest in a small hotel. Mindy has decided to buy a controlling stake in the Hotel Sunrise, a 140-room independent limited-service midscale property. Mindy has 80 percent ownership and her silent partner owns 20 percent, allowing Mindy total control in operating decisions. Mindy sees a lot of potential for the hotel, which has struggled over the years to gain market share. The previous owner, an old hotelier, had refused to buy into a franchise and had cherished the hotel's independence, hoping to compete on service quality and reputation. The average occupancy of the Sunrise was about 40 percent on an annual basis for the last couple of years.

Mindy doesn't pretend to know how to run a hotel's daily operations, but is convinced that she can boost sales by embracing OTAs to sell the Sunrise's rooms. She pins her high hopes on working with Expedia. After her first two quarters of being in charge, Mindy sees her optimism justified: the monthly average occupancy of her hotel is up at 67 percent, which is a significant improvement. Her ranking for her location on Expedia searches is first-page placement since last month. Her ADR has taken a bit of a beating, though: it has decreased from $130 to $96.40. Expedia takes a commission of 27 percent out of that. Virtually all rooms are sold through Expedia, as even regular guests book on the OTA website rather than pay the $130 rate posted on the Sunrise's home page.

After her hotel manager presents Mindy with the performance metrics, it is clear to Mindy that, after occupancy gains, the Sunrise has a lower RevPAR than it had before. Mindy needs to think about room rates, distribution costs, and overall profitability, as both she and her co-investor are getting impatient.

Discussion Question

How might Mindy improve the RevPAR of the Sunrise without raising room rates?

Chapter 12 Outline

Automated Revenue Management Systems
    Capabilities of Automated Systems
    Cultural Challenges of Automation
    System-Integration Challenges
The Revenue Manager
    Task Lists and Competencies for
        Revenue Managers
Case Study

Competencies

1. Describe automated revenue management systems, including their capabilities, and the cultural and system-integration challenges they present. (pp. 169–177)

2. Describe how the revenue manager position evolved over time. (pp. 177–181)

3. Identify and explain typical tasks and competencies of revenue managers. (pp. 181–182)

12

Revenue Management's Place in Hotels

REVENUE MANAGEMENT SYSTEMS and the revenue manager position itself have grown in complexity and sophistication in the past two decades. In this chapter, we will first look at the capabilities of automated revenue management systems and the challenges associated with implementing these systems in hotels, then conclude with a discussion of how the position of revenue manager was created and has evolved within hotel companies.

Automated Revenue Management Systems

Why are revenue management systems in hotels so complex? The simple answer is that the systems are complex because the revenue management task is complex. Revenue management encompasses controlling the availability of inventory units involving multi-tiered pricing structures; selling different room types; selling bundled and unbundled items; using a variety of distribution methods and channels for selling similar units; using various capacity-management tactics; and controlling and monitoring other revenue management components, many of which are subject to constant changes. Hotel decision-makers must process a lot of data.

Accuracy and immediacy are critical expectations of hotel managers. In today's world, revenue reports and other data outputs must be accurate and available at any time, through any point of access, whenever needed. The natural response to all of these needs, once computers came onto the scene, was to automate. Computers can perform complex computations at amazing speeds, and software programming has reached a level where algorithm-based programs can deal with almost any possible set of variables in any scenario a manager can imagine, be it for a single hotel or a multiple-property company.

The two basic types of automated revenue management systems are recommendation systems and decision systems:

- *Recommendation systems* are capable of monitoring, forecasting, and making recommendations for optimum revenue management solutions. Systems of this kind need actively involved revenue managers and analysts to input data, analyze system outputs, and make and implement sound decisions.

- *Decision systems* go one step further. Beyond the monitoring and forecasting functions, decision systems arrive at solutions that they consider optimal, then put in place all of the rate and capacity allocation controls necessary to achieve targeted results. Systems of this kind need revenue analysts for data input and monitoring, plus revenue managers to supervise and override system-implemented controls if necessary.

Capabilities of Automated Systems

Both recommendation systems and decision systems are capable of performing vital revenue management tasks that are labor-intensive and tedious (as well as prone to error) if done manually, such as:

- Forecasting demand
- Forecasting availability
- Analyzing data (key metrics of measurement)
- Quoting rates
- Optimizing (rate, occupancy, channels, segments, revenue streams)
- Analyzing comp sets
- Analyzing group business (and perhaps performing displacement analyses)
- Providing user-defined consolidated reports

Some revenue management systems include budgeting capabilities as well.

Some system vendors promise a quantifiable improvement in revenue, either in the form of a 4 to 12 percent RevPAR increase or a 6 to 12 percent revenue lift, as a result of installing their system. The accuracy of such highly ambitious claims is subject to interpretation, however.

Some revenue management systems need hardware as well as software installations. Vendors offer client-server solutions for a single property or small groups of properties. A pay-as-you-go ASP (application service provider) solution is also available for interested clients. The acceptance of the SAS (software as service) approach is growing on a global scale. The recent trend toward cloud computing, under which the data that a system produces resides on a network instead of a server on the property, has promising potential since the critical issues of secure access and the protection of databases seem resolved. Training and consultation are customary components of product offerings. The market is very competitive, and today revenue management automation solutions are available for purchase for properties of all sizes and types.

Single-Image Inventory. The concept of single-image inventory is an important advance in automated revenue management systems that deserves special mention. Before this feature became available, hotels allocated blocks of their room inventory to in-house units (their front office, reservations office, and hotel sales office) and resellers (e.g., call centers, central reservations offices, global distribution systems, and travel agencies), and updated the reservations for the given blocks on a regular basis one or more times a day.

Because different blocks of rooms were controlled by different sellers, it was not unusual to experience inaccuracies, double bookings, or other forms of confusion from the operator's perspective. From the perspective of guests, different sellers meant they sometimes had to work harder to book a room. After being denied availability for a future date by the front office of a given hotel, for example, some consumers discovered that if they placed a call to the hotel's central reservations office (CRO), they might still be able to book a room, provided that the CRO's room block was not yet sold out at the time of the call. Of course, some consumers did not make the extra effort, and the hotel lost sales.

Single-image inventory means that interface technology has improved so much that availability information regarding each inventory unit, including designated room blocks, can be accessed in real time by all room sellers.

Consumers can book a room night through a variety of distribution channels: by calling the reservations office of a hotel, accessing the website of the same hotel, calling the chain's central reservations office (if the hotel is part of a chain), or accessing the website of a third-party reseller. With single-image inventory, the product availability, rate rules, and all other relevant pieces of information are drawn from the same data source, so they are identical all the time, regardless of the point of access or the channel used. Any time a room status or price point is altered (that is, a room night is booked or canceled or a discount is implemented), the whole database that holds the information regarding each room's status for each night for years ahead is updated instantly. The risk of double booking or losing a sale for lack of up-to-the-minute information is practically eliminated. When product availability information across all distribution channels becomes identical, single-image inventory (and rate parity) has been achieved.

The prevalence of this technology has helped eliminate duplication and confusion and has enabled hotels to capture maximum reservation volume while optimizing revenue.

Cultural Challenges of Automation

Both recommendation and decision revenue management systems require input from a hotel's revenue management team. The more appropriate and accurate the data that is input, the better the system's output. It happens frequently that a system forecast for occupancy for a future date provides a figure that experienced managers have a hard time accepting, and they may decide to override the system. What is remarkable is the proven fact that, in most such cases, the system's data has a tendency to be more accurate.

Overriding a system recommendation (e.g., a rate or minimum-stay requirement) is tempting for managers, and managers often have good reasons to do so. Even if the system's recommendation for a two-night-minimum-stay restriction makes perfect sense under given market conditions, managers have to consider more than just tactical measures when dealing with guests. Even when demand is strong for multi-night reservations, the patronage of a high-lifetime-value guest who needs only one night is worth a lot more than the patronage of a first-time guest willing to make a two-night-stay booking but who may never return in the future.

High-end hotels have traditionally hesitated to automate their revenue management operations, because such hotels offer personal attention and intuitive and individualized services to guests. Luxury hotel operators were concerned that if system outputs needed overrides too frequently, they would be more trouble than they were worth. Automation is a significant cultural change for such operations.

It is also not unusual to see managers who initially have a "Nintendo approach" to their new revenue management systems; that is, they play around with all the features and controls of the system and tweak settings too frequently, using a trial-and-error approach to learning about and implementing their systems.

Revenue management systems need to be given a fair chance to produce results, and patience is a very important virtue after implementation. Managers and employees have to learn gradually to appreciate what an automated system can do for them, and customize system settings only if there are strong reasons to do so. Revenue management systems are significant investments that can produce lucrative returns over time if used properly.

Having said that, it is also important to stress that the management of any business is best done by human beings. Artificial intelligence can contribute a lot to the decision-making process, but good managers never let a system take over. An optimum balance between automation and human intelligence can be achieved if managers let the systems do what systems do best, yet never let the human element take a backseat in an industry that takes pride in providing service to its customers.

System-Integration Challenges

In today's world, even the smallest hotels have automated systems to help their managers with management tasks. Property management systems (PMSs); point-of-sale (POS) systems; accounting systems; customer relations management (CRM) systems; heating, ventilation, and air conditioning (HVAC) systems; and building transportation systems are examples of the different automated systems a hotel may use. Typically, hotels acquire different systems at different times from different vendors. It is a challenge for hotels to interface their different systems so that they work together and allow for seamless data transfer.

For example, think of the integration needed when a guest returns to the hotel after a business dinner with a client, swipes his room card to gain entrance to the parking garage, parks his car on the second underground level, and then swipes his card again to enter the building from the garage, then swipes his card to use the elevator to access his floor. He swipes one more time to enter his room, where he takes a beer from the sensor-equipped mini bar as he sits down and turns on his laptop to check e-mail messages. Many automated systems were involved in this example: an access control system to enter the garage, the hotel, the guest floor, and the room; the building transportation system to direct the elevator; the POS system and PMS system to post the charge of one beer (POS) to the room folio (PMS) and the charge for Internet usage if that is not free; plus a CRM system to pull all the guest's relevant data together to build a guest profile. These systems may have been acquired at different times from different vendors, but they still need to be interfaced. As you can see, challenges lie ahead when a vendor must install a revenue management system that will have to be interfaced with all of the existing systems of the hotel that service revenue centers.

Industry Insight: Revenue Management Automation

By IDeaS
Founded in 1989, IDeaS offers industry-leading pricing and revenue management software, services, and consulting to the hospitality and travel industries. For more information, visit www.ideas.com.

Sync or Sink: The Role of Automation in Revenue Management

Five years ago, a revenue manager's job consisted of collecting and compiling data into Excel spreadsheets, analyzing the data to identify trends, and making a decision about hotel rates. Today, it's an incredibly complex process that involves online travel agencies (OTAs), mobile marketing, hyper-interactive consumers, and direct competitors who consistently undercut their prices.

With the added pressures placed upon revenue managers today, hoteliers are finding it necessary to invest in technologies that increase their chances of capitalizing on consumer behavior in order to optimize revenue and remain competitive. One solution is revenue management software, which automatically calculates, monitors and analyzes market data, freeing up a revenue manager's time to make smarter, more strategic revenue decisions for the hotel.

Let's take a closer look.

Increased Efficiency

Historically, revenue management has been defined as using a hotel's booking history and current activity levels to forecast demand as accurately as possible. During periods of high demand, revenue managers increase rates. When demand is low, they discount them, thereby maximizing revenue under both scenarios. However, today's forecasting and pricing decisions are rarely this simple. Amid heavy reliance on OTAs, flash sales, and mobile marketing, it's almost impossible to look at a hotel's booking history and identify trends because the booking patterns are changing constantly, making it hard for revenue managers to recognize changes in demand and react in time to make a profit. In such a high-speed environment, manually collecting, evaluating, and calculating data via Excel spreadsheets is not only a tedious process, it's slow and highly susceptible to error and missed opportunities.

This is where revenue management software can make a huge difference. Through a series of complex, specialized algorithms and countless calculations, revenue management systems automatically assess hotel performance on a daily, weekly, monthly, and annual basis, allowing revenue managers to quickly compare rooms sold and revenue against data at the market segment and total hotel level. The system provides updated reports every evening—though some systems can even pull data every hour. This gives revenue managers and hoteliers a clear vision of their data, bringing more accuracy and consistency—versus gut instinct—to the forecasting and reporting process. The increased business intelligence makes

(continued)

Industry Insight (continued)

it much easier for revenue managers to determine pricing strategies that optimize demand and increase revenue across their property or portfolio of properties.

Less "Number Crunching"— More Strategizing

The sheer amount of time it takes a revenue manager to collect and evaluate data via Excel spreadsheets is enormous—easily four to five hours a day. With an automated revenue management system in place, revenue managers can cut their workload in half, freeing up their time to analyze data and make better, more strategic decisions for the hotel. By automatically cranking out reports and recommendations in real-time, the system ensures that revenue managers remain in control—able to act proactively, instead of reactively, to changes in the market.

For example, in a manual environment, revenue managers generally identify a booking pattern and then take action, such as raising the price of rooms. Under this scenario, hoteliers often cannot identify patterns and opportunities until nearly 80 percent of their business is on the books. They end up only yielding the last 20 percent. But with an automated revenue management system in place, hoteliers can invert that. Imagine if trends and revenue opportunities were seen with only 20 percent of the business on the books. The hotel is now yielding 80 percent of the business. Because the system enables revenue managers to see trends much more quickly than they would otherwise, they can yield a much larger share of the business that's yet to come.

Greater Culture of Revenue Management

Perhaps one of the most significant benefits hotels have reported seeing as a result of having an automated revenue management system is a more defined and enhanced culture of revenue management. No longer faced with a mountain of work on Excel spreadsheets, revenue managers have time to conduct more in-depth analysis of the data now readily available to them. Rather than labor over creating reports and constantly changing prices, revenue managers can focus on exceptions to the forecast, such as a special event in town that may fall outside of the system's parameters.

In addition, the reduced workload frees up revenue managers' time to meet with the sales and marketing teams to align strategies and ensure that the overall marketing direction is consistent with the hotel's goals and objectives. Because revenue managers are experts in pricing, they can give marketers the pricing information they need to create offers and promotions that generate revenue. In return, marketers can clue revenue managers in about when they place offers into the marketplace so that revenue managers can create better, more accurate forecasts in relationship to demand.

However, these aren't the only teams who benefit as a result of a revenue management system. As the forecast becomes more accurate and consistent, senior executives in other departments—such as catering, front office, reservations, food and beverage, and housekeeping—will become more confident in the reports and more familiar with the language and basic principles of revenue management, which serves to maximize revenue from several different angles.

> **Industry Insight** *(continued)*
>
> **Improved Bottom Line**
>
> Ultimately, hotels with an automated revenue management system in place will be far more competitive than properties without an automated system. The sheer time it saves revenue managers alone can escalate their role from "number crunchers" to strategic partners—serious contenders for a position in the C-suite. By automating a huge chunk of their workload, revenue managers can more easily keep up with today's fast-moving pace of business to anticipate and capitalize upon consumer behavior. In addition, by working more closely with other departments, particularly sales and marketing, revenue managers can generate more business and revenue for the hotel.

When many properties at various locations need to be linked together, data has to be transmitted and shared among properties. To continue with our example, suppose the same guest is on the road again three months later. He books a room in a city he has never visited before, in a hotel of the same chain. If that hotel is provided with access to all of the information related to the guest's previous stay in the first chain hotel, a number of benefits accrue: the booking process can be simplified and sped up, as the guest's personal information does not need to be collected again, only confirmed. His personal preferences regarding bed configuration, room location, and so forth can be automatically passed on to the second hotel. As a result of the streamlined reservation process, time is saved for both guest and hotel, and loyalty can be increased as a result of the wow factor—the hotel can certainly prove that this guest's business is appreciated and his needs and wants have been noted chain-wide.

To achieve this level of integration, a hotel chain has to go beyond property-level system integration and take integration to a regional, national, or even global level. It is hard enough to smoothly integrate all of the systems and sub-systems at a single property; it is a significantly greater challenge to have all of a chain's different properties share data. The challenges of system integration are exponentially greater if the properties are in different time zones with different technological infrastructures and are staffed by people speaking different languages.

One interesting implication of data sharing involves deciding who owns the data. Data ownership can become a highly significant issue if a franchise operation (one corporation) owned by another corporation, managed by yet another corporation, is sold. Is the data with all of its precious guest information the property of the franchisor company that installed and maintained the CRS, the management company that runs the hotel and serves the guest, or the owner/franchisee of the hotel? To prevent unnecessary confusion, in an ideal world this question is dealt with contractually at the outset.

Automation can be a key component in revenue management activities. However, the experience, sensibility, and intelligence of qualified managers and the

Industry Insight: Automating the Umstead

By IDeaS

Nestled on 12 acres of lakeside grounds in Cary, N.C., The Umstead Hotel and Spa is the only Forbes Five Star, AAA Five-Diamond full-service hotel in North Carolina—making it the most expensive hotel among a sea of three- and four-star properties. In addition, the hotel's location in Research Triangle Park, one of the world's largest research and development centers, means that most of its weekday business comes from corporate travelers. To offset this during the weekends, since Cary isn't a typical tourist destination, the hotel earns revenue by attracting locals—individuals from within a 100-mile radius of the hotel—who stay at the property to celebrate special occasions, such as weddings, anniversaries, and birthdays.

"One of our biggest and toughest challenges is to both compete and not compete with the neighboring three- and four-star properties," said Jeremy Gonsalves, Revenue Manager, The Umstead Hotel and Spa. "Our rates are almost always $100 more than the competitive set, so finding that appropriate piece of business that brings us greater value is critical to our success."

Forecasting by Market Segment

Because of its distinct market segmentation—corporate guests during weekdays and leisure guests during weekends—it was critical for The Umstead Hotel and Spa to find a revenue management system that could forecast unconstrained demand by market segment. After experiencing a system that allowed for little flexibility and control of room rates, The Umstead Hotel and Spa decided to partner with IDeaS Revenue Solutions to implement the IDeaS Revenue Management System (RMS).

"Because we experience a flip in segmentation, we really like that IDeaS RMS lets us yield to certain segments," said Gonsalves. "By tracking and monitoring booking pace for each segment, the system enables me to more accurately forecast demand and determine the best pricing recommendations for each type of guest."

The system also saves Gonsalves a significant amount of time and energy. By automatically assessing hotel performance on a daily, weekly, monthly, and annual basis, the IDeaS RMS allows Gonsalves to quickly compare rooms sold and revenue against data at the segment and total hotel level—allowing more time for making smarter, more strategic revenue decisions for the hotel.

Seeing Green

"IDeaS has been a terrific resource for the hotel," said Gonsalves. "Thanks to the system, I have more time to explore and really understand our booking trends and how to manipulate demand to increase revenue. That's something I couldn't do as well prior to using the IDeaS RMS, and it's had a very noticeable, positive effect on our occupancy and bottom line."

Since implementing the IDeaS RMS in 2008, The Umstead Hotel and Spa has realized significant increases in occupancy, ADR, and RevPAR. Occupancy jumped 8.1 percent, ADR rose 16.1 percent, and RevPAR increased 25.2 percent.

Industry Insight (continued)

"Overall, IDeaS has equipped us with a more scientific way of looking at and determining guest value," said Gonsalves. "This, combined with the system's powerful reporting capabilities, has given us a stronger culture of revenue management, which we will continue to build upon and improve in the future."

"Our revenue management and sales departments have successfully used IDeaS for revenue optimization for the past four years," said Jim Beley, General Manager, The Umstead Hotel and Spa. "IDeaS helped our luxury property 'weather the storm' during the recession and has since strategically moved us toward a more vibrant RevPAR growth. Its success is proven. IDeaS is a partner you can rely on with confidence."

---

service culture they create are the true sources of success. The human component can be complemented but never replaced or bypassed with automated systems in an industry that prides itself on customer service.

The Revenue Manager

Revenue management professionals are proven to offer valuable contribution to hospitality operations. The professionals in various designations may carry any of the titles from revenue analyst to revenue manager or director of revenue. Some large corporations may even have a Corporate Vice President of Revenue. The key competency of revenue maximization has become more strategic over the years and more and more organizations consider revenue management to be mission critical for their success.

When the new position of revenue manager was created, the position's responsibilities, task lists, and list of desired candidate qualifications had to be created as well. This all evolved gradually over time as the position matured. In the beginning, candidates for the new position were drawn from among those at the hotel who already had to deal with revenue-related issues. The traditional position of reservations manager at midsize and large properties with a reservations office was a logical place to start looking for candidates. Reservations as a process requires working with dates, availability information, rates, upselling, guest history files, and a number of other issues related to maximizing revenue. Therefore, it was quite common to find former reservations managers filling the first revenue manager posts with a reassigned position and a reclassified title.

Over the years, the revenue manager position evolved as the new position's responsibilities and reporting relationships were fleshed out. The following sections discuss the stages of development of the revenue manager position.

Initial Stage. In the early days of revenue management, the newly minted revenue manager—often referred to as a revenue analyst—typically worked with the front office manager and most frequently reported directly to that position (see Exhibit 1).

Exhibit 1   Revenue Manager: Initial Stage

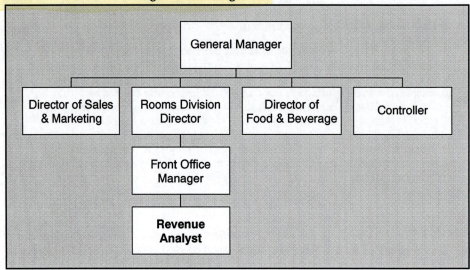

At this initial stage, the reporting structure shown in Exhibit 1 was considered acceptable for a number of reasons. Only tactical-level involvement was expected from the revenue analyst/manager at this time, and only within the hotel's rooms division. The new revenue analyst/manager was involved in historic data analysis, forecasting, processing reservations, and producing reports with a focus on internal measurement metrics. The new position was expected to perform analytical tasks and provide input to the hotel's management staff, but no significant decision-making authority was delegated to this new position at this stage.

Intermediate Stage. After the new position of revenue analyst proved to be useful, over time it started to get recognized by other hotel managers for its significant role in tactical decision-making, and a re-alignment occurred within the rooms division (see Exhibit 2). This was the result of the growing emphasis in hotels on revenue maximization as a source of profitability.

In this intermediate stage, the revenue manager position indeed evolved into a management-level position on par with other hotel department heads, such as the front office manager. In this stage, the revenue manager may or may not have had a revenue analyst reporting to him or her, based on the size of the property and the responsibilities assigned to the manager. At this stage, the job still involved mostly tactical-level activities, but it was more independent than in the initial stage, and there was a significant growth in authority. Giving the position a management title and management-level remuneration was a sign that upper-level hotel management recognized the complex nature of the job and the qualifications and experience required.

At this point, some key hospitality organizations (such as AH&LA and HSMAI) introduced specialized training and certification programs for revenue managers to complement the corporate programs and on-the-job training. A body

Exhibit 2 Revenue Manager: Intermediate Stage

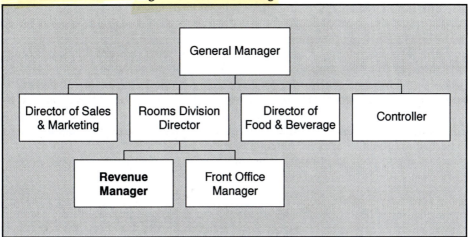

of revenue management literature started slowly getting into industry magazines, and most lodging industry conferences and trade shows began including panel discussions, workshops, or presentations on revenue management. Special interest groups devoted to revenue management started to get established within some industry associations. It is fair to say that this intermediate stage reflects where the revenue management position was for much of the first decade of the twenty-first century.

Evolutionary Stage. The next stage of the revenue management position can be classified as evolutionary in the sense that the revenue manager is no longer within the rooms division (see Exhibit 3). This evolution is the result of the revenue manager's involvement in more than rooms revenue management. Other

Exhibit 3 Revenue Manager: Evolutionary Stage

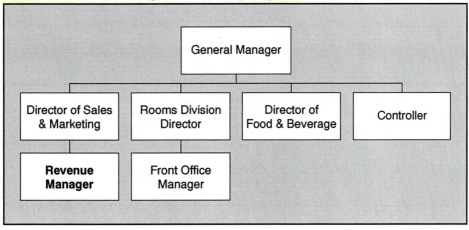

revenue streams—food and beverage, function space, gambling, etc.—are now also monitored, measured, manipulated, and controlled by the revenue manager. At this stage, the revenue management position is also considered a contributor to the hotel's strategic planning.

The revenue manager's involvement in higher-level strategic thinking comes as a result of the new discipline of revenue management having "grown up" to become a significant contributor to more than just short-term tactical aspects of hotel operation. In recent years, revenue management has become recognized as a core competency for conducting business in the field of hospitality and tourism. Today, many major international hotel corporations have revenue management expertise involved in all key management decisions. In fact, some of these companies skipped the evolutionary stage of revenue management and have already moved on to the next stage.

Fully Developed Stage. The significance of the changes to the revenue management position in the fully developed stage (see Exhibit 4) is evident: the revenue management function has been elevated to an executive-level position on equal standing with the other major functions of the hotel organization. The director of revenue management reports directly to the highest position in charge of operations, the hotel's general manager. This new organizational structure will eventually be embraced by all hotels that understand the vital role of revenue management, both on the strategic level with the inclusion of the director of revenue management position, and on the tactical level with the designation of a revenue manager on the same level as managers of other hotel departments.

The position of director of revenue management is involved in overarching strategic issues, with an emphasis on demand generation, market positioning, strategic pricing, market targeting, and promotion/advertising. The revenue manager should be involved in all of the other strategic aspects—e.g., distribution methods and channels, strategic packaging, etc.—plus all of the tactical aspects—

Exhibit 4 Revenue Manager: Fully Developed Stage

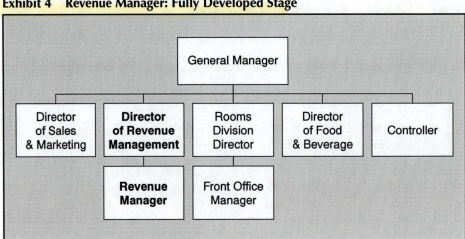

e.g., forecasting, tactical rate control, stay control, and capacity management, among others.

Task Lists and Competencies for Revenue Managers

Probably the greatest pressure on revenue management professionals is the ever-increasing complexity and variety of tasks and competencies they are expected to master in order to optimize revenue.

Just as there are differences among hotels (midsize select-service properties versus large full-service properties, for example), there are differences among the task lists and responsibilities of revenue management professionals working in the hotels. Still, some commonalities can be identified. Forecasting, rate management, the analysis and evaluation of revenue management activities, report preparation, coordination with a variety of operational units, strategy development, and interaction with other managers are on the task list of every revenue management professional.

Core technical competencies required of revenue managers include the following:

- Managing group blocks
- Managing and monitoring Internet systems to ensure rate integrity and parity
- Managing the hotel's web portal
- Maintaining relationships with third-party market managers
- Analyzing financial statements and market data
- Preparing accurate occupancy and revenue forecasts
- Developing tactics and strategies to manage group and transient market needs

The interpersonal competencies a revenue manager needs include the abilities to:

- Lead business revenue review meetings.
- Develop and deliver effective presentations.
- Establish credibility with the hotel's management team.
- Work closely with the director of sales and marketing on pricing (both short-term and long-term).
- Articulate complex strategies and other topics (both in oral and written format).
- Mentor and coach reservations and front desk personnel in revenue management strategies and tactics.
- Employ diplomatic skills to manage interpersonal conflicts.

Obviously, revenue managers need to be good with numbers, but, as you can see, their job entails a lot more than crunching numbers and producing reports. Revenue managers must be able communicators of the hotel's strategic and tactical revenue initiatives. They must be willing to take on a leadership role in helping build strong teams of co-workers committed to achieving revenue goals and business success.

The demands and expectations placed on revenue managers grow on a seemingly daily basis. However, in organizations that successfully embrace the challenges of sustainable growth, it is recognized that revenue management is not the job of a select few revenue management professionals. All of a hotel's revenue centers and support centers have to be on the same page in their understanding and support of common revenue goals. Revenue management is multifaceted, complex, and cross-disciplinary. Front-of-the house departments and back-of-the-house departments all have a part to play in helping a hotel maximize its revenue potential. It's the difficult job of the revenue manager to communicate the hotel's revenue management initiatives to, and coordinate them with, the rest of the hotel's staff.

Case Study: Override It or Not?

Hotel Byron is a small lifestyle hotel in the upper midscale category. Its capacity of 150 rooms is booked solid during periods of high demand. The upcoming week is also very close to sold out on most weekdays. The Crescendo Revenue Management system of the Front Office recommends a 3-night minimum length of stay (MLOS) for Monday arrivals that week. Discounts are not offered for new bookings, but corporate rates are certainly honored. Internet resellers (OTAs) are allocated only premium rates across all online channels. Things are looking up for next week at the Byron.

Mrs. Cornwall would like to book one single room for one night at the Byron and she needs it for next Monday. It seems like an easy decision for the Sidney, the revenue manager: reject the booking. The only reason Sidney is dealing with this request is that she got a request from Glenn, the assistant front office manager, to override the MLOS control in place for this one booking.

Sidney has searched for Mrs. Cornwall's name, but she does not show up in the guest history file. Sidney's response to the request for an override is that there is no reason to override the MLOS for Mrs. Cornwall as she has never stayed here before; further, there would be no revenue generated as the guest would wanted to use a complimentary room night gift certificate that clearly states "Subject of Availability." There is nothing much to contemplate as far as Sidney is concerned. The Byron is booked close to capacity and rooms are going for full rate. Sidney is not interested in giving away comp rooms on a high-demand week.

However, Glenn remembers well that overbooked night two months ago, when Mrs. Cornwall was walked to another hotel, The Hyatt Place. That night, the Byron issued an apology and a gift certificate to Mrs. Cornwall for a complimentary night, inviting her back, asking her if she wouldn't mind giving the hotel another chance. Glenn remembers the disappointment of the guest, the discussion they had, and that he had learned that the only reason for choosing this particular hotel at that time was the Byron's close proximity to the home of one of Mrs. Cornwall's relatives, who became bed-ridden recently.

Mrs. Cornwall indicated that she would come and visit a couple of times a year. She also revealed that she was visiting her uncle, who is the vice president of a local equipment manufacturing plant. The plant in question was in the process of planning a 3-day training workshop for 120 dealers and service supervisors at the Byron. Mrs. Cornwall had heard how nice the hotel's restaurant was and what a sumptuous cappuccino the Byron's coffee shop can offer. Glenn told Mrs. Cornwall that she would be welcome back and that the hotel would do its best to make sure the next stay would be trouble free.

Discussion Question

How would you handle this reservation?

Appendix

Many of the items in this list of the top ten revenue management mistakes will be familiar to revenue management practitioners in the field who already bear some battle scars. However, some items may be new, so the list is offered in the hope that it might help revenue managers and others avoid some pitfalls. Smart people learn from their own mistakes; even smarter people learn from the mistakes of others.

The Top Ten Revenue Management Mistakes Hotels Make

10. Seeing revenue management as a job done only by the revenue manager.
9. Allowing Internet discounting agencies to sell guestrooms at prices of their choosing, then complaining about the erosion of rate integrity.
8. Claiming to differentiate the hotel based on service excellence, then promoting discounts, "value package" offerings, free frequent-guest points, and other freebies.
7. Thinking that the hotel's weekday strategy and weekend strategy can be the same.
6. Expecting that the "flag" (brand) will fill the hotel without the hotel's management team lifting a finger.
5. Counting revenue dollars as equal, regardless of the distribution channel they came through.
4. Thinking that short-term goals must always have priority over long-term goals.
3. Thinking that artificial intelligence—the revenue management software—is superior to human intelligence.
2. Believing that the right price to charge for a room night is established solely on the hotel's costs and ROI expectations.
1. Believing that discounting is an effective way to increase revenue.

What is actually meant by the above points? We will expand on these ideas in the following paragraphs, point by point.

Mistake 10: Seeing revenue management as a job done only by the revenue manager.

A husband helps his wife parallel park: "More to the right! Now backward! A lot more to the left! All the way! Forward! Now backward! A bit more!" Crunch! "Oh my! Now get out and see the damage *you've* done."

There are a number of hotel managers of different departments around the table at the revenue meetings when the topic of forecasts, inventory, and rate allocations are discussed. There is no shortage of opinions and advice.

Everybody has a point of view and feels compelled to contribute. Therefore, when all is said and done, it is not fair to single out the revenue manager if revenue goals are not met.

Revenue management success depends on the entire organization, and team efforts are required to achieve revenue objectives: "All for one and one for all" should be the watchword. The revenue manager can be the point person, but fingers should not be pointed and blame should not be assigned to a single individual or just one operational unit if revenue results are less than desired.

Mistake 9: Allowing Internet discounting agencies to sell guestrooms at prices of their choosing, then complaining about the erosion of rate integrity.

The industry's wakeup after 2003 on this issue was necessary and somewhat overdue. Until then, third-party Internet re-sellers used the merchant model to mark up room rates by 25–30 percent and were in control of sell rates. The hotel industry had nobody but itself to blame for this, and gradually the industry wrestled back control over room rates and distribution. The direct method of selling to guests using the hotel's own web portal may not be the highest revenue producer per reservation, but it is still the most cost efficient, most controllable, and yields the highest net room rate. The most important question at rate setting: Who is in charge?

Mistake 8: Claiming to differentiate the hotel based on service excellence, then promoting discounts, "value package" offerings, free frequent-guest points, and other freebies.

An incoming call to Excellent Service Hotel is put on hold and an automated voice system kicks in: "Your call is important to us. All of our agents are currently serving other callers. Please wait until the next available operator." And the message goes on for five more minutes in a loop. When the call is finally taken, a AAA discount of 10 percent is offered from the room rate without even verifying AAA membership. Go figure.

A hotel's strategic positioning should be the foundation of tactical rate management. Once a hotel decides to compete on service quality, location, unique selling points, or anything else but room rate, that positioning should be followed through with consistency. Competing on rates is a different game and it is not necessarily going to help a hotel's bottom line. A high-ranking executive of a global luxury chain known for its service excellence famously once said, "If we ever promote rate, we're dead." This blunt statement is a great example of consistency in brand message.

Discounts, freebies, and rate incentives may be quick fixes for disgruntled customers but they will not make up for lousy service or understaffed call centers. If service excellence is promised, that should be delivered, not discounts.

Mistake 7: Thinking that the hotel's weekday strategy and weekend strategy can be the same.

If the stay pattern, booking pattern, spending pattern, and market mix are different on weekdays than on weekends, at some point the hotel has to arrive at the logical conclusion that different strategies are needed on weekdays and weekends to maximize revenue. Hotel managers should base their decisions on solid data instead of wishful thinking. Different market dynamics warrant different strategic and tactical approaches for revenue maximization.

Mistake 6: Expecting that the "flag" (brand) will fill the hotel without the hotel's management team lifting a finger.

Hotel brands differ in terms of their marketing and other support. Some brands drive more revenue to their operators than others. Some brand marketing strategies, call centers, and web sites are better than others. However, even the best brand support cannot replace good operational care and close attention to guest service. Inattentive service staff, less-than-perfect cleanliness, and malfunctioning items (dead TV remote controls, broken hair driers, dripping faucets, thermostats that won't adjust room temperature, etc.) are not going to produce satisfied, loyal customers, no matter how well a brand promotes a destination. Hotel managers must own up to their responsibility regarding day-to-day operational issues, and they can't expect the brand to save a lousy product.

Mistake 5: Counting revenue dollars as equal, regardless of the distribution channel they came through.

Not all revenue dollars are created equal, because the costs associated with generating each revenue dollar can differ tremendously. Do the hotel's managers know what costs are associated with selling a room night through the hotel's corporate call center? The hotel's own website? A GDS channel? An e-merchant? A travel agent? A direct call from a return guest? An association?

There are various methods and channels a hotel can use to sell its products. Third parties are nice to have if they can fill rooms that the hotel cannot. Distribution channel management is now a core strategic competency. To play in the smartest way the hand a hotel is dealt requires an analysis of revenue production per distribution channel, plus an in-depth knowledge of the costs associated with each and every sales transaction. Commissions, switching-company costs, royalty fees, transaction charges, and other applicable costs need to be identified and compared.

Identical room rates paid by different guests may result in different net rates, based on a lot of cost variables that each hotel has to develop a solid understanding of. If more revenue comes through the least costly distribution channels, more profit is made without increasing occupancy.

Mistake 4: Thinking that short-term goals must always have priority over long-term goals.

Hotels are not for those who need to make a quick buck. Hotels are not built to last a few years. Hotels are built to last for decades, some for centuries. The hotel business is a marathon, not a sprint. There are high barriers to entry, it is a capital-intensive business, and its cost structure cannot be changed (most of a hotel's costs, being fixed, cannot be manipulated). Therefore, a long-term perspective is the only successful approach in the hotel business. It takes time to introduce a new property, build a clientele, and earn a solid reputation in the marketplace. Decision-makers should take all of this into consideration. Short-term thinking is not the way to long-term success, and the hotel industry shows no mercy to those who can't endure. When a short-term revenue objective conflicts with a hotel's long-term revenue and strategic goals, revenue managers must take a firm stand and never let short-term gains cause long-term pains.

Mistake 3: Thinking that artificial intelligence—the revenue management software—is superior to human intelligence.

By now we've all heard the modern-day adage, "To err is human—but to really foul things up, you need a computer." Computers are great tools in the decision-making process. They are fast and accurate, and by using extensive databases they can crunch a lot of variables in a short amount of time. However, sensible managers should always carefully check any results and not blindly follow the computers' lead. The system is not the solution and the media is not the message. Sometimes we mere humans do know better.

Sophisticated software products are of great help to managers, but they should not be asked to do what they were not designed to do. Binary logic works well but only up to a certain point. Humans have lateral-thinking capabilities, empathy, sensibility, and sensitivity, and can take the human element into consideration when making decisions. Managers know that guests are more than just room numbers, covers, or accounts. In short, decisions in a service-oriented business should be made by humans, not machines. Never let a computer run a hotel.

Mistake 2: Believing that the right price to charge for a room night is established solely on the hotel's costs and ROI expectations.

Good hotel managers know that the right price to charge for a guestroom is established by the market. Hotels should charge exactly what the market is able and willing to pay—not a dollar less, but not a dollar more. Today's savvy consumer will sniff out over-pricing in a heartbeat and will not hesitate to go after a better deal for a comparable product.

The twenty-first-century customer has comparison-shopping capability at his or her fingertips 24/7. Today's consumers have the ability to find the best value like never before, and nobody likes to overpay. Therefore, hotel managers must keep their fingers on the market's pulse, keep an ear close to the ground, and be on the ball at all times. Supply and demand dynamics can change quickly, and everybody wants to be the first to know. Does that mean hotel managers should constantly jerk room rates up and down in the name of dynamic pricing? Not at all. But it does mean they should always know what their product is worth. To help gauge that, managers should know what competitors are offering and what they are charging for it. Nothing can replace a thorough knowledge of the hotel's guests and how the hotel stacks up in a crowded market of comparable products. The danger of becoming a commodity is real, and inviting customers to choose only on price point reinforces their conviction that only the price really matters. If hotels have nothing else to offer, such customers will eventually be right.

Mistake 1: Believing that discounting is an effective way to increase revenue.

Smart hotel operators, who know they are selling an experience-based, intangible product—the hospitality experience at their properties—do not discount.

Several studies on hotel discounts concluded that discounts only generate partial results, and it is only the leisure segment which may react favorably. A fact: if downward pressures on room rates force hoteliers to discount heavily (examples: markets impacted by SARS, hurricanes, terrorist attacks, etc.), it takes several years to reach the same ADR than before the price decline started.

Discounts can only grab market share on a short-term basis. Customers who can be lured away from competitors as a result of lowering rates will generate cash flow but will not help profitability. Bargain-hunter customers who are willing to switch for a marginal price difference will always go where they can get a lower rate. This means that discounting in most cases will not improve RevPAR but will merely improve occupancy by getting the business of customers that nobody can retain, as they always will follow the cheapest deals available. Such customers are here today, gone tomorrow, based simply on which hotel has a special deal or which company is more desperate for cash.

Discounting can increase revenue and market share on a temporary basis, but it cannot increase hotel profits long-term. Most of the costs are fixed for a hotel. Lower room rates mean that a lot more units need to be sold, because the costs of capital, labor, utilities, and other items are not going to change. Lowering room rates may mean attracting a clientele that is not the one the hotel was built for, positioned to serve, or best equipped to satisfy. Those operators who meant to skim the cream at the top, only to one day find themselves scraping the bottom, know all too well the difference.

Discounting is not the only way to offer more value to customers. Before a rate decision is made in the face of softening demand, it is imperative to find out the reasons for the decline. Does it have anything to do with the product? With the competition? Are there economic, political, or health and safety issues behind it, independent from the hotel? Will a lower room rate help to ease those troubles? If there are other elements that can be bundled together with a room rate in order to create value for customers, can the rates be maintained?

It is not unusual to see a problem unrelated to room rates—for example, political uncertainty—cause a decrease in demand, and see hotels use lower room rates to solve it, as if a 50-percent discount could suddenly provide the illusion of safety and security (to continue with our political uncertainty example) at a destination hit by political instability and turmoil or the danger of terrorist attacks. There are no easy answers and quick fixes for such problems.

Hotels have to have realistic expectations about prices and know which issues are price-related and which are not. There are a lot of trigger-happy revenue managers eager to pull the rate trigger and unleash a variety of discounts instead of adjusting the hotel's products and working harder to get the business a hotel needs to meet its revenue targets.

Rates are too important to be used as the first line of defense. Instead, rates should be the last line of defense, turned to only after every other avenue has been exhausted. Even then, rates should be adjusted with a great deal of care.

Index

A

Agency model, 160
Amenities, 36
Asset management, 6
Average daily rate (ADR), 20–21

B

B2C model, 158–159
Babymooners, 118
Bed configurations, 125
Behavioral segmentation, 118
Best available rate (BAR), 71
Big data, 6, 43–44
Brand affiliation, 37, 112–113
Budget, 51

C

Capacity, 124
    management, 84–89
Classification, 125
Closing a day, 83
Competitive (comp) set, 35–40
Complementary products, 56
Complimentary rate, 70
Complimentary rooms, 21
Constrained demand, 58
Consumer Price Index, 53
Contribution margin, 23–25
Corporate rates, 67–69
Costs
    fixed and variable, 9–10
    variable, 24
Crandall, Robert, 4
Currency exchange rates, 55–56
Customer relationship management (CRM), 123–124

D

Darisse, Julian, 74–75, 85–86
Decision systems, 169–170
Demand, 9
    -based pricing, 76
    constrained or not, 58
    generation, 109–113
Demographic segmentation, 117
Denial defined, 57
Differentiation, 110–113
Discounting, tactical, 71–73
Discretionary income, 53
Displacement analysis, 97–103
Disposable income, 53
Distribution channel management, 155–166
Duration control, 81–83
Dynamic pricing, 75–78

E

EBITDA, 27
Economic indicators, 53
Elasticity, 119–120
Employee rate, 70
Employment rate, 53
Event rates, 70
External measurement metrics, 35–46

F

Fair share, 40–41
Farrell, Scott, 38–40
Fixed capacity, 7–8
Forecasting, 51–60
    demand, 52–59
    room availability, 59–60
Freeman, Wendy, 162–163
Fung, Janice, 162–163

G

GDS channels, 157
Geographic segmentation, 117
Geography, 35–36
GOPPAR, 27–29
Government rates, 70
Granularity, 57
Group rates, 69–70
Growth, nominal and real, 53
Guest acquisition costs, 20, 24

H

Hurdle rate, 70
Hybrid model, 161

I

IDeaS, 173–175, 176–177
Income statement, 18–19
Inflation, 53
Internal measurement metrics, 17–30
Internet channels, 157–161

L

LGBT market, 118
Lifetime total value, 58
Location, 124–125
Long-term forecasts, 52–55

M

Marginal revenue, 26–27
Market
    intelligence, 43–44
    mix management, 124–126
    positioning, 122, 125
    segmentation, 117–121
    share, 40–42, 132–133
    targeting, 121–122
    trends, 57
Measurement
    external metrics, 35–46
    internal metrics, 17–30
Merchant model, 160–161
Meta-search engines, 160
MLOS, 81–82
Mobile, 13, 164–165
    commerce, 120–121

N

Near field communication, 120
Net revenue, 23–25
    identical, 25–26
Nominal growth, 53

O

Occupancy percentage, 20
Opaque model, 161
Out-of-order rooms, 88

191

Overbooking, 84–86
Overstays, 86–87
    defined, 59

P

Pace of build, 58–59
Packaging, 134–139
Parloring, 89
Penetration index, 41–42
Perishability, 8
Positioning, 122, 125
Pricing, strategic, 131–139
Promotion, 122–123
Promotional rates, 70
Psychographic segmentation, 117–118

R

Rack rate, 67
Rao, Gopal, 54–55
Rate, 36
    achievement factor, 67
    fences, 133
    parity, 133
    structure, 66–71
    tactical management, 65–78
    types, 67–71
Ratings, 36
Real growth, 53
Rebranding, 122
Reclaiming rooms, 87–89
Recommendation systems, 169
Regret defined, 57
Repositioning, 122
Responsive design, 121, 165–166
Retail model, 160
Return on engagement, 12

Revenue
    centers, 18–19
    defined, 18
    identical net, 25–26
    manager, 177–182
    marginal, 26–27
    net, 23–25
    streams management, 133–134, 139
Revenue management
    automated, 169–177
    challenges, 10–13
    criteria, 7–10
    history, 3–6
    marketing strategies, 117–126
    process, 3–4
    strategic, 109–182
    tactical, 51–103
    total, 12, 143–151
RevPAC, 29
RevPAR, 21–23
    penetration, 42
    total, 29

S

Search engines, 37, 159–160
    optimization, 159
    organic vs. paid, 159
Segmentation, 117–121
    and packaging, 138–139
Short-term forecasts, 55–58
Single-image inventory, 170–171
SMERF groups, 69
Social media, 12–13, 161–164
Spending per day, 29–30
Spill factor, 57
Spreadsheet design, 100
Statement of income, 18–19
Stay control, 81–83

Stayovers defined, 59
Stay-through, 82–83
Substitute products, 56–57
Summary operating statement, 27–28
System integration, 172–177

T

Tactical rate management, 65–78
Total revenue management, 143–151
Total spend, 58
Travel restrictions, 56
TRevpar, 29

U

Unconstrained demand, 58
Understays defined, 59
Upgrading, 89
Upselling, 73–75

V

Visitor statistics, 57
Voice channels, 156

W

Walking guests, 84–86
Wash factor, 57, 84
Winzer, Bill, 76

Y

Yield management, 5